OTTOLINE

OTTOLINE

THE LIFE OF LADY OTTOLINE MORRELL

Sandra Jobson Darroch

COWARD, McCANN & GEOGHEGAN, INC.
New York

First American Edition 1975

Copyright © 1975 by Sandra Jobson Darroch and Robert Darroch

SBN: 698–10634–2

Library of Congress Catalog Card Number: 74–16641

Printed in the United States of America

CONTENTS

Illustrations follow pages 96 and 224.

Acknowledgements

Acknowledgement is gratefully made for permission to include the following works or extracts from them:

Asquith, Lady Cynthia: *Diaries: 1915–1918,* edited by E. M. Horsley. Copyright © 1968 by Michael and Simon Asquith; Alfred A. Knopf, Inc., and Hutchinson Publishing Group Ltd., Publishers.

Asquith, H. H. and Violet: Unpublished letters by permission of the Hon. Mark Bonham Carter.

Bedford, Sybille: *Aldous Huxley: A Biography.* Copyright © 1973, 1974 by Sybille Bedford; Alfred A. Knopf, Inc., Chatto & Windus Ltd., and William Collins Sons & Co., Publishers.

Bell, Clive: *Old Friends.* Copyright © 1956. By permission of Chatto & Windus Ltd., Publishers, and Quentin Bell. Unpublished letters by permission of Quentin Bell.

Bell, Quentin: *Virginia Woolf: A Biography.* Copyright © 1972 by Quentin Bell. By permission of Harcourt Brace Jovanovich, Inc., and The Hogarth Press, Publishers, and the author.

Bell, Vanessa: Unpublished letters by permission of Quentin Bell.

Bennett, Arnold: Unpublished letter by permission of Mrs. Dorothy Cheston Bennett.

Brett, Dorothy: Unpublished letters by permission of International Creative Management.

Carrington, Dora: *Carrington Letters and Extracts from her Diaries,* chosen and with an introduction by David Garnett. Copyright © 1970 by David Garnett and The Sophie Partridge Trust. Reprinted by permission of Holt, Rinehart & Winston, Inc., and Jonathan Cape Ltd., Publishers.

Epstein, Jacob: Unpublished letters by permission of Lady Kathleen Epstein.

Forster, E. M.: Unpublished letter by permission of The Society of Authors as the literary representatives of the E. M. Forster Estate.

Maclagan, grandson of the late William Maclagan, 88th Archbishop of York.

Mansfield, Katherine: "Night-Scented Stocks," from *Poems* by Katherine Mansfield. Copyright © 1924, renewed 1952 by J. Middleton Murry; Alfred A. Knopf, Inc., Publishers.

Moore, Harry T.: *The Priest of Love.* Copyright © 1952, 1962, 1974 by Harry T. Moore; Farrar, Straus & Giroux, Publishers.

Moore, Thomas Sturge: Unpublished letters by permission of Riette Sturge Moore and D. C. Sturge Moore.

Morrell, Lady Ottoline: *Ottoline: The Early Memoirs of Lady Ottoline Morrell,* edited by Robert Gathorne-Hardy. Copyright © 1963; Alfred A. Knopf, Inc., and Faber & Faber Ltd., Publishers. *Ottoline at Garsington: Memoires of Lady Ottoline Morrell, 1915–1918,* edited by Robert Gathorne-Hardy. Copyright © 1974, Faber & Faber Ltd., Publishers.

Murry, John Middleton: Unpublished letters by permission of The Society of Authors as literary representatives of the Estate of John Middleton Murry.

Nehls, Edward H.: *D. H. Lawrence: A Composite Biography.* Copyright © 1957: University of Wisconsin Press, Publishers.

Rothenstein, William: Unpublished letter by permission of Sir John Rothenstein and Mr. Michael Rothenstein, Executors of the Estate of Sir William Rothenstein.

Russell, Bertrand: *The Autobiography of Bertrand Russell, Vols. I & II.* Little, Brown & Co. in association with The Atlantic Monthly Press and George Allen & Unwin Ltd., Publishers. Unpublished letters by permission of The Bertrand Russell Archives, McMaster University, Ontario, Canada. All quotations from unpublished letters copyright © 1975 by Res-Lib Ltd. Unpublished journals, 1902–1905, by permission of The Bertrand Russell Estate.

Sassoon, Siegfried: Unpublished letters by permission of G. T. Sassoon.

Spencer, Gilbert and Stanley: Unpublished letters by permission of Mr. Gilbert Spencer.

Spender, Stephen: *World Within World: The Autobiography of Stephen Spender.* Copyright © 1951 by S. Spender; reprinted by permission of The University of California Press, Publishers, and A. D. Peters & Co. Ltd.

INTRODUCTION

The fact that this is the first biography of Lady Ottoline Morrell needs explanation. Even in her lifetime Ottoline was something of a legendary figure, yet it wasn't until after her death in 1938 that the legend really burgeoned. In a growing number of memoirs, reminiscences, and other people's biographies she made rather shadowy appearances, usually as an improbable, slightly comic character. Even when her own memoirs were published more was hidden than revealed. It was an old state of affairs, in that many had heard her name but few could say very much about her. This paradox was traceable partly, perhaps even principally, to the fear in those who possessed information about her that to disclose it would hurt others—a view represented by her friend Robert Gathorne-Hardy who, when editing her memoirs in 1963, said it was still too soon to tell the full truth about Ottoline.

Two books, Michael Holroyd's biography of Lytton Strachey and Bertrand Russell's autobiography, did much to change this attitude. Holroyd's candid treatment of the Bloomsbury Group and their friends, including Ottoline, made many people realise that there was more harm in suppressing material than in releasing it. It was in this atmosphere that I approached Ottoline's daughter and gained her permission—refused to many others before me—to embark on a biography of her mother.

Very early on I became aware that this would not be a straightforward job of research. In anything touching Ottoline's reputation there seemed to be two views which I came to categorise (probably oversimply) as the pro and the anti. A legacy of feuds dating back more than sixty years, these opposing attitudes coloured—and continue to colour—most of what is written about Ottoline. Picking a way between the two camps presented difficulties and I realised that I would not get very far unless I could find sources that were comparatively neutral. It soon became clear that this material would only be found in letters and other contemporary documents.

Here I was fortunate. Ottoline's daughter gave me access to a large number of unpublished documents, most importantly the unedited type-script of the memoirs containing Ottoline's account of her affair with Bertrand Russell. At King's College Library I saw the Charleston Papers, which included much unpublished material concerning Ottoline's relations with Bloomsbury. The Strachey Papers provided me with valuable new material, as did Virginia Woolf's letters in the University of Sussex Library and the Koteliansky Papers in the British Museum. But by far the most important new source was Ottoline's own correspondence, over 7,000 letters written to her during her lifetime, virtually all of them previously unseen. When I and my husband, Robert Darroch (who thenceforth collaborated with me on the book), saw these letters at the Humanities Research Center in Austin, Texas, in October, 1972, we knew we had the ingredients for a proper biography of Ottoline. Not only were there hundreds of letters from people like Lytton Strachey, Virginia Woolf, T.S. Eliot, and many others, but the collection contained all of Russell's letters to Ottoline—more than 2,500 of them—written between 1911 and 1938. These gave an intimate account of the affair that for several years dominated their lives. They also cast new light on both Ottoline and Russell. Next we discovered that Russell, too, had kept all of Ottoline's letters and that these were housed in McMaster University, Ontario, Canada. Though Russell had laid an embargo on them until February 5, 1975, we saw these 1,500 letters on microfilm the day the embargo was lifted.

With such a wealth of unpublished documents, we decided to try to present the material as directly as possible. The fact that Ottoline, unlike Lytton Strachey or Virginia Woolf, was not a literary or creative figure reinforced this decision, as did our belief that we should try to steer a course between the positions already taken up on the subject.

There are two final points I would like to make.

As this is a story of Ottoline's life, the period in which she lived is necessarily seen through her eyes; this means that an incomplete image is often given of other people who come into the narrative. Also, not everyone will agree—or indeed has agreed—with this picture of Ottoline. Some may discover in this book a different Ottoline from the one they knew: if so, I hope they will gain an added respect and sympathy for her.

SANDRA JOBSON DARROCH
1975

WELBECK

Chapter 1

Part i

"&there used to be a great lady in Bedford Square who managed to make life seem a little amusing & interesting & adventurous, so I used to think when I was young & wore a blue dress, & Ottoline was like a Spanish galleon, hung with golden coins, & lovely silken sails."[1] That was Virginia Woolf's vision of Lady Ottoline Morrell. In fact, everyone who knew Ottoline thought she was remarkable. David Cecil called her an Elizabethan, rather like Queen Elizabeth herself; D. H. Lawrence said she was a queen among women;[2] Osbert Sitwell described her as an oversized Infanta of Spain;[3] and Dorothy Brett said she had a heart of gold and a yen for men.[4] It was Ottoline's extraordinary appearance that struck people most. She trailed, recalled Peter Quennell, like one of the peacocks that followed her, her high-arched nose, prognathous jaw, pale face, and mahogany-red hair giving her an appearance both baroque and gothic.[5] Stephen Spender was intrigued by her voice; he loved the way she emphasised syllables, transforming ordinary speech into "horn-like blasts"—an effect echoed in her unique handwriting, the exquisite loops and arabesques of which elevated mere sentences into a realm of pure ornament.[6] He conjured up a picture of her parading around Bloomsbury dressed like some aristocratic shepherdess and leading her Pekinese dogs on ribbons tied to the shepherd's crook she carried.

Leonard Woolf, Virginia's husband, also saw Ottoline taking the Bloomsbury air. He described her as looking like some enormous bird with her hair and clothes flopping and flapping around her, a bird whose "brightly and badly dyed plumage was in complete disarray and no longer fitted the body."[7] He remembered her passing a trench in which some men were working; seeing her, they roared with laughter, then whistled and catcalled, but Ottoline walked on, oblivious and impervious. "A very silly woman," was Woolf's summing up. For Woolf and his Bloomsbury colleagues Ottoline was too fantastic, too scented, too exaggerated. Vanessa Bell said she talked twaddle;[8] Clive Bell spread mali-

15

cious stories about her; and even Lytton Strachey, who was truly fond of Ottoline, couldn't resist the customary Bloomsbury gibe, once describing her as *rongée* by malevolence: ". . . every tea party in London to which she hasn't been invited is wormwood, wormwood."[9] David Garnett, a younger member of Bloomsbury, first met Ottoline in 1913 and to him she appeared magnificent: glacier blue-green eyes, masses of dark Venetian red hair, a long straight nose, proud mouth and jutting-out chin—a "lovely, haggard face."[10] But Garnett too thought her overdone: ". . . all her houses were a little too hothouse, too parrot-house. The rooms reeked of potpourri and oranges. I think in a way we exploited Ottoline. But it was awfully fun to be invited and one didn't run down invitations. It was awfully nice for a scruffy young man to go to dinner at Ottoline's. But that's only adding to the legend."[11]

It is this legend that has come down to us today, much of it through the tongues and pens of Bloomsbury. They and their friends told stories about her parties at Bedford Square, Garsington, and Gower Street; they labelled her a shallow society hostess; they ridiculed her efforts to seek out and foster young poets and painters—"lion hunting," they sneered. Yet the legend is only a fraction of the truth, and the gossip and sneers hardly touch the real Ottoline. She largely disappeared from view after 1918, retiring behind a façade that she and others erected around her declining years. But before then, at Garsington and Bedford Square, Ottoline lived an extraordinary life—much of which she kept to herself.

Part ii
1873–1881

She was born in London on June 16, 1873, into a world of class and privilege; Victoria had been Queen for thirty-six years and was to reign another twenty-eight. Ottoline's parents were paradigms of the Victorian age: Her father was Lieutenant-General Arthur Bentinck, colonel of the Seventh Dragoon Guards, a big, bearded patriarch with a deep voice and booming laugh. Her mother was Augusta Mary Elizabeth, daughter of the

Very Reverend and Honourable H. M. Browne, dean of Lismore. Augusta was Anglo-Irish on her mother's side and was the general's second wife. They had three older children: Henry, William, and Charles, and the general had an elder son, Arthur, by his first wife. A few weeks before her last confinement Augusta Bentinck, who was thirty-nine, sat down and wrote to her eldest son, Henry, who was ten:

> 5 Portman Square,
> May 19th, 1873

MY HENRY—MY DARLING,

If God takes me from you this is to bid you farewell. I pray to God to comfort you, if I go, as I pray him to spare me to you if it is His will. . . . But if God takes me, His will is best. He and your own dear Father will in time comfort you. Papa will be as kind to you as I ever was, and God will take care of you if you ask Him, and never forget my darling to read your Bible and to say your prayers, wherever you are, for God loves those who love Him. . . . Be persevering in your studies, and try when you are older to do good in the world, to make a name worthy of your ancestors and of yourself. . . . Keep my little Willie in the right path. . . . I think you will be happy at the schools we have chosen for you both, Cheam and Eton, and that you will go to Oxford.[12]

But Mrs. Bentinck was spared, and her child, a daughter, was christened Ottoline Violet Anne Cavendish-Bentinck (though the family preferred to use plain Bentinck). Ottoline—the unusual name was a legacy of her Dutch ancestry*—spent her first four and a half years cocooned in the safe, ordered, narrow way of life then enjoyed by the English upper class. They had a house in the country, a summer residence in London, servants in the basement, coachmen in the coachhouse, and Nurse Powell in the nursery. An early family photograph shows Ottoline as a pudding-faced infant dressed up in a white lace dress with a sort of junior bustle and curling hair cut in a fringe. When the family came to London for the Season her father would take her to Hyde Park where he held her broad pink sash as she galloped out in front of him. In the country he took her for rides in a pony trap down winding lanes, and on evenings when important visitors came she would hide her head on his shoulder.

The family was very comfortably off, the general's army salary being

*See Appendix 1.

supplemented by an allowance from his distant cousin, the Fifth Duke of Portland. Due to a series of dynastic mishaps the general was now the duke's heir, and as Portland was old and ailing it was assumed that at any moment Ottoline's father would become the sixth duke, inheriting the family seat, Welbeck Abbey, together with extensive and lucrative estates in Derbyshire, Nottinghamshire, Northumberland, Ayrshire, Caithness, and London. In 1877, however, these secure expectations were dashed when General Bentinck suffered an unexpected heart attack and died at fifty-nine. To Augusta Bentinck it was a double blow: Not only was she left to bring up a large family alone, but the prospect of becoming Duchess of Portland was gone, as the dukedom would go to her stepson, Arthur, now a twenty-year-old officer in the Coldstream Guards. After the funeral Mrs. Bentinck spent her period of mourning with her children in the country, returning to London for the summer of 1878 and taking a modest house in Grosvenor Crescent, off Belgrave Square. From its windows Arthur and his half-brothers and half-sister used to watch through lace curtains as splendidly dressed guests arrived at the Duke of Richmond's much grander residence opposite. Mrs. Bentinck had not been granted an army pension so the family's circumstances were reduced and there were fewer toys for Ottoline, fewer servants belowstairs.

This difficult period lasted only a year. In December, 1878, Arthur turned twenty-one and the fifth duke re-entailed his estates to provide for his succession by the young guardsman, at the same time giving him a generous allowance (which Arthur spent on a stable of hunting horses and the lease on a substantial London house, 13 Grosvenor Place, at the rear of Buckingham Palace). Almost exactly twelve months later the fifth duke himself died, and Arthur became the sixth duke. The family came down from the country and were put up at Claridges while boxes of grapes and peaches, wrapped in pink paper, were dispatched from the Welbeck greenhouses for the new owners. And six-year-old Ottoline and eleven-year-old Charlie were taken to Cremer's toyshop in Regent Street and told to choose anything they wished. Two weeks later the family travelled up to Welbeck to enter into their inheritance. Charlie meanwhile had fallen ill and had to be carried off the train at Worksop station, watched by a crowd of locals who had come out on the cold wintry night to see the young duke and his family arrive. To a natural interest in their new master was added a curiosity to see if he showed any sign of oddness, for the fifth duke had been noted for his eccentricities. Neither Mrs. Bentinck nor Arthur had ever met him, but rumours of his activities at Welbeck had filtered through and as they drove up the long drive to the squat, dark abbey they were wondering what they would find. Their worst fears were realised. Through the carriage window they saw silhouettes of decapitated trees and mounds of rubble, while even to reach the abbey entrance they had to go over a bridge of planks, as the drive had been dug up. Inside, the hall floorboards also were up and more planks had to be negotiated to reach the stairs that led to the only habitable part of the building, a suite of rooms in which the old duke had lived out his solitary routine, communicating with his servants through double letter boxes cut in the doors.

Next morning Ottoline and Willie began exploring the abbey, a thirteenth-century building which successive owners had added to over the years. It was soon apparent where the fifth duke's nickname, the Burrowing Duke, had come from: the place was riddled with tunnels. Evidently when the late duke inherited the abbey he had been eager to add to it, and rather than spoil the façade he decided to put his extra rooms underground. From there his tunnelling developed into a mania and eventually over 600 navvies were employed at Welbeck on his excavations, which he supervised personally, his tall figure crowned with a top hat and his trousers tied with string at the ankles. One tunnel was of imperial proportions. It stretched a mile and a half from the abbey towards Worksop station and was wide enough for two carriages to drive abreast. The old duke had also been installing a new plumbing and heating system, which was the reason for the trenches outside and the disrupted state within. And in an effort to improve the appearance of the grounds he had had every tree lopped. It was hardly a homely place that Ottoline and her brother explored. One subterranean passage they discovered led to a trapdoor opening into the riding school built by the first Duke of Newcastle, a seventeenth- century ancestor of Ottoline's. But a riding school it was no longer. The fifth duke had transformed the stark interior into a fairy-tale ballroom; the ceiling was painted pink and hung with chandeliers and the walls lined with mirrors. Yet no ball had ever been held there, and stacked around the room, like so many wallflowers, were Bentinck family portraits, their frames removed.

Soon the young sixth duke began to feel oppressed by his new home—

he wanted to shut it up and return to his club in London. His stepmother however was a strong-minded woman who saw that their duty lay in restoring Welbeck to its former position as one of the country's great houses; also, the welfare of the 2,000-odd people who were tied to Welbeck and its satellite villages concerned her. Not that the old duke had neglected his tenants: he had given them donkeys to ride to work on and umbrellas to keep the rain off; he had built a roller-skating rink for the servants and threw handfuls of coins to the village children. To Mrs. Bentinck such capricious philanthropy was not enough and she began a programme of visiting cottages and screened off one end of the riding school to re-introduce Sunday morning church services. With the aid of experts summoned from London she personally sorted out the Welbeck treasures, giving Ottoline lessons in the history of the family as they sifted through the heirlooms, illustrating with pictures of Talbot courtiers in Elizabethan ruffs, pantalooned Cavendishes from the court of James I, and Bentincks with severe Dutch faces. On the family's distaff side three women stood out. The first was the prodigious Bess of Hardwick, founder of the Cavendish line and one of the few people to get the better of Elizabeth I; the second was Margaret, first Duchess of Newcastle, called Mad Madge, first of the bluestockings; third was Margaret Cavendish-Holles-Harley, who in 1734 married the second Duke of Portland, uniting the Cavendishes with the Bentincks. History became Ottoline's plaything—Henry VIII's dagger, the pearl earring Charles I wore at his execution, a casket that belonged to William of Orange (and in which she kept her childish letters). Yet, despite such interesting toys, her life was strange and lonely: she had no playmates and her only companions were servants. She never even learned to dress herself; her maid combed her hair, twisted it into sausage curls, lowered her lace petticoats and frocks over her head, tied her sashes, and buckled her shoes. Cooking and other domestic skills were likewise a mystery. Her education was entirely entrusted to governesses, principally a Miss Craig, whose duty it was to drum the Scriptures into her young pupil. Ottoline learned to embroider and to read and write, but of literature, science, and politics she absorbed virtually nothing. Only when her older cousin, Cattie, came to visit did she have any companionship at all. On these rare occasions the two would go out together in Ottoline's miniature phaeton, drawn by a pair of Shetland ponies, and gallop through Sherwood Forest. Portland, as Ottoline's half-brother was now called, outwardly was kind to her, but he was inclined to be a trifle pompous and anyway was busy enjoying the role of the young and eligible duke. Her other brothers were not very interested in a younger sister—their world was Eton and military college, and when they came home on holiday she would trail around after them fruitlessly trying to join in their games and conversation. She hero-worshipped her youngest brother Charlie, but he called her disparagingly "Higgory Stiggins." Yet Ottoline was nothing if not persistent and kept on trying to communicate; when she was nine and her nineteen-year-old brother Henry was away with the Derbyshire Regiment she wrote:

MY DEAR HENRY,
    Are you very nearly drowned and how do you like it. Charly was up for the day on Saturday and was photographed in the morning and went to a cricket match in the afternoon. I bought him a prearbook and a pice of old Windsor soap and a bottle of eau de cologne.
                                                    No more to say
                                                    Your loving
                                                        OTTOLINE
Please write at once[13]

Slowly Ottoline turned in on herself. She curtained off one end of her room to make a private place where she could have her own treasures and to which she could retire when her brothers proved too insensitive; this was the first of her boudoirs.

Part iii
1881–1894

Ottoline's upbringing was designed to fit her for one purpose: marriage to an aristocrat of approximately equal rank.* Everyone assumed she

*After Arthur became the sixth duke, the then Prime Minister, Disraeli, whose political career was greatly assisted by the Bentincks, prevailed upon Queen Victoria to bestow titles appropriate to full brothers and sisters of a duke on Ottoline and her brothers (who

would become one of the tribe of ladies who now began to flock to Welbeck, accompanying the huntin', shootin', and fishin' "bloods" that made up virtually all of Portland's friends, and a large part of the English upper class generally. Welbeck's return to the circuit of great country houses was sealed in November, 1881, when the Prince of Wales, later Edward VII, paid an official visit. Like the rest of society he had heard of the amazing Burrowing Duke and his troglodyte wonderland and he was anxious to come and see it for himself. Portland ensured he was not disappointed. Edward arrived at Welbeck via the Worksop tunnel, which was gaslit for the occasion. The prince brought his usual entourage, and while the ladies preened themselves the men went out shooting (in two days Edward and his party accounted for 1,081 pheasant, 400 hares and rabbits, plus three woodcock). In the evenings everyone played cards or listened to Mrs. Reynolds singing. During the visit, which was an unqualified success, Ottoline asked the prince for a donation for a local hospital and Edward obliged with a gold sovereign and a peck on the cheek. It was on occasions like this that the utter vapidity of the life of an upper-class lady was etched on Ottoline's mind. She observed them coming down to breakfast in velvet dresses with tight waists and lace fronts. They sat, she recalled, "and gossiped all the morning, then drove out to lunch with the shooters in tweeds, had tea in pink satin tea-gowns from Paris, and dined in still more gorgeous brocades and velvets."[14] She used to hide behind some embroidered curtains and peep at them as they swept into the drawing room before dinner, composing themselves and giving their dresses a finishing pat before appearing. Occasionally Portland and his friends would forsake Welbeck and travel up to Langwell in Scotland where they would continue denuding the countryside of its wildlife before moving on elsewhere. Several months of the year were spent in London taking part in the annual summer ritual of the Season. Portland (recently appointed master of the Queen's Horse) would take his young sister riding on Rotten Row, their horses proudly wearing the red headbands of the Royal Stables

henceforth would be lady and lords respectively). Disraeli also got Victoria (as a personal favour to him and against all precedent) to create Ottoline's mother—who had remained plain Mrs. Bentinck despite the succession of her son to the dukedom—Baroness Bolsover. Nor was this the end of Disraeli's efforts: his influence helped Portland obtain the Order of the Garter and the important post of master of the Queen's Horse. (Sources: Letters of Queen Victoria and Men, Women and Things)

and Ottoline carrying a whip engraved with her initials, O.V.A.C-B. Lady Bolsover took her daughter to the opera and theatre, and Ottoline remembered seeing Sir Henry Irving in *The Corsican Brothers* and Sarah Bernhardt in *Frou Frou*. Another night she and her mother saw Oscar Wilde, sunflower in his buttonhole, at the premiere of Gilbert and Sullivan's *Patience*. There were other excursions to art galleries to view the latest works of Poynter, Watts, and Whistler. And once a week Ottoline set off in a carriage from 13 Grosvenor Place to go to dancing class, which she didn't enjoy because the other girls sniggered at her elaborate dresses.

But for an event in 1889, Ottoline would probably have outgrown her reserve and fulfilled her destiny of marrying one of her brother's friends. However, in June of that year Portland himself married, and as Lady Bolsover watched the new duchess come down the aisle she realised her days as mistress of Welbeck were over. Shortly after the wedding she left to live in a house provided by Portland at St. Anne's Hill, Chertsey, and with her into exile went Ottoline, aged sixteen. The next two years were quiet. Lady Bolsover's health was failing (she had diabetes and myxoedema) and the task of looking after her fell principally to Ottoline. During this time—probably the most impressionable in any girl's life—Ottoline retreated even further into herself, devoting her days to nursing, running the house and servants, and poring over the fifteenth-century teachings of Thomas à Kempis, whose book *The Imitation of Christ* became her guide and scourge. Over and over she read his precepts on having a humble opinion of oneself, on obedience and submission, on the inner life, on doing without comfort, and on what delight there is in spurning the whole world and becoming the servant of God. Ottoline became something of a religious fanatic herself and even the quiet, dutiful, self-denying life she was leading began to seem almost profligate. She put away her prettiest dresses and took to wearing the plainest she could find; she thought food a weakness of the flesh, so she ate as frugally as possible; books were also pleasurable, so they had to be shunned as well. Yet even these sacrifices were not sufficient. She took up a young gypsy girl, giving her the luxuries she denied herself and teaching her to read and write. Yet still she was torn by inner conflict. How could she reconcile her love of beautiful things—the countryside in spring and the gaiety and excitement of the theatre—with her hunger for a more purposeful, serious existence? The carefree life her brothers pursued at Welbeck began to appear not just hollow, but evil.

During the next three years Ottoline and her mother several times crossed the Channel to visit spas and clinics, but Ottoline derived slender enjoyment from these trips. She was shy and pious and her mother made little effort to encourage her to meet people of her own age. Besides, at seventeen, Ottoline was not particularly attractive; she was almost six feet tall and her nose, which was always strong, had become overprominent. Later her features were to blend together better, but at this time she drew no confidence from her appearance.

In 1892 Ottoline turned nineteen and despite her obvious lack of interest in society Portland and her mother decided she should "come out." Lady Bolsover rose to the occasion and took her reluctant and awkward daughter through the Season's important events: Ascot, garden parties, and the balls held at Stafford House, Grosvenor House, Devonshire House, and London's other aristocratic residences. Here, under the twinkling chandeliers, Ottoline watched handsome happy couples swirling to the latest Viennese waltz tunes—and felt totally out of place. She shrank against the wall, and when someone asked her to dance the walk across the polished floor was agony; her only pleasant memories of that summer were of the scents of the flowers arranged around the rooms.

Her brothers despaired of her. She had the choice, were she to make the slightest effort, of any number of eligible young fellows who would be happy to marry the half-sister of the Duke of Portland. One of her brothers told her, "There isn't a girl in England who wouldn't want to step into your shoes."[15] But Ottoline was growing into a very stubborn young woman; she refused to consider any possibility of marriage. Indeed she decided to devote her immediate future to her mother and Thomas à Kempis.

The following year Lady Bolsover decided to go abroad to Italy to try a new cure; in Florence, however, it was Ottoline who fell ill. Doctors diagnosed typhoid fever and for several days her life hung in the balance. Recovering, she went to convalesce with her aunt, Mrs. Scott, at a villa outside Florence. There, pampered and petted, Ottoline experienced a new way of life in which happiness and the appreciation of beautiful things were not frowned on. Later, returning to England, the two invalids stopped off in Paris where in a final burst of energy Lady Bolsover bought Ottoline some pretty muslin dresses and a valuable necklace of pearls*— perhaps at last she realized that her daughter had become too serious and dowdy. Back in London Lady Bolsover collapsed into a deep coma and died.

Ottoline was numbed by her mother's death. Her brother, Lord Henry, took her into his house in Sloane Square, but she found little comfort there. Her brothers avoided mentioning the death, preferring to act almost as if their mother had never existed. Later Lord Henry and his wife took Ottoline north where they joined Portland's stalking party at Langwell in Scotland. But instead of entering into the fun Ottoline spent most of her time closeted in her room reading religious books, keenly conscious of the growing disapproval of everyone around her. Her brothers could not understand why their sister had to go about with such a long face.

Later on, back at Welbeck, in an effort to find something more worthwhile to do, Ottoline began holding Bible classes in her sitting room for the farmhands and footmen. Some came out of curiosity, others from boredom, but in any event the classes were a definite hit. Later Ottoline was to look back on them with amusement: "It was difficult to concentrate at times with twenty young men in the room, all chosen as footmen because of their good looks."

In 1893, however, it was a serious business and twenty-year-old Ottoline followed up their success with a woodcarving class, Portland being prevailed on to supply a teacher. Many years later Ottoline would sometimes come across one of her former students working perhaps as an attendant at the National Gallery or in a department store. They would step forward and introduce themselves: "I was one of your young men."[16]

Ottoline also took to visiting cottages on the estate, distributing gifts and doing good works. Yet she herself was almost friendless. The only person she could talk to was the librarian at Welbeck, Arthur Strong, who gave her books by Browning, Locke, and Meredith. To Ottoline Strong was "a being from another planet";[17] but he was to run foul of Portland

---

*This necklace, which many people were later to call (wrongly) "The Portland Pearls," had belonged to Marie Antoinette.

later. One day he lit a cigarette in the dining room, unaware that in doing so he had breached some rule of etiquette. Portland dismissed him instantly.

Ottoline's only other relief from the unhappy atmosphere came from occasional trips to Ham Common, near London, to see her aunt, Mrs. Scott, at whose house she met some interesting people, among them little Bertie Russell. She got on well with Mrs. Scott's daughters, Violet and Hyacinth, despite their being a little too High Church for Ottoline's Evangelical taste. One day Hyacinth invited her to accompany her on a visit to an Anglican convent in Cornwall run by the Little Sisters of the Poor. There Ottoline met a nun named Mother Julian who was to be her mentor over the next few years. She discussed her worries with Mother Julian, particularly the problem of how she could reconcile the romantic and the spiritual sides of her nature, and Mother Julian assured her that to love beautiful things and enjoy life was not evil. Though not completely convinced, Ottoline began to understand her mother's last gesture in buying her the muslin dresses and pearls. This discovery was the first step towards her liberation.

Chapter 2

1895–1901

Probably the first man to fall in love with Ottoline was William Dalrymple Maclagan, eighty-eighth Archbishop of York. In 1895 Maclagan came to Welbeck to officiate at some Bentinck family occasion and while there became friendly with the long-nosed sister of his host. Being one of the Empire's principal religious leaders, he was socially equal if not senior to her brother, and as he represented a way of life that Ottoline now felt to be superior to that pursued at Welbeck, it was natural she should seek his company and support. Yet there was more to their friendship than just a common interest. All her life Ottline had a knack for attracting men years her senior; there was something in her makeup that proved almost irresistible to men like Maclagan. Soon she and the sixty-nine-year-old prelate were to be seen taking long earnest walks in the grounds of Welbeck. They made an incongruous twosome: Ottoline, just on six feet tall, towering over the diminutive, white-haired archbishop. After he returned to his palace at Bishopthorpe they corresponded regularly. Having lost her father at an early age and having been forced to rely on her brothers for advice, Ottoline turned to the kindly old archbishop as a surrogate father. She addressed him as Father and he called her My Dear Child, My Dearest, signing himself "Your Loving Father in God." Soon Ottoline was making regular visits to Bishopthorpe, so many that Maclagan had a room set aside for her in his palace, much to his wife's disapproval. He took it upon himself to supervise Ottoline's education and prepared regular readings lists for her; also he took an interest in her classes for the Welbeck staff and other good works. They exchanged gifts and she voiced her concern about his rheumatism while he asked her about her recurrent headaches. He wrote: "I truly believe [God] committed you to my care."[1] Years later Ottoline was to admit in her memoirs that Maclagan had been rather flirtatious "in a mild, fatherly way."[2] During the spring and summer of 1896 they met frequently and Maclagan often came to address her classes, which had now been extended to London during

27

the Season. Held in her brother's house at 13 Grosvenor Place, these extramural meetings were mainly for girls, possibly belowstairs staff whom Ottline befriended, or shopgirls, with whom she had a remarkable rapport throughout her life. The following year, on June 3, 1897, Maclagan wrote to Ottoline:

> I have made a note of Thursday 13th, Friday 16th and Tuesday 30th July at 5 p.m. for your little gatherings. (P.S. I was not *quite* pleased with your look today. Please be very careful & self-indulgent—if you can!)[3]

But the Tuesday date proved difficult, as he explained rather apologetically the following month:

> DEAREST OTTOLINE,
>   Alas! the Queen has fixed Tuesday next for receiving the Bishops of the Lambeth Conference at Windsor, and my attendance there is absolutely necessary. What can be done about my address to your friends? . . . Would there be any chance of my seeing you Sunday if I were to call?[4]

In 1896 Maclagan lent his support to a project that was to alter Ottoline's life profoundly. In June she turned twenty-three, an age at which her brothers thought they had a right to expect some indication of her future intentions. Yet she showed no interest in any of the activities of a normal young woman of her class and position. "One thing I was quite clear about, clear with a sort of horror," she says in her memoirs, "I could not marry any of the young men who came to Welbeck. I remember visualising myself with dread as the mistress of one of their large houses, entertaining shooting parties, and living with a man to whom I could never talk."[5] Her brothers had become used to Ottoline's absence from the gatherings they enjoyed; now, however, she intruded into their lives again. The idea came not from her but from Miss Craig, her governess, who had stayed on at Welbeck and kept in touch with her former pupil. Miss Craig, concerned that Ottoline was looking tired and unhappy, said one day, "You are being starved. You must go abroad. You must get away."[6] The idea of travelling to the Continent had not occurred to Ottoline before, possibly because her previous visit had terminated in the tragedy of her mother's final illness. Now she screwed up her courage to ask

Portland's permission. At first he raised objections: "Why do you want to go? Are you not happy here?"[7] Then there were the logistics—Ottoline could not be allowed to go travelling around Europe alone. The brothers met in a solemn conclave to discuss the problem and it was only after Miss Craig found a friend, Miss Rootes, a learned lady of impeccable respectability, as companion-chaperone, that Portland reluctantly gave his approval. The archbishop smiled on the plan and recommended Cortina in the Dolomites as a congenial destination.

Ottoline's maid, Ellen, started packing. At the last moment a fourth member was added to the party: the Honourable Hilda Douglas-Pennant, a tall, prim, fussy young woman with a prisms and prunes expression. Although Ottoline knew Hilda only slightly she asked her one day if she would like to come to the Continent and Hilda jumped at the idea. So, as the summer of 1896 faded, the party of four, laden with air cushions, clocks, smelling salts, and fans, travelled via Victoria to Dover, thence to Ostend and Brussels. Hilda was amazed by Ottoline's large red cape, which was in fact a travelling library, Ottoline having sewn pockets around the interior into which she crammed volumes of Ruskin. As they progressed, Miss Rootes, white of hair and long of tooth, commented on passing items of interest. Cathedrals were examined from nave to crypt, art galleries toured, and points of historical interest diligently described. Ottoline took notes in a leather-bound notebook. From Brussels the party proceeded at a leisurely pace by Würzburg, Munich, Innsbruck, and Ratisbon to Cortina. Ottoline travelled in a daze, revelling in her new freedom. Hilda and she became firm friends, and not even Hilda's undisguised distaste for the omniscient Miss Rootes soured Ottoline's enjoyment. In October the weather in Cortina began to close in and the women travelled south to Venice. There the friction between Hilda and Miss Rootes worsened. Ottoline was in a dilemma. She appreciated the older woman's erudition—it was she who opened her eyes, not only to classical literature, but also to the idea that Ottoline might further her scrappy education at some formal institution—but Hilda wanted Ottoline all to herself. Finally Miss Rootes understood and departed, leaving Ottoline, Hilda, and the maid to continue on deeper into Italy. As the luscious countryside drifted past, Ottoline began to blossom. Padua, Bologna, Ravenna, Urbino, Siena, Perugia, Assisi—the romance, mystery, colour, and beauty of northern Italy flooded into her parched soul. For Ottoline Italy became a pulsing symbol of freedom; the richness of the land and the richness of its past overwhelmed her. "I drank then of the elixir of Italy," she said. "I drank so deeply of it that it has never left me."[8]

Ottoline and Hilda had arranged to join Mrs. Scott and for the rest of the winter they stayed with her and her daughters in Rome and Florence. Usually Ottoline relished their company, but this time, liberated as she was from Welbeck and her past, they seemed too serious for her new mood. Even so, she enjoyed these months spent walking through cobbled streets and squares, watching sunsets and visiting galleries with Hilda.

In March 1897 the two returned reluctantly to London, the prospect of which appalled Ottoline. Now that the rash, romantic element in her personality was beginning to free itself, she felt she must "do something." In Italy she and Hilda had talked long and seriously about life, without coming to a firm conclusion. Hilda had introduced her to poetry—to Keats in particular—and now Ottoline thirsted for further mental stimulation. Back at Grosvenor Place she took up some of her old threads, reconvening her classes for young girls and inviting Maclagan to come down from York to deliver his little sermons. It was an advertisement in a newspaper that provided Ottoline with her next escape route. It gave details of preparatory courses for St. Andrews University in Scotland. Remembering Miss Rootes' advice, Ottoline resolved to go to St. Andrews for the coming academic year. This drastic step required another family conference, as it was thought no well-bred girl would want to go to university. The spectre of their eccentric sister turning into a bluestocking and becoming the source of unkind remarks among their circle haunted the family. Ottoline, however, found an unexpected ally in Portland's mother-in-law, Mrs. Dallas-Yorke, who spoke up for the plan and whose support proved decisive. So Ottoline travelled north, stopping off at Bishopthorpe to see the archbishop, then continuing on to Scotland accompanied by a retinue consisting of Hilda Douglas-Pennant, two dogs, the maid Ellen, and Miss Hurblatt, a lady tutor Mrs. Dallas-Yorke had provided for Ottoline and Hilda (who was also bent on further education). They all moved into lodgings at No. 5 Murry Park, near the university.

This was Ottoline's first real excursion outside her upper-class world and she was rather nervous about it. In the university register she entered her age not as twenty-four, but as a coy seventeen. In every way she was an outsider. Her first mistake was the subject she chose, or rather Miss

Hurblatt chose for her: logic. Ottoline's mind never had been logical and never would be. This dry, unexciting course was decided on mainly because Miss Hurblatt had heard that its professor, D. G. Ritchie, was the best at the university. Ottoline, with her debutante's schooling, was utterly unprepared for university, and even Miss Hurblatt's diligent coaching could do little in the teeth of the fact that both young women were entirely out of their depth. Worse, Hilda conceived another of her dislikes, this time for the hapless Miss Hurblatt, and this didn't assist study either. What the other students thought of the menage at Murry Park, and the sight of Ottoline's tall gaunt figure, cape flapping against her legs, scurrying around the cold, windswept town, can be imagined. She tried to make contact with them, but Hilda frowned on too much fraternising. Also, Ottoline's well-meant efforts, abetted by the local bishop, to organise Bible classes for her fellow students fell rather flat. Still, she enjoyed herself. The students had a habit of shuffling their feet if someone of whom they disapproved entered the lecture room, and Ottoline recorded, "I am thankful to say I was never shuffled at."[9] Finally the rigours of the climate and the course, plus a general feeling of ill-health (which had pestered her since the typhoid attack in Italy in 1892) convinced her that logic and St. Andrews were not worth returning to after the summer vacation. She wrote a note to Professor Ritchie thanking him and he replied that he was sorry she had found his course too dry. (Typically, Ottoline and the professor continued to correspond for some years.)

Despite her failure at St. Andrews, the experience was another step away from Welbeck, and the summer of 1898 was the first London Season Ottoline enjoyed. She went to many of the parties and helped her sister-in-law, Lady Henry Bentinck, entertain at 13 Grosvenor Place. Also, the previous Christmas, Ottoline had met a man who was to play a not insignificant role in her life: Herbert Henry Asquith, one of the chief figures in the Liberal Party. Now married to his second wife, the formidable Margot Tennant, Asquith had been Home Secretary in the last Liberal Government and would follow Campbell-Bannerman as Prime Minister in 1908. He was a handsome man of forty-five, with a fine classical intellect and had something of a weakness for women, particularly young women, a weakness he was to indulge discreetly even while at No. 10 Downing Street. Ottoline, down from St. Andrews for the Christmas vacation, met Asquith at a dinner at Grosvenor Place. He was immediately attracted by her rather austere beauty, her obvious intelligence, and her unorthodox outlook on life; also, she was twenty-four and unmarried.

After she returned to London, Ottoline saw more of Asquith. He visited her in her sitting room on the top floor of 13 Grosvenor Place and their talks ranged far and wide. An inveterate correspondent, he lectured her on the merits of letter writing, a lesson she was to take very much to heart. They used to sit together on a deep sofa against white muslin cushions that had belonged to Lady Bolsover and discuss religion, poetry, literature, and politics. He also lent her books by radical authors. Over the several months of 1898 their friendship deepened and in August he wrote to her:

> A year ago nothing cd. have seemed less likely than that, in the ebb & flow of the social tide, you & I would ever have been floated or washed into a creek of our own. But it has been so—has it not? I don't know how you feel & think about it, but for my own part I don't wish to lose touch & to be drifted away & apart again in the stream of chance.[10]

However, Asquith had temporarily to take a back seat to another middle-aged man who in July or August, 1898, swept into Ottoline's life like a comet. This celestial invader was Axel Munthe. Outwardly Munthe was not attractive—very ugly was Ottoline's description of him—though he possessed an athletic, supple figure, remarkable hands, and much charm. There hung about Munthe an air of mystery most women found almost irresistible. A Swede, he had studied medicine in Paris, becoming—so he claimed in his phenomenally best-selling autobiographical book, *The Story of San Michele*—the youngest MD in French history. Later he became a society doctor in Rome, specialising in nervous ailments, disturbances to which rich women seemed particularly prone. Munthe had also built a superb villa above Capri. That summer he was visiting London and had become the target of every society hostess. Lady Henry Bentinck managed to lure him to lunch at Grosvenor Place and it was there that Ottoline first saw this fascinating satyr. Munthe's mystery, his romantic legend, and his slightly insolent manner attracted her, and they were soon discussing the beauty of the regions around Rome and Florence. Ottoline had an added reason for taking an interest in the tall, bearded doctor: her headaches. If Munthe was an expert on anything, it was ladies' headaches; a touch of his long, sensitive fingers on the brow, a look from his cornflower-blue eyes, a few confident words, and the most recalcitrant migraine would vanish. Ottoline's cousin Violet Bentinck also suffered from headaches and this gave Ottoline an excuse for writing to Munthe and asking if he would go down to Ham Common to examine Violet. Of course Ottoline offered to accompany him. They met at Waterloo Station and during the journey found they had much in common: both were descended from Dutch families, both loved Italy, and both had a high sense of duty, though Munthe's sense was less ingenuous than his companion's. Ottoline found she could talk easily and openly with him and decided he was not what she called the "cardboard-pattern sort of person" normally encountered in London society. After the Ham Common trip he came to see her in her sitting room and at the last party of the Season he swept her off her feet, asking her to visit him at Capri. That night, for the first time, Ottoline was sorry to be leaving a party, and as she went out she flashed a triumphant smile at her sister-in-law.

Yet Ottoline could hardly let on to Portland why she wanted to go to Capri. Instead she told her family she and Hilda were going off on another trip to the Continent, to visit a French health spa, and her brothers were quite happy to let her go. In France she received a letter from Munthe repeating his invitation and offering her a villa of her own on Capri. Ignoring Hilda's objections, Ottoline resolved to go. Munthe, she reassured Hilda, was perfectly respectable and quite elderly. Twenty years later Hilda recalled what happened that hot August in 1898:

> Now—once upon a time in the Year One—long ago lost in the mists of forgetfulness, there lived a maiden Ottoline Violet Anne by name. And it came to pass that she persuaded another damsel called Hilda the Haughty to wander alone with her for many years over the face of the earth. And as they went on their way they sang for joy & lightheartedness & carried no burdens save books—many & heavy—until they came to the island of Shadows set in the midst of the Shining Sea where dwelt a great & powerful magician & weaver of spells—Then . . .[11]

No wonder Hilda drew breath, for when she saw Munthe, far from being a safe old gentlemen of at least eighty, he was obviously in the prime of life, and over the next few days Ottoline became his willing captive. The villa he installed them in was exquisite, with a floor tiled in blue marble and a fountain garlanded with flowers. Ottoline seemed in a trance, and as the days went by, Hilda and Ottoline's maid Ellen grew increasingly alarmed. Gradually, Hilda's disapproving glances began to tell. Ottoline told Munthe, "It is too good here. I must fly."[12] What happened over the next few days isn't clear, but Ottoline agreed to stay a little longer. "I knew that he loved me," she wrote in her memoirs. "I had been filled with a spiritual and transcendental desire to pour love into this man, had poured out everything in my heart to him, but now for the first time in my life, I realized the usual feelings of love."[13] They went for a trip to Sorrento and Pompeii, and there Ottoline and Munthe managed to elude Hilda and wander off into the woods alone. Ottoline's memoirs are not explicit about what they did next. She says their hearts "mingled." She wrote: "The physical side of my love was barely awake, only enough to give the abandonment of the heart with complete and passionate warmth."[14] Later they slipped back to Capri in a fishing boat with Ottoline lying covered over in the bottom.

Several days later, accompanied by a scandalised Hilda, she returned to England. Ottoline felt numbed with emotion, but on arrival in London a reaction set in; doubts about whether she should or could love such an unusual and unpredictable man assailed her. Munthe was very proud and she feared he would not face her brothers' wrath by asking for her hand. She sensed too that he harboured reservations. Before she had left Naples he held her arm and said, "I feel there is something in you that you will never surrender to me."[15] Also she began to worry about their spiritual compatibility; once when Munthe had come upon her praying in an Italian church, he made some slighting remark about the intensity of her faith. Yet despite these doubts Ottoline was deeply attracted, and she decided to travel back to Italy to see him. Arriving in Rome, she went to his surgery, taking her place in the waiting room. There she saw, left out on a table for all to handle, a white-vellum-bound copy of Browning which had been her precious personal gift to him. And when she went in to see him he was cold and cutting; he told her she was neurotic: "I could never marry a religious fanatic," he said. "I have quite enough nerve cases among my patients. To have one as my wife would be too much."[16] That was the end of Munthe.

Ottoline retreated to her aunt's villa near Florence to nurse her wounds. She spent days wandering the streets, slowly recovering her spirit. Sometimes a friend of her aunt's, Violet Paget (an intellectual who wrote under the name of Vernon Lee), took her for drives in a pony carriage. Later Ottoline returned to England and Grosvenor Place, where her fashionable sister-in-law was not especially understanding. Portland was also unsympathetic; he was thankful Ottoline hadn't run off with Munthe, but he still feared she might retreat to Cornwall and become a nun. When Ottoline later discovered that her brothers had actually written to each other discussing this possibility she was furious. "Why didn't they ask me?" she complained.[17] She would have told them it was the last thing she had in mind. In the coming years, however, they were to have occasion to wish she had disappeared into a nunnery.

Instead, in April, 1899, Ottoline decided to give education a second chance, and another family conference was convened to approve her plan to go to Somerville College, Oxford, as a home student. This time she would not let Hilda come with her, probably because of her inhibiting influence at St. Andrews. Ottoline took rooms in Oxford and attended lectures on Roman history, also being tutored by a Miss Deverell in history and political economy. This was much more to her liking. Miss Deverell introduced her to socialism and other avant-garde ideas, once taking her to London to hear the anarchist Prince Kropotkin speak. During the summer of 1899 Ottoline remained in Oxford, bicycling around the cobbled streets with a pile of books strapped on the back. Several times she was invited to tea by a member of local society, Mrs. Frederic Morrell, wife of the university's solicitor. It was at the Morrells' house, Black Hall, that Ottoline first met the man she was to marry two years later—the Morrells' elder son, Philip.

In December or January she decided to leave Oxford, giving as her reason her headaches. But that seems a lame excuse. Perhaps she had had enough of academic learning, or perhaps she had got tired of life in Oxford in winter. Yet her decision might also have had something to do with the renewal of her friendship with Asquith. As soon as she returned to Grosvenor Place she began to see a great deal of him—there is a possibility that she may have been seeing him before then, perhaps in Oxford. Though in her memoirs Ottoline doesn't go so far as to call it an affair, it is certain something was going on between them. Indeed, there were strong reasons why she should want to disguise the special nature of their friendship. For one thing, Asquith was married and she was not—an affair publicised could ruin either or both of them. Also, later, after Ottoline married, there was the additional consideration of not wanting to offend her husband. Then there was the difficulty that Asquith, though permissible dinner company, was still a prominent political opponent of the Bentincks; Portland, a member of the ruling Salisbury administration, would not have been amused at an affair between Asquith and Ottoline—and she was still dependent on her half-brother for all her material circumstances.

It is not easy to gauge when their relationship became serious. Ottoline says in her memoirs they became "really intimate" in early 1900, but "intimate" does not necessarily mean an affair.[18] In any event around this date Asquith began making regular visits to Ottoline in her boudoir at Grosvenor Place. Of course they could have been perfectly innocuous. In Edwardian times it was not unusual for gentlemen to visit ladies in their sitting rooms between the hours of four and five when servants were told not to enter unless rung for. Ottoline liked Asquith very much indeed, though she was never totally at ease with him, finding him neither spontaneous nor intuitive. She was pleased that such a man of the world should pay court to her. Later she said, "As I look back on this intimacy, I regret many things, above all that my hypersensitive conscience made me nervous about it, so that I was prevented from drinking its full pleasure and riches."[19] One Sunday Asquith took her to St. Paul's Cathedral where he assured her "of his affections"; this confession disturbed her and she began to fear she might be getting in out of her depth. Unfortunately details of this important period in Ottoline's life are sketchy. Apart from a few tantalizing references in her memoirs, our main source of information is Asquith's correspondence with Ottoline which she preserved (though there is some reason to believe several of the letters have been lost). Before August, 1898 (when she met Munthe) Asquith's letters are fairly formal; then there is a hiatus until February, 1900, when he suddenly abandons his normal didactic tone and instead of opening "My Dear Lady Ottoline" there now is no preliminary salutation and he ends his letters "Your loving friend," with no signature. Most of his letters over the next twelve months are couched in slightly coy terms with oblique references to some mutual secret, and several contain gentle pleas for her to resume a relationship which she has apparently broken off. Three or four are addressed to Switzerland and Germany where Ottoline had fled in April or May, apparently because of her health. Before leaving England she spent some time in a nursing home run by a Miss Nelson Smith in Maida Vale and several of Asquith's letters express his surprise that she had not yet left it. At Easter he wrote saying he wanted to see her especially "to talk about a—lots of things!"[20] A postscript has been ripped off this letter. In another letter he said he was anxious to see her soon: "Can I come to your retreat? or must I wait till you emerge? and when will that be?"[21] Another letter is signed, "I am always and everywhere your loving friend."[22] On June 21, 1900, he wrote to her in Switzerland:

How does the atmosphere feel up there? I write as a dweller in the plains. Does it make you feel as if you have escaped & emancipated yourself from the dim & damp & sometimes poisonous air of the plains? And do you feel that you have got above & beyond the sort of influences which—for instance—dominate Maida Vale? If so, I shd. be very sorry. For, after all, the time which you & I have spent together has been, in what Browning calls the 'level flats.' And I shd. miss something a great deal—if I were to realise that all this was something you had left behind & below! Is it so?[23]

Then there is a gap until Boxing Day, 1900, when Asquith wrote thanking her for a gift, saying, "I was glad to know from your Christmas letters that your anger had abated & been replaced by more Christian & more natural conditions."[24] This letter ends the more intimate part of the correspondence between them. Such letters and the clues in Ottoline's memoirs give scant support to a theory of an affair between them. And Asquith's biographer Roy Jenkins says he knows of no evidence to support such a theory.[25] Yet there is no doubt that Ottoline and Asquith were very close and there are other hints that they did have a physical relationship later.* There is as well an interesting reference made by Lytton Strachey in a biographical sketch he wrote about Asquith. Though Strachey was a notorious exaggerator he mostly stuck to the facts when writing serious biography. In this sketch Strachey relates how he and Henry Lamb were with Ottoline one evening when she brought out Asquith's letters, preserved in a box. She told them, "He used to come and see me in the evening—right up at the very top of the house."[26] They began looking through the letters and Strachey, after recalling that most of them seemed rather dull, goes on: "One letter, which promised to be more interesting,

*See Chapter 12.

was at the last moment (owing to Philip [Morrell]) withheld. I gathered that he had made love to her—perhaps kissed, or tried to kiss her—and that she had objected, and he had written to apologise."[27]

Indeed it seems quite likely Asquith did make some overtures to Ottoline, but how far she responded is impossible to judge. On one hand she had nothing to gain from an affair, but she also had nothing to lose. And if, as seems likely, she *did* have an affair with the middle-aged Munthe, then neither customary maidenly inhibition nor Asquith's age exclude the likelihood of something more than casual friendship. But whether it was just a kiss, or something more, we will probably never know.

In late summer or early autumn of 1900 Ottoline, accompanied by the now ubiquitous Hilda, left Switzerland to go to Germany to consult a Professor Beigel. About sixty, tall and aristocratic "like an old Jewish Rabbi," Beigel, too, fell under Ottoline's spell and after one consultation he bent down and kissed her.[28] In her memoirs Ottoline said: "I do not think anyone has ever been so devoted to me."[29]

On one thing Ottoline was now determined: she would not willingly return to London where the ashes of the Asquith business still smouldered. Nor did the thought of Welbeck and Grosvenor Place beckon; with Portland and her brothers and their way of life she was done. She was stifled by their disapproval; she wanted to escape, to be free, to catch joy on the wing. So she resolved to stay on the Continent for as long as possible. Actually her brothers were probably nowhere near as interested in her doings as she imagined. The Boer War was raging and her youngest brother, Lord Charles, had been wounded at Mafeking. Another brother, Lord William, was to die in 1903 from an infection caught during the fighting. Portland and his wife had financed a field hospital to help the Imperialist cause: None of them had much time to worry about Ottoline's wayward activities. Also, the Druce-Portland Case was brewing, raking up past family idiosyncrasies, much to Portland's annoyance.* So when Ottoline came back briefly to London around Christmas, 1900, to seek means and permission to return to Italy (a course she had talked Professor Beigel into advocating) no hindrance was put in her way. On this London visit Otto-

---

*A case, similar to the Titchbourne inheritance fraud, in which the mother of an Australian gold miner named Druce claimed that her son was the rightful sixth Duke of Portland.

line met Asquith again, probably for the first time since the previous February, and her anger at his advances had apparently cooled. They agreed to remain friends and met several times in January before Ottoline left with Hilda for Sicily.

The two travelled around Sicily for several weeks, usually in the company of a Professor Butcher and his wife. During this trip Ottoline was like a pent-up spring, releasing itself in fits and starts. In her heart she felt a driving desire to be free, but that was a negative urge. She could go round revelling in the sensual delights of the eye and mind, but what else? What about the positive side? She discussed it with Hilda. They decided that when they returned to London they would take a house and live together, leading their separate lives. But although Hilda was her closest friend, Ottoline hungered for someone else who could take a wider view. In Florence they teamed up with an intellectual friend of Vernon Lee's, Maud Crutwell, and the three went off on expeditions into the warm, romantic countryside. They made a strange trio: Ottoline, almost twenty-eight, tall, aloof, with a high-boned face, aristocratic nose, masses of titian hair, dressed always in slightly unorthodox clothes and wearing a large hat and muslin veil to shade her from the sun; Hilda, looking like a spinsterish schoolmistress out on a Sunday jaunt; and Maud, at forty-five the eldest, wearing a man's shirt, sailor hat and a blue serge suit, sitting up in front holding the reins of their pony cart, smoking a cigar, her round, pink, innocent face beaming. They toured Ravenna, Lucca, Pisa, Carrara, then back to Florence before making a reluctant return to England and, for Ottoline, the hardly rivetting prospect of setting up house with Hilda.

GROSVENOR ROAD

Chapter 3

Part i
1901–1903

Indeed, it is not altogether clear why Ottoline did choose to return to London, winter, and memories she had left England to escape. Perhaps Hilda had to come back, or perhaps Ottoline had to see her family again. Perhaps she sensed that ground tours and sybaritic exiles could not go on forever. Hilda was in a similar quandary and during their discussions the two often considered how they could satsify what Ottoline called the "inner life." Marriage—the only answer Hilda could think of—did not appeal to Ottoline: She was not prepared to exchange her hard-won liberty for a new sort of bondage. While they looked round for permanent rooms, Ottoline went back to Grosvenor Place and took over her old sitting room overlooking Buckingham Palace. Asquith came to see her several times, but things were kept on a fairly formal footing. Probably it was he who introduced Augustine Birrell to her.

An interesting and erudite Liberal, who later became Irish Secretary in Asquith's Cabinet, Birrell took a fancy to Ottoline, but she did not encourage him; she had become wary of father figures.

In those winter months of 1901 it must have been obvious to many people that Ottoline was at a loose end, and soon invitations began to arrive to dinners at which she was introduced to a wide range of bachelors. One such invitation came from someone she particularly liked: the former Welbeck librarian, Arthur Strong. Mrs. Strong was friendly with a young man who was in some ways in a similar position to Ottoline. He was Philip Morrell, and it was he who was placed opposite Ottoline at the Strongs' dinner table one evening that autumn. At their earlier meetings in Oxford Ottoline had not taken special notice of him; he was personable enough—tall, handsome with crinkly hair and a largish nose—but nothing to distinguish him from any number of young men she had met. But he had been very impressed with her. He had first seen her cycling around Oxford, and later at Black Hall he had talked to her about his interests—principally art, books, and music. Ottoline had responded politely but he was conscious she came from a higher, more rarefied world—that she was, in Lytton Strachey's phrase, the daughter of a thousand earls. His family, on the other hand, were upper middle class: one branch were brewers, while his side had been solicitors to the university for generations. Ottoline's voice interrupted his thoughts. It was an unusual voice, purring like a cat, dipping and soaring like a bird: "What, Mr. Morrell, do you think of the political situation?" He inclined to the Liberal side— unlike his family, who were solidly Conservative. His father had been Conservative mayor of Oxford and one of his brewer cousins was the sitting Tory member for Mid-Oxfordshire. But at Eton, where he had spent some of the happiest years of his life, he discovered that Liberalism was not the evil he had been brought up to believe. It was there he started collecting blue-and-white china and questioning the presumption he would go into his father's law firm. Why couldn't his brother Hugh go into the firm instead? Then Philip could study something he really wanted to, like literature. His parents were adamant: Hugh wasn't clever enough for law; it was the army for him. So Philip went on to Balliol, where he spent a miserable time acquiring a third-rate degree and a morbid fear he would die young. For the next eight years he tried to make a career of law, but his father rebuffed his efforts to reform the firm's archaic procedures. Finally, after a heated dispute, he moved to London to set up a branch of the firm in Bedford Row, next to Gray's Inn. The venture was not a spectacular success and Philip, now thirty, was left with ample time to cultivate the artistic people he had always pined to meet. With an American friend, Logan Pearsall Smith, and another friend, Percy Feilding, he was dabbling in antiques and going to Chelsea to visit artists such as Charles Conder.

So there Ottoline and Philip sat in the Strongs' dining room: both past the first flower of youth, both to some extent failures and misfits. Later in the month Ottoline invited Philip to tea and they discovered they could converse quite easily. Sometimes Asquith's visits would coincide and the three would sit and talk of life and politics, taking tea from a tray on a low stool.

No question of a serious relationship arose until several weeks later when Mrs. Morrell invited Ottoline down to Black Hall for a weekend. Here for the first time Ottoline felt Philip wanted to marry her. She recalled: "I sat up all night in my bedroom by my fire trying to push away the feeling of pressure that was closing upon me. I felt his personality almost physically elbowing in on me."[1] At first they were reluctant lovers and the letters she wrote to him were hesitant and self-deprecating. She outlined all her faults. She was deeply religious, she told him. She was strongwilled; she had a mind of her own. She also told him of her lonely childhood at Welbeck, and a little of the Axel Munthe affair, confessing she had been swept off her feet by the "boiling cauldron" of the doctor's emotions.[2] In another letter she broached more practical matters; she felt she ought to explain that she had an allowance from Portland of £1,500 a year (in those days a truly handsome sum—eleven years later Leonard Woolf found he could live quite well in London on £300 a year). By Christmas, 1901, Philip's timid courting had brought Ottoline to the point of decision. She was due to go to Welbeck for Christmas while he was going with his father to Italy. They said good-bye at Euston station where he handed her a bunch of lilies of the valley. At Welbeck she still felt unsure about marriage, but the thought of Philip gave her a comfortable glow. Soon after Christmas she returned to London and telegraphed to Italy two words: COME BACK.[3] Philip returned and proposed in her sitting room and was accepted.*

The transition from confirmed spinster to bride-to-be had taken only a few months, and yet it had been no love-at-first-sight affair. Why did Ottoline's independence crumple so swiftly? Probably the decision forced itself upon her. Marriage was virtually the only alternative to the sour, empty life single women were condemned to. She had discovered that education offered no escape, nor was travel a long-term solution, and love affairs were full of pitfalls. Besides, Ottoline at twenty-eight was as ready for marriage as most of her contemporaries had been at twenty-one; she was a late developer, both physically and emotionally. By now the rest of her face had caught up with her nose, and she was a very beautiful woman. Also, her travels and experiences had given her an air of worldliness which, combined with a certain natural aristocratic confidence, made her a challenging and alluring figure.

*From a letter Ottoline wrote to Bertrand Russell in 1911 it seems that Asquith was quite upset when she married Philip. "He was annoyed with me I don't know why because I did not tell him before I was engaged to P—& I have hardly seen him since." (OM-BR, April 10, 1911, McMaster) There is a slight hint here that Asquith might have been pressing his attentions on Ottoline again and that her engagement to Philip thwarted any further intimacy.

At the news of her impending marriage Ottoline's family were profoundly relieved. Admittedly Philip was of lower rank, but at least he was presentable. They did not suspect his liberal leanings—though one of Ottoline's sisters-in-law had a horrible dream that Philip was a Radical. At the wedding Ottoline's youngest brother, Lord Charles (the one she heroworshipped as a child), took Philip aside and told him, "I'm glad I'm not in your shoes. I wouldn't undertake her for anything."[4] Nor, noted Ottoline, did he undertake to give them a wedding present.

The ceremony took place on February 8, 1902, at fashionable St. Peter's church in Eaton Square. Two of Philip's nephews were pages and Ottoline's niece, Lady Victoria Cavendish-Bentinck, her cousin, Lady Violet Manners, and Philip's niece, Dorothy Warren, were bridesmaids. Portland gave her away and the Bishop of Rochester officiated. After the vows were exchanged, the choir sang *O Perfect Love*. Sitting on the bride's side of the aisle were the Marquess and Marchioness of Granby, the Countess of Bective, the Earl of Feversham, Lord and Lady Howard de Walden, together with all Ottoline's brothers and their wives. On the groom's side were his parents, Mr. and Mrs. Frederic Morrell, his sisters and their husbands, and other relatives and family friends. Lady Ottoline Morrell, as she now was, walked out of the church into a new life that would resemble her old existence as little as the gay, Edwardian era resembled the claustrophobic Victorian age which had finally expired with its Queen over a year before.

After a honeymoon in Italy, where Ottoline swam at the Venice Lido wearing a large hat (and where she lost her engagement ring), they returned to a modest house in Grosvenor Road alongside the Thames. During the week Philip would go off to his Bedford Row office while Ottoline indulged her outré taste, creating a pink and grey drawing room and furnishing her boudoir with silk cushions and her favourite books. Most days she would meet Philip for luncheon at a fashionable café in New Oxford Street where they watched enviously the writer Laurence Binyon and his friends talking and laughing at a nearby table. In the evenings they stayed at home reading Gibbon and Macaulay together. After the first few months Ottoline's hopes began to tarnish. Something definitely was lacking. At first she thought it was her husband's job. Philip too was dissatisfied, but he was not prepared to give up his career and become some kind of drone living off his wife's income. He rejected the idea of transferring to the Bar, as it involved trouble and risk, and he did not have enough self-confidence to chance. it. What he really wanted to do was become a writer—a journalist perhaps, or a biographer—and he believed his success with essays at university provided him with some reason for hopes in this direction. He began keeping a writer's notebook, composing little biographical pieces. But such exercises were no answer to the immediate problem of how to escape the deadening influence of the solicitor's office.

In July, 1902, a solution appeared from a direction neither had considered. One weekend at Logan Pearsall Smith's home at Haslemere they met Beatrice and Sidney Webb, who talked about the fortunes of the Liberal Party, which was still recovering from its disastrous drubbing in the 1900 Khaki election. Sidney Webb mentioned a new organisation called the Liberal League which had been formed to help finance young and likely candidates contesting Conservative-held seats. Philip and Ottoline were immediately interested; fighting the Tories and the middle-class imperialism of Joseph Chamberlain appealed to them both. Ottoline sent Philip to see Asquith, who referred him to an official of the Liberal League, who in turn advised him to see Herbert Gladstone, Liberal chief whip. To Philip's consternation the seat Gladstone offered him was South Oxfordshire, in the very heart of Morrell Conservative territory. After some initial hesitation Philip agreed that closeness to home ought not deter him if his convictions were strong enough. The next step was to be adopted by the local Liberal Association, and this was achieved in September when he addressed a meeting in Oxford. After that all hell broke loose. The local press denounced Philip for a complete lack of principle and ability, taking consolation only in the fact that as the constituency had never returned a Radical—and never would—he had no chance of getting in. Philip's family were only slightly less hostile. His father and mother were aghast, while his cousin Herbert Morrell, the Mid-Oxfordshire MP, never spoke to him again. Ottoline's family, though now more tolerant of their scatter-brained relative, were equally shocked, particularly as Portland was a past-president of the National Union of Conservative Associations.

Ignoring all this, Philip and Ottoline launched themselves into trying to win over one of the country's staunchest Tory seats. Though the next election was not due for several years they started touring the constituency in a dogcart, visiting fêtes and addressing meetings. For a while it was exciting and adventurous. Many a winter's night in 1902–1903 was spent dashing between tiny hamlets trying to convert a handful of voters, and once their dogcart was attacked and overturned by angry Conservatives. But as the months wore on the shine wore off; electioneering began to pall and Ottoline again found herself bored and dissatisfied. They still had few friends and almost their only form of entertainment—apart from dull political parties—was attending Sunday concerts at Queen's Hall where they paid 7/6 or 10/6 to hear Beethoven, Bach, Weber, or Liszt. It was not the sort of life Ottoline had dreamed about.

Part ii
1903–1904

Ottoline says in her memoirs: "The years 1904 to 1906 I will pass on one side—save to say they were disagreeable and painful, at this time they do not appear to me very significant. Perhaps I shall return to them if days and health are given to me."[5] But Ottoline did not return, and that which she found so hard to say remained unsaid. What was she referring to? The words "disagreeable and painful" could refer to her pregnancy in 1905–1906 and the death of one of her twin children, together with the period of illness which followed. That these events were sad and painful there is no doubt, but she did write about them—and at length.

Since her marriage, Ottoline had occupied herself mainly helping Philip woo the voters of South Oxfordshire. There were still regular visits to Welbeck and Black Hall, though these were less pleasant since Philip's defection. Hilda Douglas-Pennant and several other friends came to tea and there was shopping and management of the Grosvenor Road household. But most of the time Ottoline was bored. By October, 1903, she had been married for almost two years, and she was far from reconciled to domesticity. For a man it wasn't so bad—he had his clubs, his cronies, and other outside interests—but for a sensitive, intelligent woman with an aristocratic upbringing, being cooped up was irksome. Such a situation, more recognised nowadays, is the subject of a now-forgotten novel called *Cuthbert Learmont*, which was published in 1910. Its author, J. A. Revermort, describes how a tall, copper-haired woman named Mary Fotheringham breaks the bonds of her conventional marriage by having an affair with a Scottish divinity student, Cuthbert Learmont. Some of the details of Mary Fotheringham's fictional life are similar to the reality of Ottoline's life in 1903. Mary had married a reliable but rather dull husband. Finding herself expected to lead the life of a doll in a doll's house, she hungers for a more romantic existence, craving a companion with whom she can share the experiences of the soul. Cuthbert, whom she meets at a party, provides her with just such a kindred spirit; they meet again in the foyer of a theatre and agree to see more of one another. Mary, an elegant, artistic woman with a strange seductive voice and a weakness for dramatic hats, takes to having long intimate talks with Cuthbert, usually in her boudoir, where they discuss books, poetry, music, and spiritual matters. They also go to art galleries and curio shops together. Mary, who often signs her name with her initials, "an M curiously formed," suffers from intense headaches and sometimes goes off to seek cures at health spas.[6]

The parallel between Mary and Ottoline is striking—but not surprising when one learns that J. A. Revermort is the pseudonym of a Scottish-born academic named John Adam Cramb, and amongst Ottoline's correspondence are ninety-four letters from Cramb, most of them written in 1904. Were it not for these letters, which Ottoline kept in a bundle tied with pink ribbon, we would know almost nothing of her friendship with, Cramb. In her memoirs his name appears only once, when Ottoline in passing says that the writer Katherine Mansfield had once been a pupil of "my old friend Cramb."[7] Additionally there is a letter written in 1913 in which Ottoline asks Asquith to give Cramb's widow a pension (he did), also a cryptic reference to Cramb, without mentioning him by name, in a letter from Ottoline to Lytton Strachey on November 2, 1913: "Today I went to West Kensington to see the widow of a very wonderful and eminent man—who died lately—I knew him very intimately."[8]

Who was Cramb? He was not like Asquith or Munthe, still less like Philip. A middle-aged man with a magnificent walrus moustache, he spoke seven languages and littered his letters to Ottoline—written in a crabbed hand on small notepaper from 55 Edith Road, West Kensington—with classical allusions and heavy allegory, interspersed with snippets of Latin, Greek, and Italian. With Ottoline he adopted a Biblical tone, addressing her as "thou." He called himself "thine adoring Raymonde of Ruyremonde" and similar romantic names. Like his semiautobiographical hero Cuthbert Learmont, Cramb trained as a clergyman but gave up before being ordained. In 1887, at the age of twenty-six, he married Lucy Selby Lowndes and in 1892 became a lecturer in modern history at Queen's College, Harley Street, moving up to professor the following year. (He turned down a professorship at King's College, London, because it meant having to subscribe to the Thirty-nine Articles.) At Queen's college, the oldest foundation of higher learning for women in England, he taught what he called "the whole life": painting, music, philosphy, as well as history. He was a strong Imperialist and later became Lord Roberts' speechwriter. And he often visited his students in their homes.

His chief recreation was attending concerts at Queen's Hall, and it was there, in the foyer, that Ottoline and Cramb probably met sometime around the middle of 1903. He offered her a cigarette, which she accepted. They got into conversation and agreed to meet again; soon they began taking regular outings together to art galleries and bookshops, and by April, 1904, they were firm friends, planning expeditions to Richmond Park. One Sunday morning in April Cramb set off from Edith Road for a rendezvous with Ottoline on the District Line platform at Richmond. Apparently she didn't turn up, and in his next letter he chided her, calling her "stern demi-goddess."[9] On May 20 he arranged another expedition, this time to Ottoline's old home at St. Anne's Hill, Chertsey. He also sent her a copy of the Roland memoirs, asking her to turn to a certain page where she would see a picture of "a charming face."[10]

Did Cramb visit Ottoline's home? Certainly Mary Fotheringham's boudoir in *Cuthbert Learmont* could very easily be a description of Ottoline's sitting room at 32 Grosvenor Road. In the book Learmont visited Mary in her boudoir and "on afternoons separated by narrower and narrower intervals, they passed exquisite hours, in music, in reading, in strange talk, or in silences as strange."[11] In May, 1904, Cramb had an emotional outburst "by the river westward towards Kew" and buried his head in her hands.[12] Ottoline realised then that perhaps it had been unwise to encourage him. May 28 saw a crisis. Cramb wrote three letters to her and referred to a telegram of the day before. Three days later Ottoline went to Black Hall and his letters were tactfully less personal, referring to general matters like conscription, labour, and tariffs. But by early June nothing would deflect Cramb's ardour. One Saturday he wrote her a particularly florid note: "Thy letter this morning was a throb of delight. . . . O thou sweet sister . . . couldst but read my heart today how thou wouldst see there all that feeling, all that tenderness which thou didst desiderate and demand!"[13] His tight, cramped handwriting goes on, page after page: "and I accuse myself for saying that thing yesterday—for hadst thou been *well*, I feel that thou wouldst have flung it back at me or simply laughed—yet in spite of my own pain how infinitely sweet thou wert—O thou heavenliest, thou heavenliest sister—what shall I say unto thee? Thou must see, thou *must* see heaven, how coulds't thou speak that word!"

June, 1904, saw the peak of their friendship. Cramb called it "her month," probably because her thirty-first birthday fell in June. They went to more galleries together and for trips to Richmond Park. Then there was a silence from Ottoline. Cramb was distraught: "Thou hast not written? Hast thou a temper? I wish thou wouldst be *sensible*. . . . I know nothing from thy wild statements."[14] Then he asked her to dine with him—"an enchanting possibility"—and by June 20 he was happily calling her "Alvorissima." He wrote again on June 22, twice on June 23, once on June 24, twice on the 25th, and again on the 27th. He suggested a rendezvous at the Grafton Galleries to see the Manet exhibition and pictured himself as a gazelle led by Ottoline on a chain. She invited him to accompany her to Henley. By November, 1904, their friendship had cooled. In a letter postmarked November 18 Cramb hinted that Ottoline had resolved to break off. He said this made him "triste vraiment."[15] By December 15 he was no longer affectionate. However, the correspondence continued on and off in formal terms until 1910. He often mentioned the cigarettes he bought for her at Noteras, 113 Piccadilly—Ladies' No 1 Gold tipped. He had them sent to her home and in one letter he told her that so often had he done this that the assistant knew her address by heart.

Ottoline may not have been aware at the time that Cramb was writing *Cuthbert Learmont*, but after it was published in 1910 he either gave her a copy or she bought one. If she recognised herself in the novel she doesn't appear to have minded—a curious fact, for all her life she was inordinately sensitive to any portrayal of herself or her family. It is likely that Otto-line would not have approved of the ending of *Cuthbert Learmont*, in which Mary leaves her husband and children to go away with Cuthbert. If her friendship with Cramb had taught her anything it was that there was as much danger of being restricted by an affair as by marriage. Cramb had become too importunate; this may have been one reason why she decided to retreat from him. It was one thing to have a liaison with a man other than her husband, but it was quite another for that relationship to domi-nate her life. Ottoline was accustomed to the civilised ways of aristocratic affairs and she had enough affection for Philip and a sufficiently ingrained sense of duty to realise that Cramb might jeopardise the other parts of her life. As well she seems to have had a number of arguments with Cramb, most probably over politics and religion. Perhaps she poured cold water on his ardour simply because in the end she discovered she didn't really have enough in common with him. Yet Ottoline felt a great deal of affec-tion for Cramb, as is shown by what she said and did when he died sud-denly in 1913. In her letter to Strachey she said: "He was as brilliant—& wonderful as anyone I ever met—& now there is a white urn in [Lucy Cramb's] library & it holds his ashes."

Part iii
1904–1906

How much did Philip know or suspect? It is difficult to say, but the fact that Ottoline later went to some lengths to conceal her degree of involve-ment with Cramb indicates she thought Philip was largely ignorant. And even if he did know he was not the type to initiate a blazing row about this sort of thing. As she had occasion to complain later, he was infuriatingly broadminded. Ottoline's friendship with Cramb had provided her an out-let and contact with a mind that, to some extent at least, soared; but her conscience must have been sorely troubled in 1904. A constant theme in her life is the tussle between her puritanical conscience and her wild, ad-venturous romanticism. Neither side could dominate the other for any length of time and as soon as one side had its day, the other was waiting in the wings to take over. Another pattern is an escape reflex: it happened with Munthe and it happened with Asquith; in fact whenever Ottoline had an emotional crisis, a trip abroad or a visit to a nursing home was sure to follow. Though there is no question she did suffer from illnesses, they were often precipitated by dramatic events in her personal life. So after she broke off from Cramb it is not surprising to find her and Philip leaving for a holiday in Spain, returning to Grosvenor Road on a cold January day in 1905. The time in Spain, where they sat in cafés and joined in peasant dancing, was virtually a second honeymoon, and their return to London was something of a fresh start. One rainy afternoon Philip said, "We must make some friends. We haven't any friends."[16] This wasn't quite true: they knew some people—the society painter Sargent, a large number of Liberals, a few literary people, together with old friends like Hilda Douglas-Pennant and Logan Pearsall Smith—but Philip's remark may have indicated he realised that Ottoline's craving for communication and social contact, soon to develop into an obsession, had to be directed into safer, shallower channels. Perhaps Ottoline realised it too.

New friends soon appeared. One day Percy Feilding showed them a painting by an artist named James Pryde and this sparked a scheme to have Ottoline's portrait painted. Pryde, despite his name, was an extremely shy man, and when he came down from Oxford to inspect Ottoline his courage failed. Leaving her sitting in her loveliest lace dress, he fled, returning a little later with a substitute, the photographer Cavendish Morton. Later Pryde did paint a picture of Ottoline, though she didn't think it very flattering. Through Pryde, however, Ottoline met another artist, Charles Conder, whom Philip had met already. Ottoline visited Conder's Chelsea studio where the atmosphere of paint, models, and moral freedom immediately attracted her. Soon the Morrells and Conder and his wife were dining together and making expeditions to Hampton Court. (There has been a suggestion that Ottoline was in love with Conder, but there is no evidence to support this idea.) Ottoline also attempted to make new friends in other directions. She wrote to the novelist George Meredith and to the anarchist Prince Kropotkin, who declined an invitation to dine. Around this time Ottoline also got to know Ethel Sands, a cultivated American woman who painted and held a weekly salon at her home in Lowndes Place, Belgravia. Miss Sands also held court at New-

ington House near Oxford and was a friend of Henry James and his brother William. Henry James, who was also a friend of Mrs. Morrell (it is
said she was the inspiration for Mrs. Gereth in James' *The Spoils of
Poynton*), later became a close friend of Ottoline. Another friend of this
period was Crompton Llewellyn Davies, a solicitor whose humanitarian
views, particularly on land reform for agricultural labourers, were taken
up with gusto by Ottoline and Philip. It was either Davies or the Webbs
who introduced Ottoline to Charles Sanger and his wife Dora, a recently
married couple who held an open house (or rather flat) for their friends
each Friday evening. Sanger, a barrister, had been an Apostle* at
Cambridge and was friendly with several people who were later to be
members of the Bloomsbury group. On her first visit to the Sangers'
Ottoline climbed the several flights of stairs and entered their sparse,
matting-floored sitting room high above the Strand to find Charles and
Dora alone and warming themselves around a gas stove. Later Lytton
Strachey, a tall, gangling young man with a high-pitched voice, arrived
and perched his awkward figure in a basket chair, leaning forward to
warm his hands while he talked animatedly about the Shaw play he had
just been to see. The freedom and informality of such gatherings impressed Ottoline and she resolved that as soon as possible she would try to
start something similar herself.

With Ottoline's social activities burgeoning, the house at Grosvenor
Road was beginning to prove too small and towards the end of 1905 she
and Philip began looking for something larger. There was an added reason for needing more room: in October, 1905, Ottoline made a discovery
that pleased her not one little bit—she was pregnant. What to other wom-
en was a warm invasion, a fulfilment of their destiny, was to Ottoline an
assault upon her person, a burden, the breaking into her existence by an
unknown foreigner. She reacted hostilely, and this hostility could have
caused Philip to feel alienated, for Ottoline implies that there was some
strain in their marriage at this time. She said, "I felt classed with those
unfortunates who have to bear the burden of a child alone, without a husband to share the responsibility."[17] Philip did however have other matters to occupy him at this time; a general election was to be held in Janu-

*A member of the Cambridge secret society called the Cambridge Conversazione So-
ciety, better known as the Apostles or simply the Society, membership of which was extremely select and limited only to the very brightest undergraduates. (Holroyd, p. 179)

ary, 1906, and he was busy campaigning. And, much to everybody's surprise, he was elected Liberal MP for South Oxfordshire. This stroke of luck (for that is what it was: he got in on the biggest landslide in British political history) gave Philip what he craved: a role in life independent of his family and his wife.

His election coincided with the move to their new home, an imposing, spacious Georgian house, 44 Bedford Square, in the heart of Bloomsbury. This was an area that had long appealed to Ottoline—before her engagement she and Hilda had been negotiating to take rooms in a house there. A combination of Georgian elegance and Bohemian shabbiness, Bloomsbury consisted of a series of squares around the British Museum and was separated from the then-fashionable parts of London by the commercial areas of Oxford Street, Regent Street, and Covent Garden. Lately, however, Bloomsbury was beginning to look up. The cafés and restaurants of Percy and Charlotte Streets attracted artists, writers, and younger intellectuals. Also, middle-class people were moving in. Two years earlier, in 1904, Virginia, Vanessa, Thoby, and Adrian Stephen had taken up residence in nearby Gordon Square. But of all the Bloomsbury squares, Bedford was probably the most distinguished-looking—and No. 44 a not inappropriate residence for an up-and-coming MP. A pair of green double doors led into a wide hallway from which a noble staircase curved up to two large first-floor drawing rooms; there floor-to-ceiling windows overlooked the tree-filled private gardens in the square below. The rest of the house was arranged on three floors, plus basement and attic.

Here, early in 1906, Ottoline waited impatiently for her pregnancy to run its course, alternately annoyed at the prospect of becoming a mother and guilty that she should be harbouring such thoughts. Her social engagements had to be curtailed and she filled the tedium with plans to renovate her new house. She also wrote to people like Birrell and Hilaire Belloc asking them to recommend books she might read (Belloc replied dauntingly that Michelet on the French Revolution was as great as Tacitus). Finally the long wait ended and on May 18 she gave birth to twins. One was a boy, to be called Hugh after Philip's brother, and the other a girl, to be named Julian after Mother Julian. Three days later the boy died from a brain haemorrhage. Julian was christened at St. Paul's Cathedral on July 5.

The boy's death shattered both Philip and Ottoline, and Ottoline in particular took a long time to recover. But with the birth her latent maternal instinct asserted itself and she did her best to see that Julian, who was not a strong baby, got excellent care. The child spent most of her time with her nurse at Peppard Cottage, Henley-on-Thames, which Ottoline and Philip had bought as a foothold in the constituency and a retreat from the city. Ottoline tried to busy herself with redecorating 44 Bedford Square, but her old verve was lacking, and her health continued to be a problem. One of her main symptoms was a sort of nervous hysteria which made life for Philip very difficult. The doctors they consulted could only diagnose "nervous upset," but finally it was discovered she was suffering from a gynaecological condition which required an urgent operation. In February, 1907, she went into Miss Nelson Smith's nursing home for surgery. The operation meant that she was unable to have any more children, but as she had no marked aptitude for the maternal life this did not worry her; on the contrary, it gave her both an added reason for leading the sort of life she wanted to lead, and greater freedom to do so. After she recovered she threw herself into helping Philip politically, joining women's associations, helping the district nurse, and taking an interest in municipal libraries. But her heart was not in it. "I am not suited to good works," she said.[18] So she turned instead to something she was good at. She decided "to launch recklessly on the sea of London."

BEDFORD SQUARE

Chapter 4

Part i
1907

London in 1907 was the biggest, most powerful, and most so-phisticated city in the world. In fact, if British civilisation could be said to have had a peak, then 1907 has a strong claim to being its date. The long golden Edwardian summer had still three years to run, and seven more years would elapse before the outbreak of the war that would end Britain's world leadership. Already there were signs of decline; since before 1900 Britain's commercial domination had been waning, and now Germany and America were equal if not ahead in production. But the London of 1907 ignored such sordid statistics. It was the pleasure ground of the rich. Lining the spacious squares and streets of Mayfair, Belgravia, and parts of Kensington were the mansions of the privileged minority who believed the world existed for their benefit. In an inner crescent of suburbs, from Hampstead round to Greenwich, resided the only slightly less privileged middle classes, who were beginning to discover that they too could share the sophistications and leisure activities that previously had been the preserve of their betters. And, below them, in an ever-widening sea of surburban sprawl, lived the six million or more other Londoners to whom £200 a year represented riches beyond their ken.

To the fortunate one million London presented a pleasant prospect. With no income tax worth speaking of, life went on in a leisurely fashion, largely horse-drawn, and centering around the comfortable clubs of Pall Mall and Piccadilly, the well-stocked emporiums of Knightsbridge and Oxford Street, and that most civilised of institutions, the House of Commons, in which, thanks to the previous year's election, a solid rump of Liberal gentlemen was presiding over what was believed to be the transition from a stuffy, restricted Victorian England to a bright, new, modern and progressive state in which, through education and opportunity, the poor would better themselves. A spirit of reform and optimism was in the air. As Leonard Woolf said, "It seemed as though human beings might really be on the brink of becoming civilised."[1]

59

Behind this elegant Edwardian façade the ladies of the well-to-do classes presided effortlessly over the day-to-day mechanics of society. Assisted by their servants, they spent their days arranging their homes to cater for the various social functions that were the hub of Edwardian life. With few restaurants, and outside evening entertainment confined to the occasional play, opera, or ballet, most social events took place in private houses. Though less convention-ridden than in late Victorian times, society still had a strict hierarchy: morning calls, luncheons, afternoon calls, teas, dinners, suppers, and that most quintessential of Edwardian activities, the "at home." Being a hostess gave many women a chance to use talents and abilities that would otherwise have had no outlet. They turned their houses into cultural or intellectual oases, or merely centres of gossip. And a few did so in such a style that they qualified for the exalted title of salonnière.

Edwardian London had many flourishing salons. They ranged from the glittering Friday evening assemblies convened by Millicent, Duchess of Sutherland, through other aristocratic gatherings of hostesses like Lady de Grey, to the comparatively modest get-togethers of middle-class people like the Sangers. Even Bloomsbury, though off the fashionable beaten track, was not lacking in salons. Lady Prothero, one of Ottoline's Bedford Square neighbours, was a noted hostess, while in nearby Gordon and Fitzroy squares the Stephen sisters had just begun their recondite conversaziones.

Ottoline spent much of 1907 getting 44 Bedford Square in order. She and Philip planned the renovations together, Philip looking after the rearrangement of doorways and chimney-pieces and designing bookcases for the library, while Ottoline conceived a rather daring grey-and-yellow colour scheme for the drawing rooms. Around the house she placed urns of golden chrysanthemums and piled the sofas with her favourite silk cushions. The early entertainments held in these rooms were mainly for Philip's political colleagues, but soon Ottoline expanded her guest lists, hoping, she said, to "leaven the heavy political dough."[2] She had a solid core of old friends—Hilda Douglas-Pennant, Ethel Sands, Logan Pearsall Smith, Crompton Llewellyn Davies, the Sangers, and several others—and to these were added people she met when dining at friends' homes. She particularly admired the sort of people Ethel Sands mixed with. Miss Sands and her friend Nan Hudson (also a painter) held a salon in their

Belgravia town house, which was frequented by such people as Henry James, Max Beerbohm, Sargent, and Sickert—just the brand of guest Ottoline was hoping to draw into her net.

By early 1908 she had branched out and started what was to be her famous Thursday evening at homes. She chose the at home because it was a particularly flexible method of entertaining that guaranteed a wide range of guests. To be invited, virtually the only qualification was some talent or interest in the arts, and acceptance assured a pleasant evening and the chance to meet someone famous, interesting, or promising (not to mention the chance of being seen yourself). In her quest for guests she searched the highways and byways of the capital. Other hostesses' guest lists were plundered ruthlessly. She loosed showers of missives to writers, painters, and poets, praising their work and inviting them to Bedford Square. Each morning she would sit down in her boudoir and write to people she was getting to know. (She had a telephone but preferred the post.) Her letters were written in a unique script full of loops and curlicues and in a distinctive sepia ink that became her personal trademark. And at the bottom was what must be one of the most beautiful signatures ever composed. It took a cold heart—or an exceptionally timid one—to turn down one of these flattering enticements.

Ottoline didn't entertain every Thursday—some weeks she went out to other people's parties but her at homes soon became fairly regular. Arriving at No. 44 between nine and ten P.M., the guests would be ushered up the winding stairs by the parlourmaid. Twenty or more people might be there already (some had probably also dined at Ottoline's) standing in the double drawing room on the Oriental rugs in casual conversational knots or sitting on sofas drinking coffee and discussing politics, art, or the latest Shaw play. Usually there were snacks and sometimes champagne, but Ottoline was not keen on strong alcohol—it brought on her headaches—and often she merely served cider or cordials. In these early days she made many mistakes. Often her enthusiasm would run away with her and the most incongruous people would find themselves staring at one another across the carpet and an unbridgeable abyss of class, behaviour, and interest. The writers and politicians usually got on well together: Asquith, Ramsay MacDonald, Augustine Birrell, Charles Masterman, and other (usually radical) MP's enjoyed mixing with writers like James, critics like Beerbohm, and poets like Yeats. Where difficulty arose was when members of the Smart Set, inhabitants from Ottoline's old world, came to see the scallywags she was mixing with. These people tended to sit stiffly in their chairs, afraid to unbend. But as Ottoline's social technique developed she managed to sort out her guests better, keeping sticklers for formality like Beerbohm and James away from the scruffy artists and diverting any Smart Set people to the innocuous morning or afternoon visits.

Over the next seven years—from 1908 to 1915—a strange but rich assortment of people began to regard the drawing and dining rooms of 44 Bedford Square as probably the most civilised few hundred square feet in the world. For these people, some already famous, many soon to become so, Ottoline came to be a combination of friend, critic, patron, muse, and goddess. There was a unique, exotic air about her house, a heady atmosphere many people found intoxicating. And at the centre of it all was the lady herself—so extraordinary a figure as to be almost an apparition. Dressed habitually in a fashion verging on the bizarre—sometimes in a Grecian style, at others like a Cossack or an Oriental princess—she had a compulsive interest and enthusiasm for everything and everyone. She desperately wanted her guests to get to know each other, to mix, to exchange ideas. Her mind was forever busy dreaming up new combinations of people to invite. "Conversation, talk, interchange of ideas—how good it was," she wrote later.[3] Greedy for friendship, she was carried away with her new life—it was all so exhilarating, new, and exciting. And other people caught her excitement. The painter William Rothenstein was one. In December, 1908, less than two years after Ottoline's operation, he wrote her: "You have the most delightful salon in London."[4]

Part ii
1908–1909

Yet the list of famous names that fill page after page of Ottoline's visitors' book is only of marginal interest—a dozen other hostesses could boast of guest lists equally impressive. What makes Ottoline unique is the role she played in the lives and careers of a relatively small number of these people. For she was not content to remain on the sideline and watch the throng of talent that beat a path to the green double doors of 44 Bedford Square; nor was she happy just to pick up vicarious crumbs of glory dropped by the talented ones as they passed through. No, she also wanted something *from* them. Passionately, desperately, she yearned to infiltrate their lives, to help them, encourage them, champion them, to share their creative experience—her long-sought-after "experiences of the soul." In return she was prepared to give a great deal. And the extent to which she succeeded raised her far above the level of a mere hostess.

This success did not come cheaply. Later the price she had to pay proved high indeed. But in 1907 Ottoline saw none of this, although she did not lack for warnings. An explicit one came from that most fastidious observer, Henry James, who was a regular visitor to Bedford Square and took a fatherly interest in her activities. One evening, after observing a boisterous group of young people at one of her Thursdays, he put his hand on her arm and said, "Look at them. Look at them, dear lady, over the bannisters. But don't go down amongst them."[5] Ottoline commented: "I disobeyed; I was already too far down the stairs to turn back." Further warnings came from her family and their Smart Set friends. They thought Ottoline's activities bordered on the "fast." But such warnings fell on deaf ears, especially as, around Christmas, 1907, an exciting prospect loomed—a meeting with the romantic, mysterious figure of Augustus John.

John was precisely the sort of person who appalled Henry James: "He paints human beings like animals and dogs like human beings."[6] But Ottoline did not agree. She had first met John three years earlier in Conder's studio. Then John had been the epitome of the struggling artist, so poor he had to stay in bed so that his wife, Ida, could darn his only suit. Conder had shown some of John's nude sketches to Ottoline who was shocked by the expanses of bare flesh. Lately John had prospered, and, at twenty-nine, was on the verge of popularity. Ethel Sands had invited him to her home for dinner and the other guests included the painter Walter Sickert, Prince Antoine Bibesco—and Ottoline. As usual John was late and while they waited for him they discussed his scandalous reputation. Ottoline recalled his dramatic looks: his pale, bearded face, dark auburn hair, eyes "like sea anemones," delicate hands—more expressive even than Axel Munthe's—and gold earrings.[7] Someone mentioned John's torrid private life; of how his mistress, Dorelia McNeill, had moved in with

John and his wife to live à trois, how Dorelia and Ida had both had children by John and how a year ago Ida had died in childbirth. Finally John arrived, dressed to everyone's surprise in orthodox evening clothes, though still sporting his gold earrings. Miss Sands seated him next to Ottoline and the two spent most of the evening discussing John's compulsive hobby: gypsies. Though deprived of actual Romany blood, since his father was a middle-class Pembrokeshire lawyer, John had done the next best thing and adopted gypsy dress, gypsy habits, and the gypsy mode of life. He had taken his unconventional ways to the Slade art school in London where his draughtsmanship was considered second to none. Later his startling, black-cloaked figure was a familiar sight around Bohemian London.

To Ottoline, already attracted to the intuitive, relaxed world of artists, John seemed infinitely romantic, and his slightly aggressive manner and hesitating way of speaking made him no less attractive. And he was equally impressed by her. Suddenly he said, "Will you sit to me? Will you come? Tomorrow?"[8] Ottoline agreed, and next day she and Philip walked over to his studio in Fitzroy Street, not far from Bedford Square. After climbing a narrow staircase they found John, dressed neatly in a grey suit with a silk handkerchief around his neck, standing in front of a large unfinished painting.* His studio—a large room in which he also lived and slept—was clean and tidy, but there was no sign of Dorelia, who was apparently in Paris looking after John's brood of children. A little later two more people arrived, a blunt-faced man with reddish hair and a pleasantly spoken woman with Grecian features whom John introduced as Clive and Vanessa Bell. (Bell was a young art critic and Vanessa one of the Stephen sisters.) Ottoline invited John to return for tea to Bedford Square and there Philip mentioned that John might like to paint Ottoline's portrait. John agreed, but this scheme had to be postponed as he was due to leave in a day or so to rejoin Dorelia in Paris, while Ottoline and Philip were going to Peppard Cottage.

Ottoline was moonstruck, and while snowed in at Peppard she read Balzac and dreamed of John. By March she was writing long letters to him in Paris and sending him presents, including Wordsworth's poems.

*Called Seraphita, inspired by Balzac's novel of the same name, the painting, Ottoline says, depicted "a girl dressed in a tight black dress standing on a mountain top with strange ice-flowers at her feet." (*Memoirs,* Vol. 1, p. 157)

He wrote back saying, "I do not intend to allow you to forget the portrait suggested by Mr. Morrell."[9] They discussed Dostoievsky and the French primitive painters. By April their letters had become more personal; she was impatient for him to return and in reply he said London horrified him—perhaps he could transfer his studio, and her with it, to Paris? By May Ottoline was even more impatient; she wanted to know exactly when he would return and added that she feared he might be disappointed with her. He reassured her he would not be and said he was returning almost immediately. Finally towards the middle of May he did start back, telling her he was disaffected with Paris. "The gypsies have a saying," he told her. "The dog who walks finds the bone."[10] Normally Ottoline would not have appreciated being likened to a bone, but the imminence of John's return put all else out of her mind.

Within days of his getting back she was going to his studio for regular portrait sessions. It was a situation tailor-made for seduction. Few women could have resisted John—and indeed, over the years, few women did. By May 30, after several sittings both in his studio and at Bedford Square, he wrote to her dropping the formal "Dear Lady Ottoline" and signing himself "Elfin":

> At last I am alone—in bed and can write to you Ottoline—as I promised. When you were in my studio to-day I wished I could cry—I should have felt more intelligent perhaps—with the delicatest & noblest of women loving me so infinitely beyond my deserts. . . .
>
> I have always been so excessively anxious to feel myself quite alive that I have plunged with needless precipitation into the most obviously fast flowing channels where there are rocks & bubbles & foam & whirlpools & the water seems perhaps more watery if less pure. . . . Since my wife's death there have been few opportunities of excitement [or] intoxication that I have let pass and this plan has saved me from deadly morbidity at any rate if it has not improved my complexion altogether. But one doesn't meet Ottoline everyday—we *can't* go on thus, darling that you are—you will only get unhappy & I shall hate myself. Don't let us spoil a beautiful thing . . . and let us be gay like herpes![11]

Their affair was not a protracted one and reached its peak around July, 1908. They were happy months. Ottoline revelled in the spontaneity and impulsiveness of John's attentions and was flattered by his desire to paint and draw her. Between May and July they met several times a week, usually in his studio, where he made scores of sketches of her, most of which were ripped from his block and discarded on the floor (many of them were retrieved however and John subsequently sold them).

What did John see in Ottoline? It might be thought that his interest could have had commercial overtones—that he realized she could help his career. Help him she certainly did, but he was unquestionably attracted to her, as his letters to her indicate. Also, Ottoline was a very alluring woman when she fell in love with John in 1908. A snapshot taken about this time gives some idea of her appeal: It shows a long nose and strong jaw, challenging eyes, a soft mouth, and high cheekbones that betray her aristocratic background; the pose she strikes—sitting upright on a sofa, cigarette (a daring departure in those days) in her left hand—is rather militant, an impression reinforced by her military-style tunic and Cossack hat. She is certainly a figure to challenge a man such as John. Why did she deceive Philip? Indeed, why did she embark on the affair? There has been a suggestion that Philip had tended to shun Ottoline since her operation, but this is rather hard to believe; more likely he simply was busy with his legal and parliamentary activities and was content that his wife was occupied. Ottoline's motives were more complex. Apparently she had the idea that in having affairs with people like John she was not only having fun but performing a duty. She was acting as a mother and a ministrant angel to the "creative flame." She herself recognised this, and in her memoirs there is a revealing dialogue with "an old friend of John" (the friend of course Ottoline's own better self). The dialogue runs:

> "I expect he says he loves you?" she said, turning simply to me.
> "No, never [Ottoline replied]. He may feel attracted by my being strange to him, but I am far too different to him. He could only feel at ease with one of his gypsy clan. If I was one of them perhaps he would let himself go, but he is afraid of a woman such as I am."

Even so, Ottoline believed she could help John, if only fleetingly, and she tells the "friend":

> "I cannot touch his melancholy. What I can give him is not what he wants. He .calls for something strong, reckless and rampant, which will carry him off his feet, and he knows too well that it is not mine to give."[12]

The friend says that she had heard John call Ottoline an angel. This was a role that rather appealed to her, so Ottoline continued to hover over John, showering gifts on him. They exchanged rings and she gave him cushions, chocolates, books on poetry and Plato, lilies, and a small watch similar to the one she had given Asquith (unfortunately it broke down almost continuously). John was unlike anyone Ottoline had known before. His courtly, old-fashioned manner and romantic aura captivated her, and even when she wasn't with him he would haunt her thoughts. "He would appear in my imagination as if he passed through the room, suddenly making the conventional scene appear absurd," she wrote.[13]

In July John went back to France to rejoin Dorelia and his children in Paris. Ottoline continued to write, but soon the first indication of discord appeared. John apparently wrote something frivolous and she upbraided him for it. In another letter he told her she did not have to prove her generosity to him (a lament of many people whom Ottoline befriended). By October John was back in England and thinking of taking a house in Chelsea; ominously, Dorelia was with him. Despite Ottoline's efforts he was beginning to slip away. She tried to help some of his impecunious friends, including the American sculptor Jacob Epstein, who was in trouble over some figures he had carved for a building in the Strand. Ottoline and Philip went to see him and commissioned a garden statue. Epstein was overjoyed: "A garden statue sounds delightful; sculpture outdoors amongst trees and shrubs; it is reminiscent of Italy and France."[14] Ottoline also tried to help Henry Lamb, a young artist who was something of a disciple of John's; she sent a cheque for Lamb to John, but the latter returned it, saying Lamb wasn't that needy. As well Ottoline bought four sketches from John and tried to interest her brother, Lord Henry, and several of her friends in John's works.

However, by the end of November Ottoline was accusing John of ingratitude; he replied:

DEAR OTTOLINE,
Of course I like the ring & wearing it, but you give me so many things it makes me shy of accepting more and whether you like it or not I find pleasure in it—I have a natural taste for barbaric splendour; and your giving the ring doesn't make it less precious! . . . . It is more difficult to receive than to give.[15]

Now John began to miss appointments, but Ottoline was still prepared to forgive. On November 23 he denied he had found her dull and stupid the day before. In December he wrote saying he was sorry she was feeling miserable and asked if he could bring two of his boys to visit her one day. He added that a concert might be nice and hoped he would feel the right way about it when the time came. But by the ninth he could not come after all and he also apologised for having forgotten the Bells' luncheon: He had been shopping with Dorelia. In another letter, probably also in December, 1908, he told her that Dorelia was the only person he loved and added that "in loving her I am loyal to my wife" (the deceased Ida).[16] He insisted Ottoline must not feel worthless: she was wonderful and there would always be some cord between them, despite Dorelia—a cord

so fine, so fragile that to strain it would break it, or to ask more from it than from the faint zephyrs of the air, or a more audible more definable message than the glimmer of a star in flight, for ever. . . . And you will not continue to suffer too much. You will have the fortitude of great hearts & unconquerable souls—and the sweetness of the music of Heaven will teach you to smile at last with the sweetest smile of all, and the profoundest. Bless you Ottoline—Elfin.

In the contest between Dorelia and Ottoline for John's affections Dorelia held most of the cards. Ottoline might have background, title, culture, allure, and whatever, but it was Dorelia who was actually living with John; also, she was the mother of two of his children (as well as being in charge of the rest). And she was a determined woman.

From November, 1908, to March, 1909, Ottoline continued to bombard John with almost daily letters and weekly invitations. Manfully he tried to juggle the two women but in the end he was unequal to the task. The pull of Dorelia proved too strong and slowly John disengaged himself from his high-flown dalliance. Ottoline tacitly admitted defeat in March when she wrote to Dorelia asking her and John to dine and meet the Bells. Dorelia, a forthright woman with a strong streak of pride, declined: "Thank you very much for your invitation, but I can't come as I think it rather ridiculous to be introduced to people as Mrs. John. I do not know the Bells. . . . John asks me to say he will be pleased to come."[17] A few weeks later Ottoline and Dorelia met at last when Ottoline came to John's new studio in Chelsea to resume her portrait sittings. She decided that Dorelia had dignity and repose and a firm grip on the John household; the ice between them melted and they were soon on the best of terms. At Bedford Square, however, things were not so amicable. The ever-patient Philip finally had become not only suspicious but hostile. As early as December 18 John had said in a letter to Ottoline: "I was really not surprised that Morrell should have been out of humour. I felt I was cutting rather an offensive figure in your house. I should be very sorry to disturb so admirable a personage as your husband"[18] And in January he wrote: "I think it evident that your husband don't like me."[19] So Philip, for one, was relieved as it became clear that John's interests lay elsewhere. At the end of March Ottoline asked John's boys to Peppard for Easter and there she and Philip took them out on to the Common with Julian, now a lively toddler, to fly kites. The visit was a success, though Ottoline found the boys' unconventional upbringing had made them rather ragamuffinish, and when she asked one of them what he normally ate at home he replied gruffly: "Bones."[20]

Throughout spring and early summer of 1909 Ottoline continued to sit to John. She analysed his character and found it had two sides: "His direct, ruthless, animal gypsy side, loving primitive men and women, and things ugly and cruel, and his simple, nervous, sensitive side—the imaginative, idealist poet."[21] Early in May Philip, Ottoline, John, Dorelia, and a pair of American art lovers, Mrs. Chadbourne and a Mrs. Kochlin, had a day's outing at Hampton Court. Of the six, John and Ottoline stood out: John in a high black hat and looking rather sulky and Ottoline resplendent in an extravaganza of a hat (held on by a veil) and a full-sleeved Spanish-style dress, like something out of a Velasquez painting. John didn't like the rooms full of old masters, and the only time he got excited was when they saw a herd of deer on the way home. But a worse outing occurred in July when John invited Ottoline to come to visit him and his menage where they had encamped in a meadow outside Grantchester. It sounded wonderfully romantic—a day with John gypsy-style—and Ottoline eagerly accepted. John met her at the station at Cambridge in a gig he had hired, but as Ottoline made to enter the vehicle the horse let out a neigh and collapsed on the road. John dismounted, looked at the horse lying twitching on the ground, and lit a cigarette. Eventually two station loafers came and pulled the horse to its feet, allowing Ottoline and John to proceed to Grantchester. There Ottoline discovered Dorelia and her sister struggling to do the washing and cooking in the most primitive conditions and in no mood for light conversation. It began to rain. Dinner was a miserable affair consisting of a crust of bread and fresh fruit and afterwards Ottoline decided to call it a day, getting back to London damp and bedraggled. Yet their friendship survived that hapless afternoon, and two days later John wrote calling her "chère amie" and asking her to sit to him when he got back to London.[22] But as time went on they saw less of each other, though they continued meeting on and off and would occasionally dine together. For the rest of Ottoline's life they were on good terms and went on corresponding, although John confessed that he never fully learned to decipher her letters ". . . which were written in a character of her own invention, so original and precious as to be almost indecipherable."[23]

Part iii
1909

Around March, 1909, Virginia Stephen wrote: "We have just got to know a wonderful Lady Ottoline Morrell, who has the head of a Medusa; but she is very simple & innocent in spite of it, & worships the arts."[24] It may have been that Virginia met Ottoline earlier than this as her sister Vanessa and her husband Clive had been frequent dinner guests at 44 Bedford Square since their first meeting with Ottoline in John's studio just over a year before. Virginia and Vanessa had been living in Bloomsbury since 1904, moving there with their brothers Thoby and Adrian after the death of their father, Sir Leslie Stephen. In November, 1906, Thoby died suddenly and within a few months Vanessa had married Clive Bell. They remained at 46 Gordon Square while Virginia and Adrian moved to Fitzroy square to set up their own establishment. After Virginia and Adrian settled in they revived the Thursday evening at homes that Thoby had started at Gordon Square for his Cambridge friends, and it is from this time that some people date that most discussed phenomenon, Bloomsbury.

There are many views of Bloomsbury (or, to be more accurate, the Bloomsbury Group). Some argue about its membership, others about its importance, still others about its very existence.* Probably the least disputable thing that can be said is that whatever it was, it revolved around the Stephen sisters, their relatives, and Cambridge friends. Its main concerns were ideas, art, music, and literature and its principal tenet was freedom of expression, a legacy of the fact that several of its leading lights had been Apostles who at this period were much influenced by the philosopher G. E. Moore and his theories about honesty in personal relationships. In practice Bloomsbury was a very liberated group and some (though by no means all) of its members were homosexuals. Although several of the group—notably Virginia Woolf, Lytton Strachey, and J. M. Keynes—produced work of major significance, probably what distinguished Bloomsbury most was its conversation. Virginia Woolf's biographer, Quentin Bell, quotes her account of an event that happened about August 1908, which gives a flavour of the revolutionary nature of Bloomsbury talk:

> It was a spring evening. Vanessa and I were sitting in the drawing room. . . . At any moment Clive might come in and he and I should begin to argue—amicably, impersonally at first; soon we should be hurling abuse at each other and pacing up and down the room. Vanessa sat silent and did something mysterious with her needle or her scissors. I talked egotistically, excitedly, about my own affairs no doubt. Suddenly the door opened and the long and sinister figure of Mr. Lytton Strachey stood on the threshold. He pointed his finger at a stain on Vanessa's white dress.
> "Semen?" he said.
> Can one really say it? I thought & we burst out laughing. With that one word all barriers of reticence and reserve went down. A flood of the sacred fluid seemed to overwhelm us. Sex permeated our conversation. The word bugger was never far from our lips."[25]

Though Ottoline has been described as "the patroness of Bloomsbury" and the "high priestess of Bloomsbury," she was never remotely near to being a member of the group. Her relationship with its members fluctuat-

---

*Its early members included Virginia and Vanessa Stephen, Clive Bell, Lytton Strachey, Duncan Grant, Adrian Stephen, Maynard Keynes, and Saxon Sydney-Turner. Gradually its membership widened to include Roger Fry, Harry Norton, David Garnett, the Shoves, Molly and Desmond MacCarthy, Mary Hutchinson, and various others.

ed, and was deeper with some (particularly Lytton, Virginia, and, for a time, Clive Bell) than others. That she was attracted to Bloomsbury is easy to understand—their talk was a fresh gust in her drawing room and she admired their cleverness and talent—but that they should be attracted to her might seem slightly odd, particularly in light of the dismissive remarks they made about her later on. Quentin Bell, for example, appears to be speaking for Bloomsbury when he refers to her as "extremely simple and not very clever."[26] Yet he goes on to say that Bloomsbury members found Ottoline likable: "She brought petticoats, frivolity and champagne to the buns, the buggery and high thinking of Fitzroy Square."[27] Indeed, Ottoline gave Bloomsbury a chance to indulge its less serious side and she herself was most friendly with its more frivolous element: Lytton, Virginia, and Clive. The more serious ones—Leonard Woolf, and Saxon Sydney-Turner, for example—normally found her too rich for their palate. It was more or less coincidental that Ottoline and Bloomsbury moved into each other's orbits. They had friends in common—particularly Augustus John—and they lived in the same part of London. More significant, perhaps, is that they were all refugees from the smart and respectable sections of society. Thus, given her propensity for seeking out talent and intelligence, it is not surprising that after Ottoline's visit to Fitzroy Square she wrote asking for the names and addresses of all of Virginia's "wonderful friends."[28] Over the next few years Ottoline and Bloomsbury were to see a lot of each other. She and Philip—or John or Henry Lamb—would drop round to Fitzroy Square and Vanessa, Clive, and Virginia often turned up at Bedford Square to revel in what Virginia called "that extraordinary whirlpool."[29]

Probably Ottoline's strongest link with Bloomsbury was painting. Moore's philosophy was a mystery to her, but she could and did appreciate contemporary French and English art, and in this, as in many things, she was completely out of step with popular and fashionable opinion which at this time still clung determinedly to the Victorian Royal Academy style. It was for young, struggling artists that Ottoline felt special sympathy and she saw that here she might do something worthwhile. So she lent her patronage to the contemporary art scene, buying and championing such artists as John, Epstein, and Duncan Grant. Early in 1909 she met the critic and painter (and later Bloomsbury member) Roger Fry and joined with him in an ambitious project to encourage English artists.

In March, 1909, Fry wrote to D. S. MacColl, keeper of the Tate Gallery, proposing lunch with himself and Ottoline, saying: "She has been very good to me and has a real feeling for art. You know she has patronised John a good deal."[30] In April the three of them plus C. J. Holmes, a friend of Fry's, decided to launch a fund dedicated to buying works of current English artists. The fund was a success and in 1910 it was re-named the Contemporary Art Society; its first committee members in-cluded Fry, Clive Bell, Ottoline, MacColl, and Holmes. During its first three years the society bought works by John, Epstein, Conder, Sickert, and Henry Lamb, and for a short time Ottoline acted as its buyer.

The pace of Ottoline's life was quickening. Not only did she have her household to run, and parties, dinners, and at homes to preside over, but her political entertaining on Philip's behalf was becoming more important as, towards the end of 1909, it was clear that a general election would be held soon. And if, as expected, the Tories were to make up some of the ground given up in 1906, South Oxfordshire would be one of the first Lib-eral seats to fall. Not only did Ottoline support Philip on the platform at several big Liberal rallies but she also did her bit entertaining charabanc-fuls of Liberal women trucked down from Oxfordshire for afternoon tea and inspection of the baby daughter of their MP. Then there were ritual pilgrimages to such shrines of Liberal patronage as Mells, home of the Liberal doyenne, Lady Horner, where Ottoline felt distinctly uncomfort-able—it reminded her of Welbeck. A more pleasant visit took place in September, 1909, when Logan Pearsall Smith took Ottoline and Philip to Bagley Wood, near Oxford, to see Bertrand Russell who was married to Logan's sister, Alys. A year older than Ottoline, Russell also came from an old aristocratic family and was the co-author of *Principia Ma-thematica*. He was also something of a prig and had for some time har-boured a poor opinion of Ottoline, mainly because he believed her use of scent and powder indicated she was a flibbertigibbit. However, his friend Crompton Davies, with whom Ottoline and Philip had worked improving the lot of farm labourers, caused him to revise this opinion. Recently Rus-sell had interested himself actively in politics, becoming a courageous supporter of women's suffrage and only avoiding being adopted himself as a Liberal candidate through his prospective supporters' last-minute dis-covery that he was a practising atheist. Nevertheless he resolved to aid the Liberals somehow and, disliking his local Liberal candidate, offered to help Philip in South Oxfordshire. In the course of the campaign he had many opportunities to get to know Ottoline, discovering as he says in his autobiography, that she was "extraordinarily kind and much in earnest about public life."[31] But both his and the Morrells' efforts were in vain and when the results came out early in 1910 Philip's seat was lost.

Meanwhile Ottoline's friendship with Dorelia had led to the two women going off together in October, 1909, to Paris where they stayed with the rich Mrs. Chadbourne and went to see an exhibition of Postimpressionist paintings. Later Ottoline accompanied Mrs. Chadbourne to Matisse's studio where the artist showed them—rather commercially, thought Ottoline—some of his work, an example of which Mrs. Chadbourne wisely purchased. Then Philip came over and he and Ottoline visited Gertrude Stein, an occasion Miss Stein recorded in her *Autobiography of Alice B. Toklas,* describing finding Ottoline on her doorstep looking like some "marvellous female version of Disraeli."[32]

Chapter 5

Part i
1909–1910

ALTHOUGH Ottoline didn't realise it, her separation from John did not occur entirely of its own accord. It had received a distinct nudge from Dorelia. Perceiving that John was quite content to let the affair drift desultorily along, Dorelia took matters into her own hands and cast about for some way of diverting her aristocratic rival. And in September, 1909, she hit upon a brilliant idea. One day towards the end of that month she prevailed upon Ottoline to go with her to see a school she was considering for John's boys. On the way there they stopped off at John's old studio in Fitzroy Street. Dorelia left Ottoline waiting in the taxi while she went inside, explaining that she wanted to leave a message for Henry Lamb, who now lived there. As she waited in the cab Ottoline's mind drifted to memories of previous visits to Fitzroy Street. Suddenly a voice interrupted her reverie. "Won't you come in for a moment? Dorelia sent me."[1] Ottoline looked up and there, standing by the taxi window, was a figure that seemed to have escaped from a vision of Blake's—a pale slim young man dressed in an old-fashioned mustard-coloured coat, a green-and-yellow silk scarf round his neck, and pale golden hair swept back off his forehead. It was Henry Lamb.

Ottoline followed him into the hall, up the steps, and into the studio she knew so well. There Dorelia was waiting—an innocent look on her face no doubt—with another young woman, Helen Maitland, Lamb's current mistress. Ottoline invited Lamb and the two women to return to Bedford Square for tea. (Apparently the visit to the school was shelved.) Lamb was, if possible, an even more romantic figure than John, and Dorelia, who had been Lamb's mistress in Paris, was right in believing that introducing Ottoline to him would produce the result desired. Ottoline found Lamb immensely attractive, and he was equally taken with her. But for the moment their mutual interest had to wait on the election campaign and Ottoline's trip to Paris; in the meantime she and Lamb exchanged polite notes. Fortunately Ottoline kept all Lamb's letters and it is from them that

the story of their friendship can be pieced together. (In her memoirs Ottoline usually omits the details of such matters. She has a genteel disdain of
anything that even remotely approaches crudity, and when, for example,
Lamb later refers in a letter to having spent two days with her she irritably
crossed out the words, as if the very ink offended her.) The first of
Lamb's letters—undated, but probably late 1909—is quite innocuous. He
addressed her as "Dear Lady Ottoline" and said he was off to Cornwall
and hoped to see her on his return. The second (possibly February, 1910)
is more friendly, but not yet intimate. He thanked her for some tulips
("You are far too angelic") and referred to a hurt he had given her, perhaps over the nature of his relationship with Helen Maitland, for he said:
"You say my friends can be yours, if I will—yes, but are you ready to
make enemies of my enemies? Do not be rash!"[2]

The next letter (probably March, 1910) is plainly one only a lover
could write: "I am insatiable for more life with you & in you," he told
her. It is evident they are having trouble meeting, for he says: "I am sure
it is folly to add to the circumstantial difficulties of seeing you: do let me
see more of you, I pray you most earnestly (less often if it must be so, but
longer)." We don't know if she was going to his studio, but it does not
appear so: perhaps Helen Maitland was ensconced there. He writes:

> All the recent happy memories are of our free times together & all the
> horrors spring from interruptions: don't for ever postpone our privacy be-
> cause of future possibilities. . . . I get congealed in your armchairs & the
> multitude of visitors distracts me. Must I wait for the age & fame of a
> Henry James before I am allowed the general concession of private
> attention?[3]

And he asked her to the opera. From this and another letter (probably
March or early April, 1910) it seems clear that most of their meetings
were in cafés, and during walks or at Ottoline's Thursdays. Brentie, Ottoline's maid, was ferrying notes between them and they were looking forward to some seclusion when Lamb joined Ottoline at Peppard. Also obvious is that Philip was suspicious. Since his defeat in the January election Philip had been busy running a new Liberal organisation called the
Gladstone League, of which he was secretary. (Ottoline also was involved—in the unlikely capacity of office dogsbody, opening letters, sort-
ing papers, and looking after the stationery.) Philip was well aware his

wife was incurably addicted to romantic figures like John and Lamb. He could not do anything to alter this, so in all probability he said nothing. On the other hand Ottoline did not want to do anything overt to hurt either Philip or her marriage, so she tried to be as discreet as her nature would allow. Thursday evenings, secretarial duties at the League and the rest of her varied life went on, with Lamb fitted in where possible.

Lamb was ten years younger than Ottoline. His father had been a mathematics professor and Henry was expected to follow him into the academic world. He began studying medicine but, finding he preferred a brush to a scalpel, he threw up his studies to go to the Chelsea School of Art. Later he eloped and went to France where he fell under the influence of John. There his wife Euphemia left him after he began associating with a female friend of John's, possibly Helen Maitland. He had only recently returned to London. It was Lamb's boyishness and immaturity that particularly attracted Ottoline and there was obviously a maternal element in their friendship, as she admitted:

> I was much older than he, and I had the instinct that I had something in me which would supply what he needed, some ingredient in which he was lacking. It was perhaps a half maternal instinct that pushed me towards this twisted and interesting creature.[4]

Lamb had been too long in the shadow of John—apeing him, painting like him, taking up with his mistresses—and was insecure, and Ottoline was good at boosting the confidence of insecure people. Yet Lamb was also temperamental and resented too obvious or too generous a dose of assistance or sympathy.

It seems likely that Lamb and Ottoline had two days together at Peppard in mid-April, and a longer period in May or June. Ottoline had been at Peppard quite a lot lately, partly because Julian, who was still frail, was staying there with her nurse, and partly because Ottoline's doctor had urged the peaceful country life on her as a cure for her headaches and ill-health generally. As cottages go, Peppard was not particularly striking—two storeys, brick and tile, with casement windows opening onto the garden. Ottoline likened it to a "bathing box" and complained that it was too small to entertain guests properly. But Peppard had compensations: the countryside and the common were pretty, there were some pleasant walks, and London seemed a long way off. As the warm weather advanced, so did their friendship. They went for expeditions into the woods and picnicked under the beeches. Ottoline found Lamb a complex, moody man, difficult to manage. For half a day he would be a charming and delightful companion, then he would change and pour out accusing words at her. But sometimes after his wild rantings he would break down and sob, clinging to her. Sitting under the trees on Ottoline's silk cushions they talked about art and books. Then they would have lengthy, agonised discussions about the ups and downs of their relationship. After one such debate he wrote to her: "Divine Ottoline, Have we not the principal treasure? These endless discussions as to what may or may not be lacking seems mean & belittling sometimes: forgive me for raising them so often."[5] A regular topic was the amount of time Ottoline spent with Philip and her other friends, which he begrudged her; but she had no intention of giving up the other parts of her life, no matter how delightful a companion Lamb was.

In April, 1910, another meeting occurred that was to give a new perspective to Ottoline's life over the coming years. This one took place in a setting very different from the pleasant surroundings of Peppard. Up in the Lancashire industrial belt the Burnley Liberal Party executive was meeting to discuss a minor crisis in the affairs of the local party. For years Burnley had been a fairly secure Liberal seat but in the recent election the Liberal candidate had been narrowly defeated and was not standing again, so the Burnley Liberals were in the market for an up-and-coming Liberal to contest the next election. They wrote to Liberal headquarters in London explaining their problem and received the name of the former MP for South Oxfordshire as a suitable candidate, after which they sent a deputation to London to interview Philip and ask if he would be agreeable to stand. For Philip their arrival was timely. The Gladstone League was proving less a means of helping the Liberal Party than a way of helping the circulation of the *Daily News,* the newspaper which sponsored it, so the scent of political battle was welcome to him. He met the Burnley delegation in his study at Bedford Square and told them he would be willing to stand. When he showed them a photograph of Ottoline, their leader said, "Yes, she will suit the Burnley democrats all right."[6] So while Lamb made plans to holiday with John and his gypsy menage in France, Ottoline and Philip made the long train trip up north to inspect and be inspected. In Burnley they were put up at a house belonging to Lady

O'Hagan, a local Liberal bigwig. The visit was a success and on April 12 Philip was unanimously endorsed as Burnley's next Liberal candidate.

Ottoline went back to Peppard in a state of nervous exhaustion. She had put up a good show in Burnley, visiting local textile mills, attending meetings, and generally playing the part of a conscientious candidate's wife. But the effort, together with the poverty and misery she saw there, were too much, and she retired to her bed for several days, enjoying her solitude and catching up with Lamb's letters. From France he wrote saying Dorelia was very ill and that the hotel John had recommended was (literally) lousy. Turning to more personal matters he said that what he really wanted was a new leaf to his life with Ottoline at his side. In reality, however, it was Helen Maitland who was at his side. He suggested, surely playfully, that Ottoline and Philip should come to France to form a *ménage à six,* a proposal he illustrated with a diagram showing Ottoline, Philip, John, Dorelia, and Helen spread around the boundary of a circle with Lamb, a bee, flitting from one blossom to the next.

On May 16 he was back in London but couldn't see much of Ottoline due to the difficulty of avoiding Philip and because he had a five-week commission to paint a Brazilian woman's portrait. Ottoline came down from Peppard several times for rendezvous in a coffee shop in Connaught Street, after which they went for strolls in Hyde Park, Lamb looking most dashing in a new, pink, square-topped hat. When he could spare himself from the Brazilian lady he and Ottoline would catch the train to Putney or Richmond and walk and talk. At the end of May he was looking forward to going to Peppard again. But obviously Philip was getting anxious, for, after another city rendezvous, Lamb wrote to ask if there had been "a great storm waiting" for her at Bedford Square.[7]

In June Lamb went to Cambridge to see his brother Walter, who was a don. He didn't enjoy the visit, nor did he enjoy the fact that Ottoline was putting restrictions on the time she could spare him, and he returned to London feeling out of sorts and suffering from headaches and stomach pains. "Obviously," he wrote to her, "I can only look forward to rare & short spells of that enchanted existence we enjoyed a few days ago & in the intervals I only waste time crying for the moon. Therefore I must marry Ethel Sands & have no more worry about my material future. Does this conclusion convince you?"[8] Ottoline in reply sent him tickets to the theatre.

On June 18 he wrote asking her to accompany him to Brest with Boris Anrep, the Russian ceramic artist. Ottoline was tempted but Philip apparently placed some restrictions on the plan, for Lamb wrote: "If he could be made to be serious about sending you with a chaperone surely one could be found."[9] Instead Ottoline and Philip themselves went off to the Continent together, intending to go to La Bourboule in France where Ottoline was to take the waters. Before they set off Lamb wrote telling her he had been riding on the downs in Sussex. "I got so wild with joy I shouted your name out loud," he told her.[10] August, September, and part of October Ottoline and Philip spent on the Continent, travelling from La Bourboule to Aix-en-Provence where they joined John and Dorelia, whom they found sitting outside a café, John looking very dissipated with a square-cut beard and bloodshot eyes. Later, on the way back to London, Ottoline and Philip stopped off in Paris where they encountered Roger Fry.* Afterwards Fry wrote to his friend Goldie Lowes Dickinson at Cambridge: "Lady Ottoline was with us in Paris, she is quite splendid. She talks of coming to Cambridge to see you. Will you get them lodgings & may I come too? We should have some real good talks; she'll face anything. I think she suggested Nov 6."[11]

At Cambridge Ottoline and Philip spent a not especially exciting weekend meeting, apart from Dickinson, people like Russell, Lytton Strachey, E. M. Forster, Fry, Russell's colleague A. N. Whitehead, and Jane Harrison, head of Newnham College. At Miss Harrison's Ottoline suggested to Strachey half jokingly that he might like to come to stay at Peppard. He pondered, drifted away, then came back and said, "Do you really mean me to come to Peppard?" Ottoline replied: "Of course I do."[12]

Part ii
1910–1911

Lytton's acceptance of Ottoline's invitation began a friendship between them that ended only with Lytton's death in 1932. Yet his initial reasons

---

*Desmond MacCarthy was also there and recalled Ottoline entering in a hat "like a crimson tea cosy trimmed with hedgehogs." (Desmond MacCarthy-OM, nd, HRC)

for accepting were selfish: partly he wanted to escape from London and the trammels of his family, and partly he was filled with desire for Henry Lamb, whom he knew to be a friend of his hostess and a likely fellow guest. Indeed, Ottoline, who probably knew of Lytton's penchant for his own sex, may have used Lamb as bait to lure him to Peppard, a ploy she was to make some use of later at Garsington. At any rate for Lytton the invitation was timely; he was in need of a little patronage.For most of the previous year he had been plagued by illness; "Mahomet's coffin," as he whimsically called his frail physique, had been particularly tiresome, forcing him to take several rest cures at Scandinavian health farms. In a continuing effort to find salubrious surroundings he had been compiling a list of friends with suitable rural retreats to which he could propose himself for as long as their owners would take him; Peppard fitted nicely into this roster. Lytton had first seen Lamb at one of the Stephens' Gordon Square functions and had been captivated. He wrote afterwards to Leonard Woolf: "He's run away from Manchester, become an artist, and grown side-whiskers. I didn't speak to him, but wanted to, because he really looked amazing, though of course very very bad."[13] But hardly had his appetite been whetted when the object of his admiration was snatched away by Euphemia, the art student with whom Lamb eloped to Paris. Now Lamb was back, and with Ottoline, so a visit to Peppard was doubly attractive.

Almost as soon as she issued the invitation Ottoline began to regret it for she still didn't have much confidence she could mix on equal terms with such clever people as Lytton. And, on the face of it, she didn't have much in common with this archpriest of the Bloomsbury Group. He was an intellectual who had dominated his contemporaries at Cambridge; he was also a homosexual and renowned for making terribly witty remarks and being cruel to people who weren't as clever as he. Now, at thirty, he was beginning to make a name for himself as a writer, particularly of biography and criticism, and he was currently working on a survey of French literature. As Ottoline returned to London she wondered how she would possibly entertain him.

At Bedford Square Ottoline and Philip found Lamb waiting for them. The plan had been for him to accompany them to Peppard where a studio had been prepared for him and accommodation arranged at the local inn, The Dog (Philip having vetoed his staying at the Cottage itself). Lamb had brought with him a large quantity of luggage—paintboxes, canvasses, clothes, etc.—and Philip, observing the pile, ventured to suggest that a separate taxi might be engaged to carry it while they followed in another vehicle. To this sensible idea Lamb replied: "Why do you object to travelling with my luggage overhead?"[14] It was not an auspicious start. But things improved, and the day after the trio's arrival Lamb was established at The Dog and Ottoline was waiting for Lytton's arrival. She had written him confirming the offer of the spare room at the Cottage, ". . . which I hope you will prefer to Mr. Lamb's Public House. He is here. I cannot answer to his temper . . . but the thought of seeing you makes him very happy today."[15] A few days later Lytton arrived and proved to be a model guest. His appetite perked up and in the extensive woods around Peppard Common he indulged his love of walking. He proved easily amused and Ottoline relaxed after it became evident that Lamb was steadfastly heterosexual, although enjoying Lytton's doe-eyed attentions. At night she would listen to the two men's voices in the sitting room beneath her bedroom; "I heard the duet of their voices underneath, laughing and joking, Lytton playing with him like a cat with a mouse, enjoying having his own sensations tickled by Lamb's beauty, while his contrariness adds spice to the contact."[16]

After a week or so Philip had to leave to go up to Burnley to begin campaigning for the election due in January, and a little later Ottoline left to join him. Lytton and Lamb stayed behind, Lamb setting about Lytton's portrait. Lytton described the setup to his younger brother James:

> Fortunately Philip is absent, electioneering in Burnley. Henry sleeps at a pub on the other side of the green, and paints in a coach-house rigged up by Ottoline with silks and stoves, a little further along the road. She seems quite gone—quite! . . . How does the woman do it! Every other menage must now seem sordid . . . Ah! She is a strange tragic figure (And such mysteries!).[17]

Lamb wrote to Ottoline in Burnley, telling her he could get on with his work much better when she wasn't there; but he missed her nonetheless: "I burn to embrace you & cover all your body with mine."[18] Shortly before Christmas Lytton left Peppard, returning briefly to London before going to France where he was to spend the next four months with his sister Dorothy and her husband, the painter Simon Bussy. Lytton wrote to thank Ottoline for his stay, which he said had been perfect bliss,

". . . an interlude from the Arabian nights."[19] He called her "Chère Marquise" and also thanked her for the orange vellum-covered notebook she gave him to copy his poems into (a gift she repeated with other writers down the years).

Up in Burnley Ottoline took to electioneering with gusto.* She spoke at meetings and helped distribute a campaign photograph that showed a curious tableau—Ottoline sitting stiffly at a piano, Philip looking fatherly, and little Julian standing angelically in the foreground. She toured several of the cotton mills where the noise of the clacking looms was so deafening the mill girls could only communicate with her by kissing her on the cheek. Each morning Ottoline was awakened at six A.M. by the sound of thousands of iron-soled clogs rat-tat-tatting up the cobbled streets to the mills. The election was expected to be a close fight and Asquith, now Prime Minister, came up to make two speeches in support of Philip. One meeting on December 5 attracted the biggest political audience in the town's history—11,000 in the hall and several thousand more outside. Altogether Philip and the local Liberals spent £953. 3s. 1d. on the campaign, an outlay that had its just reward when Philip was elected with a majority of 173 over his Tory opponent.

Soon after their return to Peppard a whole posse of guests arrived. First was Roger Fry, who was becoming increasingly friendly with Ottoline. Fry's wife Helen had gone mad and several times Ottoline had been to his house to help him cope with domestic problems. Fry had been very busy lately arranging the first Postimpressionist exhibition to be held in London and several other people involved in this project came to Peppard. Later Boris Anrep arrived to see Lamb, accompanied by Helen Maitland.† Then Clive and Vanessa Bell, also close friends of Fry, turned up, and so did the critic and Bloomsbury member Desmond MacCarthy.

Lamb was beginning to cause Ottoline many heartaches. While the Bells were at Peppard he took it into his head to be odious to her, mainly,

---

*At one meeting Ottoline made what the London press described as a violent attack on her Tory brothers and their "worthless way of life." It was probably these speeches which led to the almost certainly apocryphal story that went the rounds of Bloomsbury in which Ottoline was pictured stretching out her arms to a meeting of Burnley mill workers and saying, "I *love* the people—I married into the people."

†Among these four guests—Fry, Lamb, Anrep, and Helen Maitland—there were to spring up some complex relationships: Helen was soon to leave Lamb, become Anrep's mistress and then his wife before going off to live with Fry.

she thought, because he was jealous of the attention she was diverting from him in the presence of critics like Fry, MacCarthy, and Bell. Ottoline wrote of him: "His temper grew more and more unreasonable, and the more I suffered from it the more he delighted in tormenting me."[20] She likened him to a vampire, sucking her life away—away from Philip and Julian and the important things in her life. But she could not bear to let him go; he had a charm and a mystery about him that she found in nobody else. Early in 1911, after a display of temper, Lamb took himself off to Paris with Anrep. From there he wrote to say he had found Dorelia and one of the John children, Pyramus, both ill in a hotel. A week or so later he wrote again complaining he had not received any letters from Peppard—Ottoline was using her aloof tactic, something she maintained had a beneficial effect on Lamb's behaviour. But a day or so later she did write, telling him she felt very depressed. He replied rather callously and on the back of his envelope Ottoline jotted, "No imagination . . . momentary pleasure . . . like a child."[21] She wrote to him saying he must go his own path without her; yet in her diary she said, "My weakness hopes for him not to obey, for I long for his affection and companionship."[22] Virginia Stephen also stayed at Peppard for a weekend in February and told Ottoline how the Bells were forever going on about copulation, a topic that bored her. She and Ottoline discussed artists and both agreed they were rather brutes: writers and poets were much finer, said Virginia.

Soon Lamb was back in England and seeing Ottoline frequently. But he was still acting ungraciously and after one tiff he wrote explaining that "something made me do & say the opposite [to what he really felt]."[23] Towards the end of February he still felt unsettled and apologised for his sulky behaviour. Ottoline did her best to help by plying him with gifts of tobacco, pipes, sweets, and biscuits and installing electric light in his coachhouse studio at Peppard, but all this did was to make him feel even more a kept man, and when she went off for a few days to Black Hall he asked his friend George Kennedy to come and stay; he knew Ottoline disliked Kennedy and this gesture of rebellion appealed to him.

On February 22 Ottoline went off for a seaside holiday at Studland in Dorset where she walked barefoot on the beach and shared jokes with her maid Brentie. Philip came down from the House of Commons to join her and, though at first she was disappointed with his company, after a while they reestablished their rapport. On the way back to Peppard they called in on Roger Fry, who did a sketch of her in what she described to Lamb as "indifferent colours." Lamb told her he couldn't imagine anyone painting her in indifferent colours. He was sorry his letters nowadays seemed so settled in comparison with a year ago, but added: "When we are both 50 you won't scorn the expressions of the sedate contentment you so largely procured for me."[24] At Peppard Ethel Sands turned up for a brief stay and on March 9 Anrep's wife, Junia, arrived and chided Lamb for criticising Ottoline, whose portrait he was now working on. As the weekend of March 18–19 approached, Ottoline was relieved to be able to escape from Lamb and Peppard and return to London, where an important engagement awaited her.

Chapter 6

1911

ON Sunday March 19 a small dinner party was held at 44 Bedford Square. It was arranged because Bertrand Russell, who was teaching at Cambridge, wanted somewhere to stay the night on his way to Paris where he was to lecture. Though he wasn't a particularly close friend of the Morrells he had an open invitation to stay with them. Yet now that he had taken up this invitation, Ottoline felt misgivings. Even to a hostess of her experience the prospect of having so eminent an intellect staying in her house was a little forbidding, especially as Philip at the last moment had been called away to attend to some urgent constituency business in Burnley.

Believing she might have problems conversing with a man whose razor-sharp mind had earned him the name "The Day of Judgement," Ottoline cast around for some other guests to make up a scratch dinner party for the evening. Fortunately she found two people who were ideal. One was Ralph Hawtrey, a contemporary of Russell's and fellow Apostle at Cambridge, and the other was Ethel Sands, a practised hand at easing dinner table difficulties (and a good friend of Russell's brother-in-law, Logan Pearsall Smith). Russell arrived around four thirty in the afternoon and the dinner went off pleasantly. Russell relaxed in the congenial company and his already enhanced opinion of Ottoline was further advanced by her obvious taste and amiable manner. He felt happier than he had for a long time. Around midnight the party broke up, taxis were called, and Hawtrey and Miss Sands departed. Ottoline and Russell returned to the drawing room for a few moments before retiring. But neither made a move to go to bed; instead they sat by the fire and continued to talk—about Paris, politics, about Philip's recent success in Burnley, and so on. Gradually the conversation became more personal. Ottoline was well known for her facility for drawing people out—particularly people with problems—and she sensed in Russell a problem of some proportion. The last time they had met, in July, he had turned to her at dinner and said intensely, "There is always a tragedy in everyone's life if you know them well enough to find it out."[1] Now, finding Ottoline receptive, Russell suddenly began to talk about his own personal problems. He sat on the edge of his chair, his hands clenched and his back ramrod stiff. His face was distorted with emotion. He was desperately unhappy, as unhappy as any man could be . . . for nine years he had been living with a woman he did not love . . . he was starved of love, starved of sexual fulfilment . . . his existence was bare, he was sick of his puritan way of life and longed for beauty and passion. For nine years he had dammed up his emotions, and that night in Ottoline's drawing room the dam burst.

Ottoline's sympathetic reaction surprised Russell, but he was even more surprised to find she didn't repulse his timid advances. Suddenly he was overcome with love and realised to his delight that she would allow him to make love to her. They spent the remainder of the night talking and embracing, though, as Russell says, for "external and accidental reasons" they did not have full relations that time.[2] For both it was a crucial encounter. Later Ottoline pleaded she had been stunned and overwhelmed, but for the moment she was carried away by Russell's torrent of emotion, and everything else—Philip, Julian, her other friends—was swept aside. They agreed to become lovers as soon as possible and, around four A.M. retired to their separate beds.

To understand fully what went on that night under the calm, logical surface of one of Britain's greatest minds it is necessary to go back to 1902. In his autobiography Russell describes how, while bicycling one day near Grantchester, he suddenly realised he no longer loved his wife, Alys. She was five years older than he, a Quaker, and, although somewhat puritan in outlook, devoted. Very soon she perceived the change in his attitude and was grievously hurt by it. Russell relates how every now and then Alys would come to him in her dressing gown and beg him to spend the night with her. "Sometimes I did so, but the result was utterly unsatisfactory," he says. "For nine years this state of affairs continued."[3]

Stark and brutal as is Russell's description of this incident and what followed, it barely touches on the misery he—and the hapless Alys—went through. A more accurate idea can be got from one of Russell's notebooks which Ottoline somehow acquired and kept. Dating

1902–1905, it is in two parts. At the front are twenty or so pages of close- ly packed mathematical symbols—some of Gauss' theorems which Rus- sell was simply going through and working out to his own satisfaction. At the back are another twenty or so pages containing his diary of this period in his life. Here, with cold mathematical precision, he sets down the day- to-day horror of the destruction of his marriage.

He started by adopting a cold attitude towards Alys, "in the deliberate hope of destroying her affection."[4] In June, 1902, his wife asked him di- rectly what was wrong and he told her his love for her was dead. All that night he worked on *Principia Mathematica* while in the bedroom next door he could hear Alys' heartrending sobs. He noted in his diary:

Oh the pity of it! How she was crushed and broken! How nearly I re- turned and said it had all been lies. And how my soul hardened from mo- ment to moment because I left her to sob. In the middle of the night she came to my door to say she was calmer now and would hope—poor, poor woman.[5]

A little later he adds:

I do not believe, in my soul, that I was justified; and I don't know wheth- er I am justified now. But I have certainly effected a great moral reforma- tion in her, and that depends upon keeping her hopes alive but unfulfilled. This requires vacillation—occasional great friendliness, occasional cen- sure.[6]

In November, 1902, he wrote: "When I got home Alys had a crying fit; I know it is my fault, and I must manage better, but it is hard; she is too lonely—good God, what a lonely world it is."[7] A few weeks later he recalled an incident earlier in the year when he had picked a bunch of primroses and offered them to her as a little token of love. Both were "touched, deeply touched." He continues:

. . . for a moment hope whispered honeyed words; but in our hearts we knew they were lies; we knew that never again would the sun shine. . . . The pathos of her love lived in my imagination in that moment, and I longed, with an infinite tenderness, to revivify my dying love. Almost I succeeded, but it was too late. The spring of which those poor flowers fondly dreamed never came, and will never come; in human lives there is but one spring, and winter, when it comes, is not thawed by gentle winds from southern seas, but deepens slowly into Arctic night.[8]

And deepen it did. On December 13 he wrote: "Last night when I went to bed Alys asked the time, which was 12:40. After the light was out she asked if I remembered the date—I had forgotten it was our wedding date. . . . Her misery was uncontrollable."[9] On March 18, 1903, he wrote: "Last night for the first time I made the last possible sacrifice. In return I am to have three weeks' liberty."[10] And on April 8: "The last sacrifice to Alys was not adequately carried out, and failed totally. . . . She hated it and didn't want a repetition. I shirked my duty on that occasion. I ought to have been more self-forgetful."[11] Around May, 1903, Russell reached the depths of unhappiness. He was struggling with *Principia*, meeting mental obstacles he could not surmount, while his personal existence was a torment. He wrote: " . . . day by day I wonder how another 24 hours of such utter misery can be endured. . . ."[12] But slowly Alys came to live with her misery and the new conditions under which she and Russell occupied separate bedrooms but were outwardly still happily married. In April, 1904, he says Alys has improved greatly. In January, 1905, he is no longer miserable all the time, and improvement he attributes to the "modus vivendi" he has adopted with Alys: "I never look at her."[13] In March, 1905, he wrote: "I feel that continence will become increasingly difficult, and that I shall be tempted to get into more or less flirtatious relations with women I don't respect."[14] Three weeks later he noted: "She has given up kissing me morning and evening, which is a great gain. . . . I look forward to a gradually increasing separation."[15] Russell wrote in his autobiography of the ensuing years: "During all this time she hoped to win me back, and never became interested in any other man. During all this time I had no other sex relations."[16]

Of all this Ottoline knew nothing, so it is understandable what a shock she experienced when, in her own words, she lifted the lid from this boiling cauldron. For, in spite of his unattractive exterior and inexorable intellect, Russell was a passionate man. His subsequent career provides ample proof of how, despite the power of his mind, the power of his heart was greater. In the space of a few hours that evening at Bedford Square, Russell had fallen deeply and irrevocably in love—probably more deeply than he ever was to again. After all those years of abstinence and misery he was prepared to overcome any obstacle to achieve his end. Ottoline too was a passionate person. She was also ruled by her heart not her head. Unlike Russell, however, she had much to lose: she was married to a man she loved and had a child whose welfare she would not ignore.

The next morning Russell went off, dizzy with love. Though they didn't see each other for several days, they wrote by almost every post—the first letters in a correspondence that was to prove prodigious even by Ottoline's standards. Over the next few years he wrote more than 2,000 letters to her and she wrote over 1,500 replies. Russell's letters, almost all of which Ottoline kept, give an idea of the change that had come over him. No longer the cold, calculating machine, he was like a young swain, revelling in the joys of first love (despite the fact that he was thirty-eight and Ottoline thirty-seven). His first love letter to her was postmarked March 21, 1911:

> In the train
> Tuesday
>
> MY DEAREST,
>   My heart is so full that I hardly know where to begin. The world is so changed in these last 48 hours that I am still bewildered. My thoughts won't come away from you—I don't hear what people say. All yesterday evening Bob Trevi babbled on; every now & then I woke up & wondered who he was talking about just then. Fortunately *yes* & *quite so* & *ah indeed* were enough for him. . . . I love you very dearly now & I know that every time I see you I shall love you more. . . . It is altogether extraordinary to me that you should love me—I feel myself so rugged & ruthless; & so removed from the whole aesthetic side of life—a sort of logic machine warranted to destroy any ideal that is not very robust. . . . In Paris I shall have to try to collect my wits—it won't do to be thinking of you while the philosophers are making objections to my views. . . . Goodbye, my Dearest. I grudge the hours till I am with you again. With all my love,
>
> B.[17]

By Wednesday, March 22, Russell was in Paris giving his lectures and staying at the Hotel Corneille where a letter was waiting for him from Ottoline. As usual, after the first ecstatic surrender to emotion, she was beginning to have reservations. She told him she felt the hand of fate holding her back and wondered if her love could really mean something to him. He brushed aside her doubts: "Dearest I love you, & everything else is dross." He told her that her love could give him happiness and peace:

> All my life, except for a short time after my marriage, I have been driven on by restless inward furies, flogging me to activity & never letting me rest, till I feel often so weary that it seems as if no more could be borne. You could change all that if you were willing. You could give me inward joy & expel the demons.[18]

In her next letter Ottoline tried a different tack. Realising the seriousness of his protestations, she now insisted they must either keep their affair secret or break it off altogether. But Russell, his logical mind reasserting itself for the moment, saw the perils of subterfuge:

> My serious & intended view is that our love would be degraded if we allow it to be surrounded by the sordid atmosphere of intrigue—prying servants, tattling friends, & gradually increasing suspicion. All this is inevitable if we attempt secrecy; we cannot hope to succeed in it. If your love were not so precious to me, I should mind less; but I cannot bear to have it degraded.[19]

As to her alternative, that was even more out of the question:

> But to sacrifice you altogether, just when I have found you, is too much; I can't face that. If you will tell Philip & let me tell Alys, I can acquiesce in your staying with him; then the deceit & sordidness is avoided. And then you can still help him politically. That seems to me the right course, as well as the most likely to minimize scandal. But whatever you say I shan't give up the hope of everything. I have been told, & I believe, that your obstinacy is incredible; so is mine.

Ottoline also had misgivings about her brain. Wasn't she a trifle out of his class? He replied: "No woman's intellect is really good enough to give me pleasure as intellect. . . . It is plain to me that I love you—absolutely, devotedly, with all the passion of a fierce nature long starved & lonely." He would hear no more of her doubts: "A great love is a great responsibility; do not degrade us both by not living up to the best. . . . My life is bound up with you; it is my last chance of real happiness, or of a life that brings out my best."

Russell returned to London on Friday, March 24, and the next morning went to see Ottoline on his way to Haslemere where he and Alys had taken a house during the university vacation. At Bedford Square he met a very worried Ottoline. In an attempt to dampen his ardour she managed to get him to agree that they would not meet for a few weeks, during which time they would both have the opportunity to reflect and see if they still felt the same way about each other. Russell reluctantly agreed, but in return he extracted from her a promise that they would spend some time alone together at the end of the separation period. Ottoline would be going down to Studland again soon and she agreed that as soon as she could arrange things he could come down and stay with her. In the meantime he would break the news of their affair to Alys, and Ottoline would tell Philip. After Russell had gone Ottoline felt she might have been too strict with him, so she wrote him a note explaining that she was not trying to kill their love, merely trying to do the right thing by everyone.

At Haslemere Russell found Alys entertaining two of her young relatives, Ray and Karin Costello (Russell was coaching Karin in philosophy), so he decided to wait until Monday when the two visitors left before telling Alys about Ottoline. It wasn't an enjoyable weekend. He did his best to put on a happy face but was feeling miserable. On Saturday night he wrote to Ottoline saying he feared she would choose duty before love; he assured her, however, that there were occasions when duty meant choosing one's own happiness rather than other people's. He went on: "There have been things in my life which I should have wished to tell you, but that I am not at liberty to do so; they would have illustrated why I am so certain of what I think right."[20] He ended the letter on a low note: "I cannot understand the wish for a future life—it is the chief consolation that in the grave there is rest." On Monday Russell told Alys about Ottoline and either on that day or the previous one Ottoline told Philip about Russell. In her memoirs Ottoline relates what Philip's reaction was: "When Philip returned, I told him all that had happened, and I was terribly hurt by his saying to me, 'Do you want to go? You must if you want to.' "[21]* Ottoline was very upset by this, for she had no intention of leav-

---

*In a footnote by Philip Morrell in *Memoirs* (Vol. 2, p. 267) he says Ottoline's dating of this quote is incorrect: it wasn't said after his return from Burnley but "some weeks later at Studland." He adds: "When I returned to London from Burnley, so far from telling me 'all that had happened,' she told me very little: merely that Bertie Russell had said

ing Philip and Julian, regardless of what Russell might believe. What Alys said when Russell broke the news to her is not recorded; all he told Ottoline was, "I have told Alys who took it very well."[22] Both Philip and Alys probably realised there was little point in taking it otherwise.

If Ottoline was upset at Philip's reaction, Russell was dumbfounded. She told him that Philip had agreed to let the status quo continue. This meant in effect that Russell and Philip would be competing for Ottoline's love. Russell found this very curious: "The situation is one I have not known of before in any case I have ever heard of."[23] Perhaps, he said, he might come to understand in time; meanwhile all he asked was that Philip should not share her room; this meant a great deal to him, as he explained:

> I dread my nature—I can do much with it in many ways, but where passion comes in it is difficult. I will not put myself where hatred would come to me, & I will not let its poison come into our lives. If I can overcome that, or if you can cease to share a room with him, all will be well. If not, it will be better to part.[24]

But Ottoline would not forsake Philip. Screwing up her courage, she wrote to Russell agreeing that the best thing would be for them to part. She proposed that they should have a final meeting at the Whiteheads' house in Carlyle Square, Chelsea. Russell agreed. But the meeting did not go off as intended. As soon as they saw each other their fears evaporated and they fell into each other's arms. All Ottoline's firm intentions, so carefully nurtured in private, disappeared. Their love blazed up again, if anything stronger than before. That night Russell wrote to her: "Dearest, my whole soul is flooded with joy—your radiance shines before me, & I feel still your arms about me & your kiss on my lips." He saw now that she could not leave Philip and said: "I will accept whatever of your time you feel you can rightly give, & will not ask for more."[25] He told her he was glad they were not going to snatch at happiness by the ruin of others and he asked her for a snapshot of herself. She sent him a picture

how unhappy he was with his wife, and asked for sympathy and support which she felt she ought to give him, and to this . . . I rather reluctantly consented." Indeed, Ottoline may have misled Bertie into thinking she had revealed all to Philip; nevertheless, taking Lamb and John into account, there can be little doubt that Philip was to some degree resigned to allowing Ottoline a measure of freedom in her relationships with other men.

he found "delightful"—though he might not have found it quite so charming had he known it was taken while she was on honeymoon with Philip in Venice. He had gone back to reading poetry, he told her, and was happy that beauty had come back into his life. Ottoline, however, was anything but happy. On all sides she was beset by problems and felt very ill and tired. Not only did she have Philip and Julian to worry about, but Lamb. And, as we shall see later, she had at this time yet another emotional crisis on her hands—one she could not divulge to anyone, least of all Russell. Little wonder she had a severe bout of crisis headaches.

On Saturday, April 1, Russell returned to Haslemere in a slightly better frame of mind and he discussed with Alys what their future would be. It appears he told her that the shell that was their marriage would have to be broken up further, leaving only the merest form. She would not, he informed her, be returning with him to Cambridge when the Easter vacation ended on April 24. That night he wrote to Ottoline:

> She is behaving very well. I do not think she is suffering much. All the real pain was nine years ago, when I told her I no longer loved her. . . . Alys has great kindness, whenever there is competition, and she has times of real nobility—just now nothing could be better—I shall tell people that her rheumatism doesn't allow her to live at Cambridge. She seems to prefer to give the reason that we can't get on together, but except to intimate friends I don't feel I can say that.[26]

The following day Alys was being less noble. The implications of her husband's decision were beginning to sink in and she spoke to Russell "in a most harrowing way," as he reported that night in another letter to Ottoline. Her pain, he wrote, "is like the pain of a wounded animal. . . . At times I have thought I ought never to have told her I no longer cared for her, yet I feel that a life of active & constant hypocrisy would have been impossible and wrong. But giving pain deliberately is very terrible."[27] His truthfulness was relentless; in the same letter he confessed that he had recently kissed a woman whom he had "known a long time." This confession was apparently activated by a letter the woman had just written him, asking him to come to see her. Of course he would not go. He told Ottoline that he was telling her about this because, if it ever came to mind when he was with her, he should feel guilty, which would be unbearable. He admitted that this was a very egotistical attitude, but he wanted to be sure Ottoline would love him "without illusion."

Russell returned to London on Monday, April 3, to attend a function at the House of Commons—an occasion he was dreading for fear of bumping into Philip. But Ottoline had promised to meet Russell on Wednesday, and this balanced the former dread. In a letter to her he expanded slightly on the "harrowing way" Alys had spoken during the weekend: "I am afraid that if a serious scandal is to be avoided it may be necessary for me to remain on terms with her."[28] Alys apparently had written to Mrs. Whitehead demanding sympathy and an interview. Russell said that he had offered Alys half his income but she indignantly refused. "This looks like trouble," he commented. Alys had agreed however to a three-month separation—on the condition that Russell would make no final decision until after the three months were up. She had also resigned from the various charitable committees she was a member of. "Altogether there may be much difficulty," said Russell. He was also worrying about where he and Ottoline could meet. He had thought Mrs. Whitehead might lend her Chelsea house for a rendezvous, but there were problems in this as Mrs. Whitehead didn't want her servants or her teen-age son to know. ("He is very perceptive, & if he saw you he would guess at once.") Other possibilities also had their disadvantages:

> I think it is better to avoid places like Kensington Gardens, where we should meet all our friends. The only plan I can think of is to meet at some underground station exit, & take a cab to some out of the way place like Putney Heath.

At the House of Commons on Tuesday Russell and Philip did see each other, but only at a distance. Russell dared not look him in the eye, but he did observe that Philip seemed upset at seeing him. At three P.M. the following day Russell and Ottoline met at Bedford Square; again it was a happy reunion, smoothing out problems and recharging the friendship. Back at Haslemere that night, Alys sat up after dinner, forcing Russell to retire to his bed to write to Ottoline in privacy: "I feel she is meditating something," he said.[29] Before he went to sleep he kissed Ottoline's photograph. On Thursday Alys seemed to have come to a decision and left for London—to see Mrs. Whitehead, Russell assumed. But she wouldn't find much sympathy in that quarter: "Mrs. Whitehead dislikes her—but Whitehead hates her."[30] Alys' absence gave him the chance to write a really long letter to Ottoline, who was about to leave with Julian for her holiday at Studland. He told her:

> I went [for] a long walk alone to-day. I felt so full of happiness and life that I hardly knew how to contain myself, I [wanted] to shout and sing like the morning stars and the Sons of God. Even the East wind seemed delightful. You won't like me if I become boisterous and jovial.[31]

Before going to Studland Ottoline went to see Mrs. Whitehead, who alarmed her with talk of public scandal and the possibility of Alys committing suicide. Ethel Sands had somehow heard of the affair and Ottoline was concerned others might soon know. Russell told her he understood her fears but tried to play them down. He said Alys was becoming resigned to the situation, ". . . and will behave well in return for very small amounts of my society."[32] He thanked Ottoline for a box she had sent him (to keep her letters in) and looked forward to joining her at Studland in about ten days' time. He wrote (April 8): "Tomorrow when you get this it will be three weeks since we found each other. . . . O my heart, don't let us be kept by other people from what is possible. I love you, I love you, love you. We have had to wait for complete union, and if not at Studland it might be a long time." Later the same day he wrote again to tell her he had had a satisfactory talk with Alys. They had agreed to preserve appearance; he would spend occasional weekends with her during which they would have visitors and be seen together. She had also agreed to go on taking his money. Most importantly he had made her understand that if there came to be much scandal it would become impossible to even keep up these appearances. "Pride and prudence will combine to keep her silent, and though her family will guess that something is up, I feel sure she won't breathe a word, and I don't believe they will think of you."[33]

This last point was important to Ottoline. Alys's brother Logan was, after all, an old friend and she shuddered to think what would happen if he were to discover that she was the woman for whom Russell had left his sister. (Ottoline's concern was to prove well founded.) Russell tried to allay her fears: "She is I think now loyally anxious to do her part."[34] He

Ottoline Morrell.
Drawing by Henry Lamb. Courtesy Lady Pansy Lamb

Philip Morrell, 1903.

Ottoline Morrell, 1903.
Radio Times Hulton Picture Library

44 Bedford Square, Bloomsbury.
Courtesy Y. Ismail

Careless of money . will have this devided between two or

three other sisters . ~ She . doesn't want riches .

but I hope she can get some . . .

She said you liked the pictures . . I thought you

might advise her . . . She is in ~~England~~ London

for a few days . . then returns to Venice > .

Lawrence is a great loss . . he was a very wonderful .

Man . — Did you see a little Article Dorothie on his

in last week's Nation . Do read it — .

How are you ? . I heard you were rather very well .

Yrs .
P. Ottoline Morrell .

Ottoline's handwriting.

Above: Ottoline at St. Mark's Square, Venice, *c.* 1902.

Below: Ottoline on her honeymoon in Venice, 1902.

At Lido, Venice, 1908, left to right: Byard, Goldie Lowes Dickinson, Ottoline, Robilant, Baroness Meyer.

Ottoline, *c*. 1910.

Augustus John, 1902.
Photograph by Beresford, Radio Times Hulton Picture Library

Ottoline and Dorelia John.

Ottoline, Augustus John and Mrs. Chadbourne at Hampton Court.

Philip reading to Ottoline.

Left to right: Ottoline, John Rothenstein, Helen Anrep, Leslie Hartley, W. Porce-Stead and John Strachey.

Ottoline at Studland, *c.* 1911.

Ottoline and Julian Morrell.

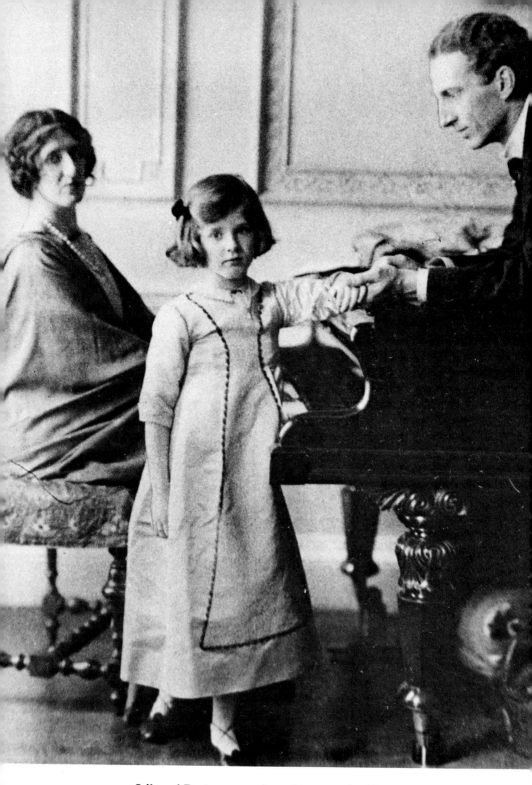

Liberal Party campaign photograph, 1911.

Ottoline Morrell, 1912.
Photograph by Cavendish Morton

Above: Ottoline in the garden at Garsington.
Opposite: Philip at Garsington.

Garsington Manor.
Courtesy Lady Wheeler-Bennett

also tried to put to rest Ottoline's fears about their spiritual compatibility. He was an atheist and she was still deeply religious. He said: "Dearest, there is no vital difference between us as regards religion. It is true I shall sometimes publicly attack things which you believe, but it will be for the sake of other things that you will also believe." On Monday, April 10, he got a note from Ottoline saying that if he wished he could come to Studland that day rather than Tuesday week. After some soul-searching he opted for the latter date, explaining: "I would rather come when you are rested as I fear you may find me not conducive to rest. I should have felt more certain [of the later date] except for the feeling that there's many a slip. . . . But that seems only a superstition." The next letter he received from her said she had been ill, so he was glad he had made the right decision. "I do hope you will soon be better. Only why should you imagine I should think you a 'wretched poor creature'? I believe people with really good health are never nice. My health is invariably perfect."[35] On a more serious note he talked about some of his personal misgivings:

> It is a dreadful thing to cause so much pain. I am oppressed by the thought of all the pain I have caused in the course of my life, and by the foreboding that I shall cause more. Dearest I do most earnestly hope I shall not cause pain to you, beyond what the situation must involve. But sometimes I think I am fated to cause misery. . . . But for all your firmness I might had done incalculable damage to you and P. and Julian—all this is obvious to me now, but at the moment I felt utterly reckless—the suppressed ego rebelled and clamoured for its desires.

Over the next few days they exchanged long letters about their early lives. Russell said he had been almost always sad: "My natural view is that all human happiness is a mere interlude, & that sorrow is the normal lot of man."[36] Ottoline told him of her unhappy childhood and of a man she had once deeply loved (probably Axel Munthe). She also told him of a serious complication that had arisen at Studland: Logan had arrived to stay. "It is a nuisance about Logan," Russell wrote. "You must manage to get him away before I come." (She did.) Neither Ottoline nor Russell, however, was going to let Logan spoil a meeting both were looking forward to. Russell wrote (April 12): "O my Dearest, I do love you with all my strength, with all possible love—I love dearly your outward beauty, and more dearly the beauty of your mind—your shy thoughts that you hardly dare speak of are wonderful. Goodbye my Dearest.'' Russell took to going for long walks around Haslemere, trying to exhaust himself so as to get some respite from the physical and mental anguish of not being at Studland. He was almost frenzied with longing for Ottoline. He wrote thirteen times during this week and she wrote almost as often, telling him in one letter that she had changed her hairstyle. He replied: ''I should like to see you with your hair in two plaits and looking very wild. Oh how happy we shall be when I come—I shall feel like a boy fresh from school for the holidays.''[37] Russell's good spirits were infectious: ''I know it is hard on Alys to see it, but I have been so full of gaiety these last two days that even she has been carried away and has grown almost gay too.''[38] His mind had also been affected: ''Reading over the great philosophers, as I have been doing, I seem much quicker than usual to see what they mean.''

On the Saturday before he was due to go to Studland, Russell, as he recounts in his autobiography, visited a dentist who told him he might have cancer of the mouth. But he told Ottoline none of this. Nor did he tell her what happened when he left Alys at Haslemere to go to Studland. In his autobiography Russell implies that when he took his leave Alys flew into a rage. He says that later he gave a lesson in Locke's philosophy to her niece Karin. ''. . . I then rode away on my bicycle and with that my first marriage came to an end. I did not see Alys again till 1950, when we met as friendly acquaintances.''[39] Actually he did meet her again before 1950, but he is right in saying his marriage ended with this melodramatic leave-taking.

At one forty-nine on Tuesday afternoon, April 18, Russell arrived by train at Swanage. He hired a pony cart and drove out to where Ottoline was waiting for him on the hill under a group of fir trees.

Chapter 7

Part i
1911

OTTOLINE had not been altogether honest with Russell. She had told him nothing of John, and only the barest minimum about Lamb, whom she painted as a weak creature in need of her support. Also she told him nothing of another attachment which had been developing for some time with Roger Fry. Over the past years she had often visited Fry to help with his wife, Helen, who was mentally unstable. Ottoline did not relish these harrowing visits but continued to go because she knew Fry was suffering greatly. In the early months of 1911 their friendship grew more intimate as Fry's admiration and gratitude deepened into affection. Ottoline admired the intellect of her Contemporary Art Society colleague and welcomed his friendship. Although Fry, who was forty-four, could seem rather stiff and dry—like some medieval saint, Lytton Strachey thought— he had a marked sympathy and understanding of women. Moreover, he was at this time especially lonely and vulnerable since his wife had just been put into a mental asylum. In March, 1911, a week or so after the Russell eruption, Fry visited Ottoline at Bedford Square. He was just about to go off to Constantinople for a holiday with Clive and Vanessa Bell and a mathematician friend, Harry Norton. We have no record of what happened at this meeting, but something obviously did, for around March 31 Ottoline received this letter from Fry:

> MY DEAR,
>   I'm still all amazed and wondering . . . can't begin to think—I can only know how beautiful it was of you, how splendid—only how terrible to learn it like that. What terrifies me is that you should suffer for it—regret it in any way—you mustn't indeed dear, it was altogether beautiful and right.[1]

He told her he might be able to see her again before he left London, as Vanessa had suddenly taken ill, which could mean a postponement of the trip. He went on: "but Oh Ottoline—no I can't fathom it yet or say anything clear or right or see the way for us, only it shall not be hard or bitter shall it my dear, it must mean more hope and love for us somehow." But Fry couldn't alter his travel arrangements, so next day he and Norton departed for Bruges where they were to wait for Clive and Vanessa to catch them up. From there he wrote to Ottoline (April 3, 1911):

> MY DEAR OTTOLINE,
>   I wish we hadn't come and stuck here, except that I may get a letter tomorrow. I don't think I can wait till I've heard from you, not properly. I'm still dazed and have only a sense of immense wealth which I don't touch or investigate.[2]

And he signed it "Yr. Roger." The next day he wrote again, this time calling her "My dearest Ottoline":

>   I know you will decide right for us . . . that now we can be much more to each other than would have been possible before, that our friendship will be more perfect, more precious, more complete, and that is after all the greatest value for us—tho' it hurts to think how much more it might be if life were not so difficult, so entangled with ties.[3]

He said he found it difficult to understand why she should think him wonderful—but it made him feel good that she did. ". . . and the best is that it isn't based on some fancy of yours because you are too dear and serene in mind for that so I needn't dread to lose it." But serene in mind at that moment Ottoline was not. She had gone down to Studland to await the arrival of Russell, with whom she was maintaining an emotion-charged correspondence. Henry Lamb was hovering nearby at Corfe and Philip was due as soon as Russell's promised three days were up. Logan Pearsall Smith was also in the vicinity, as yet unsuspecting. Now, to further complicate a tangled skein of relationships, here was Fry pouring out love letters from the East. No wonder Ottoline complained of headaches.

As Ottoline and Russell walked together through the gorse and heather to her seaside cottage, their feelings for each other, strained by separation and the pressures on them from many quarters, burst into flame again. On his side this wasn't unexpected; for weeks he had been looking forward to this day and he was prepared to take any risk for just a few hours' bliss; and a few hours could be all he might get if his doctor confirmed the diagnosis of cancer. In his autobiography he describes the next three days spent with Ottoline in Studland as "among the few moments when life seemed all that it might be, but hardly ever is."[4] On Ottoline's side the abandonment of any resolve to discourage Bertie was less understandable. By now she must have realised how strong was Russell's love for her and what any encouragement would do to it. She must also have known that she wasn't dealing with a lover like Lamb or John for whom an affair meant little more than a brief flirtation; Russell was competing with Philip not for her love but her life. She was courting the destruction of her marriage and family, the obloquy of her relations and friends, probable unhappiness, and an uncertain future. She had every reason to put a damper on Bertie's ardour. Especially, as she says in her memoirs, she did not take to his rather clumsy ways: "He assumed at once that I was his possession, and started to investigate, to explore, to probe. I shrank back, for it was intolerable to me to have the hands of this psychological surgeon investigating the tangle of thoughts, feelings and emotions which I had never allowed anyone to see. I felt like a sea-anemone that shrinks and closes at the slightest touch."[5] Yet during these three days she succeeded in making Bertie ecstatically happy and it seems from her letters to him that she too enjoyed their seaside idyll. If there is any explanation for Ottoline's dual attitude it is probably to be found in that fundamental split in her character between her romanticism and puritan conscience. When she paused to think, her conscience could find any number of reasons why she should not love Bertie, but during those days at Studland her heart gave her little pause.

At first she was shy with Bertie, but by degrees her defences fell and she relaxed. Julian, now almost five, was still at the cottage, as was Brentie, so things had to be fairly discreet. Mostly they went off for long walks or sat under the trees and talked. They exchanged details of their childhoods and Ottoline told Bertie about her unhappy adolescence at Welbeck while he imparted a little of the misery he had suffered in the past nine years of his marriage to Alys. He also tried to explain to her his mathematical and philosophical work.

Ottoline was very flattered that a mind such as Russell's should come and beg to commune with her. She knew Russell was an important man, probably a great man, and she believed him when he told her she could help him achieve greater heights in his work. But, as always with Ottoline, there were problems. Apart from the ones already mentioned there was the matter of Bertie's appearance. Ottoline said: "to my shame, however much I was thrilled with the beauty and transcendence of his thoughts I could hardly bear the lack of physical attraction."[6] Not only was Bertie strikingly unhandsome, he also lacked charm and gentleness and sympathy, qualities Ottoline always regarded as desirable in her intimate friends. In some ways this matter of unattractiveness was mutual: in his autobiography Russell described Ottoline as having "a long thin face something like a horse," although he added that she had very beautiful hair and a gentle, vibrant, voice.[7] Ottoline recognised Bertie's good points too. She described him as "rather short and thin, rigid and ungraceful, and would be unremarkable in a crowd. Then the exceeding beauty of his head would arrest me, for it gave the impression of perfect modelling: the skull thin and delicate, and the shape, especially when looked at from behind, always gave me a thrill as a very beautiful object."[8] Then there was the matter of his breath. Unfortunately Bertie suffered from acute halitosis, which made kissing him something of an ordeal. Ottoline couldn't bring herself to tell him about it and he, lacking for the past nine years anyone to apprise him of the state of his breath, was oblivious to it. There were some formidable obstacles to their love.

Finally it was time for Bertie to depart. He left in a pony cart and Ottoline stood on a hillside waving to him until he was out of sight. At Swanage he had to hide in a teashop because the train he was to catch back to London was also the one bringing Philip down to join Ottoline. In the train he wrote:

My Dearest Life—It is absurd to be writing to you now but I can't do anything else. You fill my heart and mind so completely that I can't take my thoughts off you for a moment. Our three days were an absolute revelation to me of the possibilities of happiness and of love. Each moment our union seemed to grow more complete and perfect.[9]

When he returned to his room at Trinity College, Cambridge, he continued to inundate Ottoline with letters, interspersing romantic outpourings with details of his earlier life and dissertations on philosophical subjects. And Ottoline wrote diligently back, alternately joining the exchange of endearments, then fetching up the many doubts that assailed her. They visited each other whenever practicable and their affair continued in varying degrees of warmth for the next five years. Soon a pattern began to emerge, a sort of mathematical ratio: Ottoline's love for Russell was inversely proportional to the distance between them. In her memoirs she admitted she had been swept a certain distance by Russell, but claimed her response had been as restrained as she could make it:

> What was I to do? With all his intense passionate conviction and eloquence he urged it upon me as my walk in life to leave all and go forth with him to a new life. "I will give you a life that is worthwhile," he kept saying. He refused to realise that I would not consent. It was a nightmare.[10]

Looking back Ottoline believed that if she had neglected Russell—if she had refused to "take upon me the burden of this fine and valuable life"—he would have just as easily found someone else to be the excuse for leaving Alys.[11] In this she was probably right: Bertie was ready to break out. But things appeared very different in March and April, 1911. And when many years later Ottoline asked herself what she would have done if she had to choose again she admitted she would not have acted differently.

What was Philip's view of all this? Again we have to guess from the attitude he adopted. It seems he and Ottoline came to an understanding that she would remain his wife and live a normal married life except in one respect—she could do what she could to give Russell the comfort and happiness he was so sorely craving. It might not seem a satisfactory arrangement from various points of view, but it was, to use Russell's phrase, a practicable *modus vivendi,* and disturbed the lives of the various participants least. Even so it was a precarious compromise—and one that could be disrupted at any moment by the wrong door being opened.

While Russell had been having his three days of bliss, Henry Lamb was staying nearby with Lytton, who was about to succumb to the mumps. Lamb also visited Ottoline while she was at Studland but she managed to arrange things so that Lamb's and Russell's visits didn't clash. Lamb and Ottoline were still very involved with each other, though their changeable temperaments continued to make their relationship a stormy one. Before she came down to Studland, Lamb, expecting to see a lot of her, wrote to ask if she could attend to:

1. Tea
2. Black currant jam
3. Dirty ties[12]

Somehow despite her problems, Ottoline managed to see to Henry's needs. She sent him clay pipes and socks and some bacilli for making sour milk. He was grateful for the gifts and apologised for appearing cold earlier. He said she mustn't feel hurt if he didn't mention his love for her every time, or forgot to call her "Ottolinotchka":

> Why my good creature you have only to reflect that in something like a year's time you have managed to envelope me in every possible sense with your benevolence, you have clothed me from head to foot several times over in your livery: fed, doctored, nursed, housed, studioed & beflowered me; (nay have you not penned, papered, inked, chalked, painted me even?); you have advertised, secretaried, wire-pulled, bargained, heckled, haggled, persuaded, bewitched for me—in short, you have put me on such a footing that I can look at all material & most moral difficulties straight in the face; I can chirp, grow fat, live where I will & paint what I like:—Yet can you reflect on all this & then be hurt by my chirping?[13]

A difficult decision now faced Ottoline. Assuming she continued to see Lamb—as she fully intended to—how much more should she tell Russell about him, and, more importantly, how much about Russell should she tell Lamb? She eventually opted for a policy of minimal disclosure. To Lamb she said she was helping Russell, who was a tortured soul in need of a strong white arm around his neck. To Russell she gave an almost identical story about Lamb. Fortunately the existence of Philip in the middle, so to speak, helped her to juggle Lamb and Russell so that this illusion was maintained. For the moment, however, Lamb was about to depart to France to stay with Boris Anrep, so when Ottoline arrived back at Bedford Square towards the end of April Bertie was her main worry. Throughout April and May Russell averaged one letter a day and one meeting a week. At first he came to see her at Bedford Square, but this soon became embarrassing and they took to meeting in railway waiting rooms, then going to hotels around Bloomsbury. Ottoline also had other things to think about. Julian was ill again and it looked as if she would have to be taken to the Continent to consult a specialist; also Bedford Square was proving expensive to run and Ottoline was contemplating moving to a smaller house. Meanwhile she decided for the moment to hold fewer of her Thursday entertainments.

Early in May Lamb wrote begging Ottoline to come over to Paris to visit him. He told her he was overwhelmed by her sublime strength, beauty, courage, and love; he wanted to submit to her and obey in everything; her flame and brightness dazzled him: "Though you know that what I am feeling for you at this particular juncture could only be expressed in our endless abandoned embrace. I kiss your face & your body all over."[14] Ottoline wanted to go but Philip demurred, again insisting she must be chaperoned. In the end she managed to override Philip's objections and told Lamb she would leave around May 10 so as to return, as Lamb phrased it, "to be brilliant to Winston (Churchill) on the 18th."[15] In Paris Ottoline found a changed Henry Lamb: gone was the morose and difficult man she had become accustomed to in recent months; now he was gay and charming. News of Russell's rivalry had acted as an electric shock on him, but she told him his new attitude was to no avail . . . at least that was *her* story of what took place in Boris Anrep's Paris apartment. Lamb, in a letter to her a few weeks later, mentioned another version in which she lay on a couch in "that incredible little room where you, holy woman, lay . . . & received me."[16] Their farewell at the Gare du Nord was fond.

On her return to London on May 17 Ottoline went straight to meet Bertie in a hotel off Tottenham Court Road. They spent the afternoon there and he told her later that her economical soul would be glad to hear that the hotel only charged 2s. 6d. for the room when it found out they were not staying the night.

The next evening, the eighteenth, Ottoline held a scintillating dinner for Churchill at Bedford Square. The other guests included Massingham (editor of the *Nation*); Desmond MacCarthy and his wife, Molly; Virginia Stephen; Jos Wedgewood and his wife; and, back from Constantinople, Roger Fry. Winston arrived dressed for a court ball he had to go on to later and entertained them all with talk of high politics, which to Ottoline was rather like Bertie's talk of higher mathematics. But the other guests enjoyed meeting the dashing, glamorous Churchill, and Virginia made a note: "Winston Churchill very rubicund all gold lace and medals on his way to Buckingham Palace."[17]

A few days later Ottoline sent Bertie a telegram and a large bouquet of roses for his thirty-ninth birthday and Russell had some difficulty in explaining away the flowers to his bedmaker at Cambridge. That night he came down to London to meet Ottoline and see a show. Between meetings they kept up their correspondence and Russell made a detailed study of the postal service, particularly box-clearing and delivery times, so he would know the exact moment to post each letter. He was now beginning to worry about the practical problems of having walked out on his wife and he told Ottoline he had discussed it with the Whiteheads until he was "sick of the whole sordid coil."[18] The Whiteheads thought he should offer Alys the chance of a divorce with bogus evidence and he told Ottoline that if she felt she ought to break with him while there was still time, she should. Either Ottoline didn't take this proposal seriously or decided that she was not prepared to give up Bertie. Her own doubts were of a different kind: She feared Bertie would find her mentally so inferior that he would soon tire of her. He tried to reassure her that her taste was "very exact" and her mind better than she realised: "At first I was afraid there would be a softness, & a fear of hard sharp outlines in your intellect, but I was wrong. I don't find any difference of intellectual taste."[19] He informed her that Alys now knew of their Studland, Carlyle Square, and Bedford Square meetings—but nothing more. He had been trying to find somewhere to spend the summer and had at last found rooms at Ipsden from where he could easily come over to visit her at nearby Peppard. They would study Spinoza together. It would be an idyllic summer.

Part ii
1911

Since Roger Fry had returned to London at the end of April, Ottoline had seen him several times, the latest being at her gala dinner for Churchill. He had written several times from Turkey and it was from these letters, still friendly and intimate in tone, that Ottoline learned of the disaster that had befallen the party in Byzantium. A day's journey from Constantinople Vanessa collapsed, becoming so ill that Virginia had to hurry out from London to help Fry nurse her back to health, Clive apparently being useless, and Norton in despair. It was mainly Fry's commonsense and organising ability that got the party safely home. Ottoline did not have much of a chance to speak to Fry on the eighteenth, but neither then nor at their previous meetings did she detect any change in his demeanour. She was, however, secretly glad that he had made no attempt to follow up the intimacy of their meeting in March.

On Saturday morning, May 20, Ottoline went with Russell to Heals store in Tottenham Court Road to help him choose a table for his rooms at Cambridge and after lunch Fry came to see her at Bedford Square. Ottoline described in her memoirs what happened:

> He suddenly turned on me with a fierce and accusing expression, commanding me to explain why I had spread abroad that he was in love with me. I was so utterly dumbfounded, for this thought had never entered my head—and I had certainly not uttered such an absurd thing to anyone.[20]

No wonder Ottoline was dumbfounded, for she had every reason to believe, despite her protestations to the contrary, that Fry *was* in love with her: she had his letters to prove it. What she didn't know was the reason why he had suddenly become so sensitive on the subject. While in Turkey he and Vanessa Bell had fallen in love and had begun what was to be a long liaison. So Fry would have been very angry indeed were Vanessa to hear that he was also in love with Lady Ottoline Morrell. And obviously he believed that Vanessa had either found out or was in danger of doing so.

From whom? The obvious sources of such gossip in Bloomsbury were Virginia or Lytton, both archgossips who would have delighted in spreading such a juicy morsel. Both had been at Bedford Square recently and Ottoline would not have seen much wrong in letting slip that Fry had made overtures to her; it would have provided a convenient smokescreen for Russell. In any case the gossip was out and could have come through Lytton or Virginia from one source only: Ottoline. No matter how hard she tried to expostulate, Fry's anger would not be appeased. Finally, after two hours, the interview ended with Fry stamping off and Ottoline in tears—a rare state for her. In one stroke she had now gained in Fry and Vanessa two formidable enemies. They were a powerful influence in the Bloomsbury Group and their enmity was to do much to sully Ottoline's name in that quarter.

Shattered by the terrible scene, Ottoline told Russell. He said he was sorry to hear of it but he was unable to get very indignant. Fry, he said, was overwrought and Vanessa had a lot of power over him. Anyway Bertie had other worries at the moment: Alys was threatening to expose him as a public menace. Also he felt that he ought to speak to Logan about Ottoline. (Apparently Alys had promised not to tell her brother.) By May 23 Logan knew all. He went straight to see Ottoline and they had a bitter argument. He told her he was greatly pained by her behaviour. He was, he said, the helpless brother who had for many years witnessed his sister's misery, and there was much on his heart to say; but he would not say anything more unless she wished it. Obviously she did not, for next Logan went to Philip and discussed the matter with him. In her memoirs Ottoline says Logan forced him into "denouncing" her and to promise that she would not spend another night with Russell. (Oddly, Ottoline agreed to this condition and, from now on, she and Russell spent only afternoons together. Perhaps, however, this arrangement suited her anyway.)

Meanwhile, from Cap Finistère in France, Lamb was writing passionate letters recalling their last night in Paris. He said that the night after she left he had lain down in her bed and plunged his face into the pillow, breathing himself to sleep in her scents. "It was like dying—& the following night an attempt to repeat it resulted in something like an unsuccessful suicide! The smell of your hair was fainter & the perspective of our separation much clearer."[21] Ottoline told him of her troubles with Bloomsbury and he replied that he was sickened by their squalid gossip; he was also sorry to hear of Logan's outburst. Four days later Lamb was drawing himself nude in front of the mirror, bewailing his lack of chest muscles but admiring his feminine skin.

Logan paid another visit to Bedford Square and spoke to Ottoline very coarsely about the sexual side of her friendship with Russell. Logan's homosexuality, and the fact that he believed Ottoline had lured Philip, who was his best friend at Oxford, away from him, made his disapproval all the more venomous. Pressure was now mounting on all sides. The Whiteheads advised Russell to resign his tutoring post at Newnham immediately—apparently it was thought that the young ladies there might be contaminated by the presence of a secret adulterer. Next Ethel Sands joined Logan to harass Ottoline; she invited her and Philip to come to Newington for a conference on the affair. Logan came too and for two days these two New England puritans pried into Ottoline's morals and behaviour. They were in their element and Ottoline felt herself the victim of some Salem witchhunt. They made her out to be a scarlet woman and told her she was killing Alys. Then Logan threatened that Alys would start divorce proceedings, naming Ottoline as co-respondent, thus ruining both Russell's and Philip's careers. While this inquisition was going on, Philip was out on the lawn playing croquet with Desmond MacCarthy. Finally he came in and stood up for Ottoline as best he could. That evening in their bedroom Ottoline and Philip stood by the window overlooking the moonlit garden and discussed what they should do. Ottoline said she felt as if she were covered in mud. Was she really the cause of Alys' unhappiness? Surely not, for Bertie hadn't loved Alys for many years. Eventually they decided that Logan's friendship must be given up and Ethel's behaviour overlooked. Ottoline persuaded Philip that Russell was still suffering deeply and needed her support. Her amazing husband agreed, and they left Newington next day closer than they had been for some time.

But if she and Philip had come to an understanding, Ottoline's relationships with others had taken a definite turn for the worse. She had now added to her list of enemies Logan Pearsall Smith. He was to prove an implacable foe whose spite was to dog her for the rest of her life. It had not been a good week for Ottoline.

Chapter 8

1911–1912

BACK in April, before she left Studland to return to London, Ottoline had travelled over to Corfe to the Castle Inn where Lytton was in quarantine with mumps. She stood under his window and called up and when he leaned out she saw he had acquired a beard. Of this beard he was very proud ("It is a red-brown-gold beard of the most divine proportions," he confessed to a friend) and he did not need much encouragement to be talked into retaining it as a permanent feature.[1] After an exchange of pleasantries Ottoline blew him an elaborate kiss and departed. As soon as his mumps abated he came back to London and over the next few months Ottoline saw a lot of him. In some ways they had much in common—Henry Lamb not the least. In fact Lytton would have liked to be even more like Ottoline, free to flirt with young men, to dress up in silks and rustling petticoats, and be frivolously feminine. "What a pity one can't now and then change sexes," he said, "I should love to be a dowager Countess."[2] Failing that, the next best thing was to be with Ottoline. Lytton's biographer, Michael Holroyd, says Lytton and Ottoline were at their best alone together: "Each seemed to fulfil a real need in the other; one hungering after secret confidences, the other so eager to impart them. By themselves they were natural and gay; but introduce a third person into the room and their friendship was immediately made subject to an uneasy strain." Together they carried on like a couple of high-spirited teen-age girls—all giggling and high heels and titillating gossip. "Occasionally they would step outside the drawing-room to play at tennis in Bedford Square Gardens, their slow, huge lobs over the net being accompanied by such convulsive shrieks of laughter that a large crowd of passers-by and residents would quickly assemble to behold these hysterical performances."[3]

Undoubtedly there was an element of flirtation in their friendship, for, despite Lytton's homosexual leanings, Ottoline believed he might yet be saved for the female sex; after all he did propose to Virginia Stephen. At

one time there circulated around Bloomsbury a rumour that Ottoline and
Lytton were romantically involved. Michael Holroyd cites one item of
evidence in support of this: Henry Lamb once caught the two of them
locked in a passionate embrace, and as they sprang apart he observed
blood trickling down Lytton's lip. It is just possible Lamb did observe
something like this, however the story is rendered rather suspect by its
similarity to another story that later circulated around the Bloomsbury
Group. In this version it was Henry Lamb whom Ottoline was surprised
with and as they sprang apart Ottoline allegedly explained, "I was just
giving Henry an aspirin." Also, given Lytton's innate shyness, any romance between them was probably more stagy than real, what Michael
Holroyd called "good pseudo-robust Elizabethan stuff, flighty and
rollicking."[4] There is no doubt that Lytton got on very well with Ottoline; she the dominant, masculine sort of woman he liked. Ottoline recognised this and told him once: "I often wish I was a man for then we
should get on so wonderfully."[5] As it was she worked assiduously to
convert him to more heterosexual ways until, realising her task was hopeless, she abandoned it and playfully joined him in discussions on the relative merits of the groom's brother and the young postman. She was one of
the first women to whom Lytton revealed his private thoughts on sex. Ottoline says:

> He talked a great deal about his friendships with young men. It is hard to
> realise that this tall, solemn, lanky, cadaverous man, with his rather un-
> pleasant appearance, looking indeed far older than he is, is a combination
> of frivolity, love of indecency, mixed up with a rigid intellectual integrity.
> He is, I think, frivolous about personal life and serious about his-
> tory. . . . The steeds that draw the chariot of his life seem to be curiously
> ill-matched: one so dignified and serious, and so high-stepping, and of the
> old English breed, so well versed in the manners and traditions of the last
> four centuries; the other so feminine, nervous, hysterical, shying at imagi-
> nary obstacles, delighting in being patted and flattered and fed with sugar.[6]

Russell didn't like Ottoline's friendship with Lytton and though they
were brother Apostles his hackles rose whenever Lytton came near. In
June, when Lytton was spending a weekend closeted at Peppard with Ottoline, Russell wrote irritably: "Can't you make Lytton Strachey go
Wednesday morning? Your guests can't expect to stay longer than they
are asked for."[7] But Ottoline needed someone like Lytton to neutralise

the stiff doses of passion and reason that were issuing from Upper Wyche, where Russell had taken temporary rooms before·moving on to Ipsden. At last, to Russell's relief, Lytton did go, travelling up to Cambridge to inspect the current crop of undergraduates. From there he wrote back to tell Ottoline he had felt like a pirate when he left in a taxi with the box of chocolates and pot of marmalade she had pressed on him. He reported on his progress at Cambridge: most of his days were spent lying in a punt beside King's College "propped up by innumerable cushions" and holding a sort of pastoral court:

> Various nice young men are around me, and I have won their good-will by giving them langues de chat to eat. I wish you could look at the scene for a minute or two—it's really rather pretty with willows, sunshine, parasols, blue skies, and white flannels. But even I (such is the progress of my education) feel it would be still nicer if there were also some lace petticoats. . . . Do you know though, that as my education progresses, my Terror also grows? The female sex—! Oh dear, how alarming![8]

That summer Ottoline made one last attempt to convert him, and in doing so went more than halfway to meet his tastes, suggesting as a possible spouse Ethel Sands, who was a Lesbian. Lytton gracefully declined: "So kind of you to think of Miss Sands for me. If only one could marry houses, it would be very convenient. As it is . . . I think I'll wait a little."[9]

While Ottoline was at Peppard receiving visits from Lytton and Russell, back in London lurid stories of her affair with Russell were circulating. Ottoline blamed Fry and Vanessa for this gossip—and indeed they had started it—but the real villain seems to have been Virginia. An inveterate gossip, she delighted in embellishing and propagating stories of how the eminent philosopher was infatuated with the famous Bloomsbury hostess. Vanessa had to caution her not to say too much because of the harm it could do Russell at Cambridge. Vanessa also wrote to Fry warning him to be particularly discreet with Virginia, who had already told her brother Adrian, "which means Duncan [Grant]."[10]

But Fry had little reason to be discreet; like Alys and Logan he came of Quaker stock and strongly disapproved of what Russell had done to Alys. In June he went to see the Whiteheads (who were acting as go-betweens for Alys and Russell) to discuss the matter. Mrs. Whitehead construed what he said as jealousy and reported to Russell that Fry was still fond of Ottoline. Russell, passing this on to Ottoline, added his own opinion that the trouble was that Fry had been hurt and was hitting back. Meanwhile the Whiteheads and Alys were putting more pressure on Russell to give up his tutoring post at Newnham. Finally, faced with the threat of a public scandal, Russell did resign; but he refused to give up his post at his beloved Trinity College. This wasn't enough for Alys and Logan and they again threatened a gory public divorce, with Ottoline's name brought in. This goaded Russell into action and in June he gave Alys an ultimatum— either she cease bothering him or he would throw himself under a bus. Alys had reason to believe this might not be just an idle threat, so she gave up her harassment, retiring into a role which, according to Russell, she actually preferred: that of the silent, long-suffering martyr. On June 6 Russell was able to tell Ottoline: "We need fear Alys no longer."[11]

In spite of the split with Fry, Ottoline still played an active part in the Contemporary Art Society and in the middle of June she arranged a large party for several hundred guests at Bedford Square to publicise its work. Some of her committee duties, however, were less onerous and during meetings she found time to write to Henry Lamb in France. He pictured her sitting with her pince-nez (she had recently discovered she needed reading glasses) giving him a few moments between items of business.* He also asked when he could see her—July? Or perhaps she could come over to Brittany to Anrep's little pink house by the sea (Anrep sent a sketch of it). Ottoline replied that she had no room for him in July and playfully (or perhaps sarcastically) asked for details of what housekeeping duties would be required of her should she decide to come to Brittany. Lamb assured her she would not have to make any beds. What about August? he asked; could he come to see her then? No, she replied, he would have to wait until September. Apparently Ottoline had pleaded duties and responsibilities to Philip as an excuse for not seeing Lamb, for in June he wrote: "I'm sure P can't demand it"; he scolded her for entering the houses of "publicans and sinners" (perhaps a reference to rich Liberal supporters) and for leading a worldly life.[12] On each page of his letter Ottoline scrawled "ROT" and "Superior H.L."

---

*Ottoline told Russell that she had been trying some "tortoishell" spectacles and commented to him: "You will never be able to kiss my eyes now—a great tortoishell [sic] rampart to protect them." (OM-BR, July 2, 1911, McMaster)

Most of the summer of 1911 Ottoline spent at Peppard. She wrote later of this time:

> It was one of the few English summers that are day after day hot and cloudless. Bertie was staying at lodgings at Ipsden and came over every day to see me. We grew more and more accustomed to one another and more intimate.[13]

Looking back, both of them regarded this period as one of the happiest in their lives. Each day they went out into the woods around Peppard, walking down shady paths and sitting under the trees, the hot sun beating down on them through the leaves. As they sat and talked Ottoline began to realise that here at last she had come across an intellect so powerful and expansive that not even *her* thirst for mental stimulation could exhaust it. Russell gave her daily lessons in philosophy, reading Plato and Spinoza to her and setting her exercises in logic. Perhaps, he told her, when she was sixty he might think of trying to show her how to apply logic to some of the simpler problems of life, such as "business is business" and "boys will be boys."[14] Ottoline believed her friendship with Russell was leading her back to a more natural and serious world of thought from which she had drifted away trying to please Henry Lamb, who liked to feel intellectually superior to his female friends. Ottoline felt Russell's superb intellect sharpening her mind, pruning away the fuzziness and forcing her to grasp things firmly and examine them in depth. She believed that with Bertie's help she could soar into that ethereal world of ideas and ideals she was always seeking: "The beauty of his mind, the pure fire of his soul began to affect me and attract me . . . his unattractive body seemed to disappear, his spirit and mine united in one flame, the flame of his soul penetrated mine."[15]

Mostly Philip stayed in London attending to his parliamentary duties. Once Ottoline went up to hear him speak in the House and a second time to join him in Westminster Abbey to watch the coronation of George V. Occasionally Philip would come down to the cottage and Russell had to be careful to time his visits accordingly. Yet there were occasional slip-ups. One occurred on the weekend of June 7–8 when Bertie accidentally met Philip face to face for the first time since the affair began. Philip was polite and asked him to stay to tea. Russell told Ottoline later: "I thought that Philip felt my presence almost unendurable, and thinking so, I admired his behaviour very much indeed. I felt a sense of shame in his presence—not reasonably but instinctively. I am glad the first meeting is over—it will be easier another time."[16] It must have all been rather strange for Julian—this man who was not her father turning up and staying with her mother, the two of them going off for long walks and having such intimate, intense discussions! But perhaps Julian was by now unsurprised by the comings and goings around her.

One day Ottoline gave Russell a heart-shaped locket containing a lock of her hair. She told him she was shy about appearing sentimental but he assured her he was just as sentimental. They discussed the subject of children and he said he was very keen to have some. But when she told him she was unable to have any more he asked her not to give another thought to the matter: it was probably more convenient if they did not have a child. Despite his protestations Ottoline came to realise he wanted children desperately and that things might have been different had she understood this better at the time. Another problem that kept cropping up was religion; no matter how much Russell tried to minimise the differences between them it was something that continued to lurk in the shadows, threatening to jump out any moment and cause bitter exchanges. There was also Russell's constant worry that no matter how happy they were he knew she was not his. Once he overheard someone refer to Ottoline and Philip as "such a devoted couple," always putting their arms around each other and calling each other "darling."[17] This caused Russell to be tormented by jealousy, and there was very little Ottoline could do to ameliorate his torment. She tried suggesting that he might cultivate other women friends apart from herself. He rejected this. "Believe me," he told her, "I *know* I am right in saying it is better I should avoid intimacy with other women. You will make a grave mistake if you go against this knowledge."[18] Ottoline had another reason for suggesting other women friends. She was finding that Russell's demands on her were more than she could cope with. To her, sex was a means to an end: to Bertie, it was an end in itself.* He tried by analogy to convey how much he needed her: "Young men who want to live decently have a frightfully hard time, it

---

*However, Ottoline did apparently derive some enjoyment from her relations with Bertie and told him once: "I feel shy of speaking ever about *our* physical union—but it *is* most divine & today it seemed so almost more than ever before." (OM-BR, January 9, 1912, McMaster)

must be difficult for women to know how hard. At that age one's instincts never give one any rest night or day. All one's thoughts and feelings are coloured by them."[19] The question of their physical relationship continued to cause discord and would dog their future just as much as the matter of religion.

One of the main excuses Ottoline gave Russell for not wanting to make love as frequently as he wished was her ill-health. Excuse it may have been some of the time, but it was also the truth: Ottoline's health throughout the entire period of her friendship with Russell was exceedingly poor. That summer at Peppard it seemed that she was almost constantly plagued by headaches. The Contemporary Art Society party in June had exhausted her and beneath the surface she was close to emotional and physical collapse. Throughout June and July the entries in her diary reflect moods alternating between joy and despair. Bertie did his best to cheer her up with quasimathematical jokes; for example:

> The attraction between myself and another person is directly proportional to the merit of the other person and inversely proportional to the square of the distance between them; O. is an object of infinite merit; the distance between me and O. is zero.[20]

He also told her that she was now often featuring in his dreams. In one dream she had a small, insignificant face and a snub nose; in another she was a man and he was a woman and the dream went on to "the point where the difference was of the most importance" (he added that as a woman he behaved very sensually in the dream and remembered thinking it was lucky for her he was not a man or he should have been brutal.)[21]

In July Ottoline's doctors put her on a course of injections to help her rest and ordered her to get more sleep. Bertie told her: "I hope you will get 14 hours' sleep on all possible occasions—these do not include occasions when you have visits from eminent philosophers, do they?"[22] But the injections didn't help and in August her headaches became so acute she decided to go to Marienbad for a cure. She came down to London for a few days and at Bedford Square Virginia visited her, reporting back to Vanessa that Ottoline had told her she still wanted to be friends with Roger Fry, but that it was hopeless because Fry didn't want to be friends with her. Vanessa wrote Fry urging him to make a friendly move: "Couldn't you write to Ottoline?" she asked.[23] But Fry did nothing. At the end of August Ottoline left for Austria while Philip remained behind in London and Russell prepared to quit Ipsden, first calling at Peppard to say good-bye to Julian. He reported to Ottoline that Julian had told her nurse: "Mummie's gone and Daddie's going. It's a queer world."[24]

Russell was hoping to join Ottoline in Marienbad as soon as possible and wrote her almost every day asking when he could come. In one letter he revealed that his friends were beginning to make sly digs at him over his "secret" friendship with her. It was funny, he said, how many people mentioned her name. Not everyone, however, knew and his bedmaker at Cambridge told him that the current theory around Trinity was that he was having an affair with a local Cambridge woman.

Finally Ottoline told Bertie he could come and join her. When he arrived he ran foul of the manager of the hotel, an officious Prussian who frowned on this strange Englishman paying visits to the titled lady with the different name; also he complained about the way they got cigarette ash all over the sofa. Eventually he banned Bertie from visiting Ottoline's room, a decision against which she appealed to Rufus Isaacs, the British Solicitor-General, who was also taking the waters. Alas, he could do nothing. Finally, around September 18, Bertie left, to be replaced almost immediately by Philip, who had arrived from London. The Prussian went out of his way to inform Philip of his wife's misconduct and was most put out when he smiled and told him how pleased he was to hear it.

Back in England Russell found trouble waiting for him; somehow Alys had learned that Ottoline had gone to Marienbad without her maid and that Russell had been with her. (He suspected she had been using detectives.) Alys' wrath—vented, apparently, by letter or by way of the Whiteheads—was not pleasant. While Ottoline was in Marienbad she received the sad news that Mother Julian had died. Russell telegraphed his sympathy, but she was inconsolable. A few days later she travelled on to Vienna where her depression was too deep for her to enjoy sightseeing. Russell also wrote telling her that on her return to London they must meet in the first-class waiting room at Euston Station, not Kings Cross, as planned, to avoid the Cambridge travellers, some of whom might recognise them. Ottoline wrote from Meran in the Tyrol telling Russell she was concerned that she was keeping him from his work (which idea he pooh-poohed) and that she was too weak a person to support him in his needs. Russell replied that there was nothing physically wrong with her a winter in an African desert wouldn't cure. In Paris Ottoline and Lamb had a brief and pleasant reunion. While still in Paris she received a letter from Russell relating how his friend Whitehead had asked to borrow a cake of soap she had given him; he couldn't bear to part with it and instead scrounged up a small piece to give him. Later Whitehead remarked that Russell seemed to have more hair than usual and asked if he had been using hair restorer. "It nearly made me blush!"[25] Russell reported—apparently oblivious to the fact that he was being gently teased. Before she left, Ottoline did some shopping in Paris and told Bertie, "I . . . bought myself two petticoats which *you* shall see!"[26]

After a reunion at Euston Station Bertie and Ottoline went to room 28 on the first floor of the Grafton Hotel in Tottenham Court Road, which Russell had booked for two days. But so unsatisfactory did this arrangement prove that he promised to begin looking immediately for a more permanent rendezvous. First he tried Chelsea but the Whiteheads advised against this area as Alys and Logan planned to move there soon; they suggested Bloomsbury. Near Gray's Inn he thought he had found an ideal flat—until he discovered that opposite was the firm of solicitors that had inherited a parlourmaid from him and Alys. Finally he found a flat in Bury Place, around the corner from the British Museum, in a building named (of all things) Russell Chambers.* He told Ottoline of his delight: "It will be very nice—we shall have a great sense of liberty & I can have books there & means of making tea, & even peppermints in some secret recess!"[27] (Ottoline was addicted to peppermints.)

Over the next three weeks they had a lot of fun fitting out the little flat in the crowded, rather ordinary red-brick building. Ottoline bought a rug and filled the rooms full of carnations and lilies of the valley while he moved in his most precious material possessions: his grandfather's desk and a small table made from Doomsday Book oak that had belonged to his mother and on which he had written most of *Principia Mathematica.* Looking back on these days in late 1911 Ottoline said:

> How much emotion those little rooms in Bury Place held—intense and burning and very tragic! Bertie demanded so much, and I could give so inadequately. He would stand at his window looking for my coming, grow-

---

*Much of Bloomsbury was owned by the Russell family and most of the area between it and Oxford Street was owned by Ottoline's family. Almost every street and square through which Ottoline and Russell would walk had names like Russell, Bedford, Tavistock; or Bentinck, Cavendish, Bolsover, and Welbeck.

ing tenser and tenser, counting the minutes if I was late. As I hurried along the street I dreaded to look up and see his face, pressed against the panes, looking for me.[28]

And after she left him "unsatisfied and tragically lonely" she would return home to Bedford Square and skip for joy: ". . . often I dance round my bed-room and fling my arms out and sing, 'Free, free'." Bertie, however, was very happy. On November 13 he wrote: "What a deliciously absurd time we had in the flat—I don't know when I have felt more silly."[29] A few days later Ottoline had to accompany Philip to Burnley where they attended a ball and she addressed several meetings. She wrote to Russell asking him to send her his views on the Persian situation and women's suffrage. Russell replied saying that until a woman had a vote she could not hope to have any dignity. (Ottoline may have agreed with this, but she was never an ardent advocate of votes for women and she opposed the suffragettes later on when they pelted Asquith with rotten eggs.) While in Burnley she wrote to Lamb, who was now back in England, inviting him to meet her when she returned to London. They met on the platform at Euston and spent a happy day together, after which he wrote to her (November 21): "It has all been so very wonderful, so revealing, transfiguring; I can still only ponder in bewildered joy." He concluded:

> I kiss
> your feet in reverence
> your knees in trust
> your hands in troth
> your mouth in courage
> & your heart in fiery penetration.[30]

But three days later he was sulky again and apologising for his behaviour; it was caused by jealousy he said. Later Ottoline went back to Burnley feeling ill and dispirited. That Christmas was spent at Black Hall where Ottoline suffered from a cold, headaches, and a liver chill—and the disapproval of Mrs. Morrell, who had found out about Russell. Ottoline wrote telling Lytton her troubles and he did his best to cheer her up. On Boxing Day she was sitting at the Jacobean table in the dining room when the maid brought her a letter from Lytton: "If it wasn't for . . . circumstances, I believe this letter would jump up from the breakfast-table, and throw its arms around your neck. As it is, a few tender glances are all that it will allow itself, while your hostess is engaged with the tea."[31] This letter was a contrast to the sort of mail she was getting from Russell during the festive season. They had had a bitter disagreement over religion. "What I don't understand," he had told her, "is the purely intellectual parts—how you can think that it is true."[32] But he soon regretted his outburst and begged her forgiveness; he would improve if only he could get the fanaticism of reason out of his soul. But it refused to be silenced:

> I must go on writing—it is impossible to do anything else. I can already see better how it is. You do not believe that reasoning is a method of arriving at truth; I do. That is the root of the matter. Reduced to that, it does not much matter. You are wrong in thinking it will crop up worse & worse as time goes on; hitherto I have never said the worst; & so it kept on growing. Things unsaid are poisonous in my mind. When once I have grasped fully how your beliefs are incompatible with truthfulness I shall hardly wish them changed.[33]

Ottoline then accused Russell of unworthy bigotry. He agreed abjectly and strove mightily to reconcile their differences. "Do you know," he told her, "that there is scarcely a word that I disagree with in your confession of faith. The only practical difference is that things which we both think possible but not certain seem to me rather less probable than to you."[34] Ottoline's sojourn in Marienbad had done little to cure her headaches and in February she decided to go to Lausanne to see a Dr. Combe who was said to be an expert on neuralgia. Before leaving she had another crisis with Lamb, this time over his semiserious courting of Ka Cox, a motherly young woman who was a friend of Rupert Brooke. But just before she left for Switzerland they spent two heavenly days together after which he waved farewell at the station. Lamb told her to take plenty of rest and, when she was running her finger down her present list of adorers, to stop and reflect a little on her youngest and former *"esclave favori"* who still hoped and loved.[35]

Despite Dr. Combe's drastic treatment in Lausanne (her nose was probed with a red-hot needle) Ottoline's headaches did not vanish; moreover her surroundings annoyed her. She complained to Bertie that the person in the next room at her hotel smelled. Then she had a tooth extracted. Then she suffered liver trouble. To make matters worse, Dr. Combe put her on a strict diet of starch and chicken. All she could do to relieve the tedium was read Spinoza and do her embroidery (Lamb had specially designed her a "Deirdre of the Sorrows" picture to sew). Russell wrote telling her he was pining for her and kissed her locket every night before bed. On March 19 she received another letter from him reminding her it was exactly one year since their first momentous evening together at Bedford Square: "You and I, dearest, belong to each other in a very eternal way: we are of those who are not passive to the world, but resolved to stamp it with the seal of divinity whenever it is possible. The flames of our inmost fires meet and mingle. I know your springs of living water, and my spirit drinks at them."[36]

While Ottoline was away Lamb had been getting to know Philip better and went riding with him several times along with Ka Cox and Leonard Woolf (who was soon to marry Virginia Stephen). Lamb told Ottoline that Philip was charming and mellow but "unbelievably naif. He has a way of making his weaknesses appear virtuous—by excessive frankness! I do like him so very much."[37] He asked Ottoline why it was Philip didn't have any friends, adding, "I suppose people are either too suspicious or patronising, & if neither *you* absorb them! What a sad sacrifice!"[38]

Ottoline had not allowed Bertie to join her in Lausanne, and he had been counting the hours until she returned. But instead of hurrying back to London to see him, Ottoline stopped over in Paris for an extra day "not to rest, but merely for pleasure," as he later indignantly complained.[39] This "oversight" joined with "a host of things I have overlooked before" to produce a coldness in Russell that he expressed in a letter in April, 1912:

> There is one thing you could do for me if you have time, and that is to look through my letters since the latter part of your stay in Lausanne, and see if there is anything in them worth remembering, and if so bring some of them round with you. I should like to talk about the things in them.

He sounded like a stiff schoolmaster. He said her judgment about sex was "morbid and maladif. . . . It seems to me one can only say that to some

sex is spiritually important, to others not. Unfortunately you and I belong
to different camps in this respect. But today I can hardly imagine what
sexual feelings are like, as they are utterly dead in me."[40] Ottoline ignored the sarcastic tone and at their next meeting smoothed down his
ruffled feathers. A few days later he sent her two poems he had composed. A stanza of one went:

> My love is a burning fire
> From the flaming heart of mankind,
> The heart of a vast desire,
> Restless and ruthless and blind.[41]

Russell told her that talking to her helped him gain an insight into how
to explain his philosophy to his popular audience. This was the sort of
work he was really interested in now, he told her; he would be happy to
leave the "technical" work to others. Around this time he started writing
his autobiography, which he proposed to publish under the pseudonym
Simon Styles. They went to concerts together and after one he told her
that her beauty was like the effect of a Beethoven melody. But the matter
of sex continued to cause problems. At the end of April he drafted a letter
saying it might be better if they parted but he didn't send it. Later Ottoline
asked how he would feel if either of them took another lover. He replied
that it wouldn't help *him* and that if *she* took up with someone else he
should suffer untold torments. However, he believed that their love might
survive if the person she chose was someone he admired and respected,
like Henry James.

A few weeks later Russell was very depressed: he was still mulling
over the Paris business yet threatening the direst consequences should she
decide to drop him. In May he wrote: "I feel that if we parted . . . the
moment would come when in a sudden impulse I should put myself under
a motor for the pleasure of hearing my backbone break. And if I avoided
that, I should not avoid sexual crime, from mere desperation."[42]

In April Lamb and Lytton went off together for a holiday in Dorset.
Earlier they had had a tiff (possibly over Lamb's refusal to set up house
somewhere together) but they made up, and from an inn in Dorset Lamb
pleaded with Ottoline to join them. She declined but offered to show him

some dances she had learned at the Easter fair on Hampstead Heath. He replied, "I will learn anything which involves you hugging my neck!"[43] But their relationship was beginning to show signs of succumbing to its inherent strains. In May there was a misunderstanding over a painting which either she or her brother Lord Henry had commissioned from Lamb. Apparently Ottoline accepted it as a gift, then decided she didn't like it and sent it back with a cheque for £30. Later Robbie Ross bought it for the Contemporary Art Society and Lamb returned the cheque to Ottoline. He also gave her another picture that was to lead to even greater trouble. Then he returned a ring Ottoline had given him, a gesture for which she took him to task. Lamb replied (May 27, 1912), addressing her as "Dear Ottoline"—a form of address he had not employed for years: "The returning of the ring was not an act of hostility, as you seemed to take it: indeed I should not have risked it if I hadn't thought the moment propitiously free from misunderstanding."[44]

In June Ottoline went off again to Lausanne to consult Dr. Combe. This time Russell accompanied her in order to see if their friendship could improve, as indeed it did. Bertie spent his mornings reading or writing in the garden of his hotel and in the afternoons he and Ottoline would go for walks together and read poetry. She found that he was more gentle and imaginative, less positive and definite, and they were happy again. While she was undergoing yet another of Dr. Combe's Draconian treatments— drinking for thirty days a daily dose of radium in milk—she received another of Lytton's morale-boosting letters. It was dreadful, he told her, to think of her in Lausanne without a maid:

> I should love to come out and be your maid—I'm sure I'd make a very good one. I believe my real rôle in life would be that. I should arrange your petticoats most exquisitely, and only look through the crack of the door now and then. . . . When are you coming back?—I'm afraid not for ages. I wish I could send you wireless telegrams of affection and laughter, dearest Ottoline. But really I do send them—Don't you see them glimmering in your radium? Oh yes, and dancing up your flight of stairs, and running into your room at the oddest moments? They don't even stop to knock at the door.[45]

On her return to London Ottoline had a frightful scene with Lamb. The incident that sparked it concerned the other painting he had given her. Ottoline had accused Lamb's dealer of delivering the painting at an inconvenient moment; Lamb then told her that in sending the cheque for the first painting she had been trying to remove the painful associations it had for her. He told her to return the second one if she didn't wish to accept it as a gift. She went to see him and afterwards he wrote a bitter note, saying he now pitied her and signing "ever your 'little' . . . Henry Lamb."[46] (This was a reference to Philip Morrell's earlier comment that Henry was Ottoline's "little lamb.") Lamb's next letter was formal and cutting. She had insisted he accept her cheque and he replied sarcastically that it was much too big. He said he was sorry she had such bad headaches but he couldn't see her, as he was off to Donegal, perhaps for a year. However, he did see her once more and at this meeting Ottoline took him bodily by the shoulders and shook him. Later she felt sorry and wrote to apologise, but he replied curtly:

DEAR OTTOLINE,

Many thanks for your advice & renewed protestations.

I also venture to say that I know *you* well, & in my turn make you a few recommendations—gratis, like yours.

Just try & keep for your own benefit a little of all this overflowing soul, spirit & help; you will really be surprised to find how they will have their work cut out for them. And when you have made a little progress towards manufacturing some self-control, you will perhaps be better prepared for the éclaircissement which you seem so anxious to get from me.

As for the "outburst"—Don't worry—Lobelia [Euphemia] used to use plates & dinner-knives—: Meanwhile I shall go on my way cheerfully— and slightly weathered, yet enormously wiser as to the validity of feminine assistance in Life.

Yrs,
HENRY L.[47]

With that Lamb ceased to communicate with Ottoline for several months and went off to tramp around the Highlands of Scotland with Lytton.

Chapter 9

1912–1914

IN the summer of 1912 Ottoline took up residence at 44 Bedford Square again and reopened her salon. Though she had been out of circulation for over a year all her old friends—Asquith, Birrell, Henry James, Ethel Sands, Hilda Douglas-Pennant—flocked back and once more the grey-and-yellow drawing rooms came alive with laughter, gossip, and argument. Nor had her flair for spotting and attracting new talent deserted her, and mixing with the more familiar faces were a number of new ones: the novelist Arnold Bennett, the painters Wyndham Lewis and Frederick Etchells, and the mathematician (and budding Bloomsburyite) Harry Norton, whom Ottoline had recently befriended. Bloomsbury itself was represented by Duncan Grant, Adrian and Virginia Stephen—and of course Lytton, by now almost part of the furniture. (Roger Fry and Clive and Vanessa Bell stayed well away.)

But for Ottoline undoubtedly the most exciting new faces at Bedford Square belonged to Vaslav Nijinsky, Léon Bakst, and Sergei Diaghilev—for this was the summer of the Russian Ballet, and Ottoline had discovered a new setting in which to sparkle. Nijinsky she had met in Paris in 1910 without being overly impressed and when Diaghilev brought his troupe to London the following year she had been away at Peppard reading Spinoza in the woods with Bertie. At first she rather dismissed the Ballet Russe, probably because everybody else was making such a fuss about it. But in July, 1912, she went to Covent Garden and became a convert overnight. She was entranced with the wild music of Stravinsky, the bizarre Oriental sets and costumes of Bakst and, above all, the faunlike genius of Nijinsky. Night after night she returned to drink in the excitement of *Thamar*, the splendour of *Scheherazade*, and the elegance of *Giselle*. In the intervals she and her friends gathered at the refreshment bars to argue the merits of one dance over another, Ottoline's tall figure draped with a gorgeous cloak and her dramatic outfit topped by a large leghorn hat decked with ostrich feathers. Through her friendship with the

Ballet's patron, Lady Ripon, she was able to invite Nijinsky and Diaghilev to Bedford Square and soon she became one of the few people in
London whom the highly strung Nijinsky would trust. Sometimes he and
Diaghilev would come to tea and afterwards wander round the gardens in
the square. One evening they happened upon Duncan Grant and Adrian
Stephen playing tennis in the twilight and at the sight of their lithe bodies
flitting over the shadows Nijinsky exclaimed, *"Quel décor!*[1]*"* Another
time he was discussing Ottoline: "Lady Morrell is so tall, so beautiful,
like a giraffe."[2] Fearing Ottoline might be hurt, Diaghilev tried to correct
him, but the dancer insisted: "No, no, giraffe is beautiful—long, gra-
cious . . . she looks like it." Diaghilev, too, was impressed with Ottoline's appearance and once toyed with the idea of designing a ballet in
which she would appear as herself—on stage and in person.

That summer Ottoline met everybody and went everywhere. And, perhaps to compensate for the comparative dullness of her private life, she
also went out of her way to wear outfits that were especially colourful and
striking. Her entrance at a garden party given by Asquith caused a mild
sensation, though she later confessed to Lytton: "I was awfully shy and
cut most of the people I most wanted to talk to from sheer fright, but some
came up and [were caught] in my magic ring."[3] Perhaps Nijinsky was
right in likening Ottoline to some tall, slightly improbable inhabitant of
the veldt; certainly whenever she went out for a stroll passersby would
stop to gaze, and she discovered that it was not wise to travel by bus because of the stir her appearance created. She told Lytton, "What an odd
life I have, continually acting on the different stages of London."[4]

Another face absent from Ottoline's public functions was Bertie's (and
a much more interesting face it was too, now he had taken Ottoline's
advice and shaved off his prim moustache). Though his meeting with
Philip at Peppard had been cordial it was still embarrassing for him to be
seen at Bedford Square, and with Ottoline preoccupied with her social doings their meetings had to be restricted to occasional afternoons together
in 34 Russell Chambers. He couldn't even go to see the Russian Ballet
with her and had to go instead with a male companion. Even so, an embarrassing incident occurred. Just as he was sitting down he caught sight
of Alys sitting only a few seats away. Jumping up, he dragged his protesting colleague out into the street; but Alys had seen Russell and followed
them out. They met face to face and she gave him a look which, Russell

told Ottoline, "was intended to pierce my heart, and did so." He was so upset he had to lean against some railings. "Darling, I can't tell you how awful it was," he added.[5] When he first saw Alys in the auditorium he had been struck by her good looks, but the second time she seemed old and tragic. Later he decided her intense stare was not all tragedy but was also "partly to see how I looked without my moustache." Throughout 1912 Russell's letters to Ottoline reveal a slight but distinct change in tone. His disillusionment when she stopped over in Paris had done irremediable damage. He worshipped her still, but his devotion was not unreserved; reason had reestablished a toehold. He began to think more about his academic and technical work and in August at a philosophy conference in London he enjoyed being praised and feted, particularly by the Americans there. Yet he was still deeply in love with Ottoline, and there were times when desire overcame him:

> My Darling My Darling—People were with me all the evening and now it is too late for the post. I had gone to bed not meaning to write till tomorrow, but the longing for you is too great—I must write a word of love, my dearest Heart—a sudden flood of yearning has overwhelmed me—such a hunger for you as is hard to bear. Dear Dear Love, I do try to be contented away from you, and to think how soon I shall see you again, but it is not easy.[6]

At other times his mind was occupied with things entirely flippant—his appearance, for instance: "My HAT has come. Do you like the crown pressed down or sticking up? This question is *very important*."[7] But on other occasions he would grow maudlin and write: "Sometimes I think you and Aunt Agatha are the only people who really care for me."[8]

Ottoline and Philip had sold Peppard in 1911 and since then had been looking around for a larger country house. While they searched, Philip's parents offered them the use of Broughton Grange, their country house near Banbury outside Oxford. Philip talked Ottoline into spending a month there in August, 1912. It was an unmitigated disaster. Most of the time it rained, Ottoline felt even more ill, and Mrs. Morrell spoilt Julian. Ottoline wrote: "It is secure and quiet, but deadly . . . purely hunting country."[9] Still, there were diversions. On August 19 she received a telegram: SHALL ARRIVE TOMORROW WIRE TRAIN LATER. IN NEED OF YOUR CORRAGIO AS WELL AS MY OWN. LYTTON[10] It came from Ulster where

Lytton and Lamb had ended up after an exhausting and progressively less comradely holiday. Earlier, Lytton, already weak from privations suffered in Scottish guesthouses, had written from Ireland, where he and Lamb had gone to recuperate: "Don't be surprised if I suddenly arrive at Broughton pale and trembling."[11] On August 20, duly fragile, he did arrive, falling into Ottoline's arms an emotional and physical wreck. Ottoline set aside some rooms and did her best to resuscitate him. They spent hours together gossiping, then Lytton would put on her high-heeled shoes and totter around the room, both of them getting more and more giggly. Mrs. Morrell did not approve, nor did Russell, who came down to Broughton for a day and told Ottoline he liked neither Lytton nor Mrs. Morrell. "Nevertheless," he told her, "I think loathing for him quite pardonable, whereas I don't see why he should loathe her. . . . He is diseased and unnatural, & only a very high degree of civilization enables a healthy person to stand him."[12] Russell's visit was not a success and all Ottoline remembered of it was a melancholy walk in a local churchyard.*

In September she went to stay at Churn, Berkshire, in a house lent by her brother, Lord Henry. There she took up watercolour painting and had another visit from Lytton, who was making a walking tour of the downs. He warned her of an exciting new development in his appearance:

> Very exceeding secret. I shall be . . . in earrings! Yes! HUSH! It was the maddest lark—perhaps too mad for me even??—but I was in a mood for *anything* so don't jibe and think me quite grotesque or a mere imitation of John or anything else—only a very young youth on a gay holiday—reckless & debonair & not caring a brass farthing for the rest of humanity.—Do you understand? Oh, *I* like them very much—so far—. But of course civilized society—imagine its comments!—I shall therefore arrange my locks so that Pipsey shall not observe them.—and you are *not* to tell him or anyone else.[13]

He signed the letter "Your eighteen-year-old Lytton" (actually he was thirty-two). When he arrived, sporting a bright-yellow coat and orange waistcoat, he tried to persuade Ottoline to soften towards Lamb, whom he likened to a cat: "How I should stroke him!—And then up would come a

---

*That may have been all *she* remembered, but the walk stuck firmly in Russell's memory and from it he was later to date the beginning of his withdrawal from Ottoline's influence.

soft pad onto my thigh—oh so soft & caressing!—and then—the sudden
stiffening, and the claws starting out and drawing blood right through my
trousers!''[14] Ottoline thought the simile very apt. Russell also paid a visit, but again it was not a success. "I felt wild and heartless," she said.
"He was self-absorbed and unhappy and sentimental about himself."[15]
They went out on the downs and he broke down completely and sobbed
and sobbed, and though she tried to be sympathetic she couldn't melt to
him. His breath, which was almost overpowering, did not help and her
broad hints about mouthwash and dental treatment went unheeded. To
Lytton Ottoline moaned that she had lost her youth and vitality and he
tried to cheer her up by telling her it was only temporary—he suffered the
same thing from time to time. "Of course," he said, "you have a splendid and glorious and vivacious and perpetually youthful future before
you, *ma plus chère de toutes les marquises*—you mustn't doubt that.
Your humble servant will always be there to assist you to the best of his
ability—and you will do the like by him, I hope. Our great-grandchildren
shall see us gallivanting down Bond Street as nonagenarians, and gnash
their teeth with envy."[16]

In October Ottoline's health forced her to return to Lausanne for
another session of Dr. Combe's radium cocktails. Lytton was deeply concerned: "Tea and radium!" he exclaimed. "A horrid mixture! One day
there'll be an explosion on your balcony, if you're not careful. The boots
will rush up—too late! too late! Miladi will have been dissipated into a
thousand fragments, and the reputation of Dr. Combe at last ruined for
ever."[17]

Russell also wrote. He had had another dream about her and this time
she had turned into a cat . . . a very nice cat, very affectionate, purring
and rubbing soft fur against him. He hadn't minded the strange transfor-
mation until he began to regret that she had lost the power of speech. Less
happy was a letter from Lamb, who was still in Ireland, accusing her of
having given Clive Bell the wrong picture to hang in an exhibition at the
Grafton Galleries. Apparently Clive had gone to Bedford Square to get
some of Lamb's paintings and had taken the wrong one. A week later
Lamb wrote to apologise, Clive having told him the error wasn't Ottoline's. Nevertheless rumours of the mixup had already spread round
Bloomsbury and Molly MacCarthy wrote to Clive Bell: "What *is* the Ottoline scandal? I am so distressed if she is being gossiped about, as I do

love her, & don't mind what she does; she is a rare muddler I fear in her intense affairs. Don't let people say unkind things about her.''[18]

In November Ottoline returned to London with the first decent piece of advice she had received from the medical profession: she was to rest in the country for at least two years. Now she and Philip began looking in earnest for a suitable country house and in the meantime Ottoline retired to Cholsey, where Philip's sister had a spare house. Lytton was devastated by news of her impending exile. How would he survive without her parties? Bedford Square was the one place where he could go and mingle with the *beau monde*. She reassured him she wasn't shutting up house just yet.

Ottoline remained at Cholsey for most of the winter of 1912–1913, which meant she saw Russell, who had duties in Cambridge, only irregularly. Though he was more or less reconciled to the necessity of her staying in the country he still missed their afternoons together and wrote several times a week. In one letter he told her he had heard that Philip was one of only four men in the House of Commons willing to speak out against the foreign policies of Sir Edward Grey. In another he defined the current state of their relationship:

> Dearest, do believe that my real deep love is not less. I know passion is less, but that can't be helped. You explained before once how you have to keep me on an island in your life; for a long time I kept you in the centre of mine, but in the long run that was incompatible with one's duties, and I had to put you on an island too.[19]

Russell's main duty at this time was trying to keep his star student, Ludwig Wittgenstein, from going mad, a task that was causing him some worry. Wittgenstein had met Maynard Keynes and several other Apostles who wanted to recruit him for the Society. Russell argued against this, but was overruled. Later Lytton and others put it about that Russell had been trying to monopolize Wittgenstein.*

In November Russell accepted an offer of £600 to go to the United States in the spring of 1914 to lecture at Harvard. He told Ottoline that though he was looking forward to seeing what America was like, he be-

*From Russell's letters to Ottoline it seems that this accusation was groundless: Russell was trying to shield Wittgenstein from all excitement to preserve his delicate mental stability.

grudged not seeing her for three months. Actually she was relieved Bertie would be absent for a while, for although her letters to him speak of her shortcomings and weaknesses, her diary gives a different picture: "I wish I knew why he is not sympathetic to me. . . . His hands are the hands of a bear. They have no expression in them, only force. . . . I find it exhausting to keep in step with his intellect all the time, and also satisfy his heart. But after all one's spirit can endure and press on—stagnation is what I fear."[20] A little later comes another outburst: "Bertie has been very much annoyed with me lately for desiring quiet times in the day for reading, he expects me to be entirely at his disposal morning, noon, night, and becomes very angry if I am not. He told me that I could never accomplish anything important in life by *my* reading while I could help him by being with him."[21]

Ten miles away from Cholsey Lytton was staying in the Chestnuts, a farmhouse Ottoline had booked him into as a paying guest. He had now discarded his earrings and was starting work on what was to become his most famous book, *Eminent Victorians*. As he delved into Cardinal Manning and the Oxford Movement, Ottoline kept his spirits up with gifts and pep talks. In January he felt low and came over for a heart-to-heart talk. He was depressed about his writing, he told her, his voice was too thin for politics, and he was no good in company. Ottoline reassured him that writing was his real *métier* and he should concentrate on that. But Lytton couldn't stay down for long and soon he was learning to ride: "I shall come galloping into Bedford Square," he warned Ottoline, "in a peaked cap & striped silk breeches."[22] Especially was he proud of his appearance in breeches: "Full many a leg is born to blush unseen," he told her. In March, partly for want of anything better to do, he returned to Hampstead where Lamb began work on a new portrait of him.* Ottoline was by now having some regrets about her estrangement from Lamb, and for Christmas, 1912, she embroidered him a silk picture to hang over his fireplace. He thanked her for this and also for sending him a cheque and added that he hoped the country air would restore her to health.

Ottoline and Philip's search for a country house ended in March, 1913, when they learned that Garsington Manor, a Tudor and Jacobean house just outside Oxford, was coming up for auction. Philip went to Oxford to

*The famous Lamb portrait, now in the National Portrait Gallery in London, showing Lytton draped limply in an armchair.

bid and returned with the news that he had bought the house and farm that went with it. He fancied himself a gentleman farmer and planned to start work on the farm immediately, but the house itself would not be vacant for another two years. Lytton was pleased at the news but wondered about the two-year wait: "And then—2 years hence!—where shall we all be by then?—and what?—infinitely grey-haired, respectable, crutch-supported antiquities—or bankrupts—or exiles with ruined reputations—I shudder to think of it. Or do you think we shall be altogether rejuvenated & sprightly? Or just the same as ever?"[23]

Russell could not work up much enthusiasm about the purchase as he knew it would involve even more difficulties seeing Ottoline. To make up a little for this she visited him several times in March. He cooked scrambled eggs on toast for her and told her the past year had taught him to accept the fact that she would not leave Philip and that he must be satisfied with what time, age, and health permitted her to allow him.

Ottoline returned to London in April and resumed her Thursday levees. Henry Lamb wrote asking to be allowed to attend, but Ottoline, fearing trouble, gently put him off. She did, however, attempt another reconciliation. At the Sickerts' one night she found herself talking to Vanessa Bell and later they shared a taxi home. Vanessa reported to Fry that Ottoline was making friendly overtures. Next day Ottoline telephoned Vanessa and invited her to Bedford Square, where they had a touching reunion, Ottoline telling her that the whole quarrel had been dreadful. "Then," Vanessa told Fry, "she kissed me passionately on the lips!"[24] When Vanessa got up to go Ottoline pressed a silk handkerchief on her. "I think she is really very nice," Vanessa said, "though muddle-headed. One mustn't expect her to be over clear about anything." But hardly had Ottoline dealt with Vanessa than Lytton began to fret; he was jealous over the interest "Our Lady of Bedford Square" was taking in Gilbert Cannan, a young writer who had been to school with Henry Lamb in Manchester. Ottoline wrote to Cannan praising his latest novel and soon he became a regular visitor to Bedford Square, sometimes staying the night in the spare room. Bloomsbury tongues wagged but there is no evidence the gossip had any substance. Nevertheless it was indicative that Ottoline was beginning to seek younger friends.

In April Ottoline went north to Burnley to preside over a local bazaar. She tended a stall and raised £70. 17.5 for local Liberal coffers, reporting to Lytton: "I sat & sold at the Bazaar for 4 days until 10:30 p.m. & altogether they made nearly £5000 . . . *can't we go* into commerce?"[25] In May she went off to Lausanne again, this time taking Julian, who was still frail. While there Ottoline transferred her allegiance to a Dr. Vittoz, a psychiatrist whose specialty was eliminating unnecessary thoughts from the mind. Her concentration did wander for a moment, however, to Lytton to whom she sent some pressed flowers and a letter: "You really must be dead. So I send you a few flowers to scatter on your grave. Where are you buried I wonder?"[26]

Throughout the summer of 1913 relations with Russell fluctuated. He was busy writing a long book on the theory of knowledge and most of his letters to her, though still regular, were shorter and less intense. But whenever a meeting was in the offing his passion would return. On May 2 he wrote:

> The last two days I had been rather sad and listless, but today has been *quite* different. It seems odd that the prospect of an hour with you can alter the whole aspect of the universe—but it is so. You must prepare yourself for a dreadful blow! Thinking I shouldn't see you for six weeks, I have had my hair cropped quite short—it will horrify you, but I thought it would please all my relations.[27]

A little later the forty-one-year-old philosopher's thoughts wandered to lighter matters: "My Darling Love. . . . The night is hot and delicious, with just a sound of summer breeze in the treetops—a night that seems made for love—ah me. . . . "[28] But Ottoline was in Lausanne so he reluctantly returned to William James' theory of consciousness. A few days later, on May 28, he made a disconcerting discovery. After spending months on his new book he ventured to show Wittgenstein a crucial part. "He said it was all wrong," Russell told Ottoline. "I couldn't understand his objection—in fact he was very inarticulate—but I feel in my bones that he must be right, and that he has seen something that I have missed. . . . Well, well, it is the younger generation knocking at the door—I must make room for him when I can, or I shall become an incubus. But at the moment I am rather cross."[29]

From Lausanne Ottoline wrote breaking the news to Russell that he couldn't come over to see her as he had been hoping. This, on top of Wittgenstein's criticism, depressed him severely. Caught between the hammer of Wittgenstein's keener mind and the anvil of Ottoline's insensitivity, he had a miserable summer and when Ottoline returned he was a bundle of nerves. Just before she arrived he told her: "I can hardly let myself think of holding you in my arms once more and hearing your voice and kissing your dear eyes. . . . O my loved one my Ottoline my soul is yours. I love you love you love you."[30] But after she arrived things didn't go at all smoothly, and Russell got so low he again contemplated suicide. "I must get myself in hand," he wrote to her, "and I will. Till then I am not fit for you to associate with."[31] He took himself off to Cornwall to try to piece together the jigsaw of his emotions.

For Ottoline probably the most important event of the summer was her meeting with Joseph Conrad. When Henry James heard she intended to go down to Conrad's house at Ashford in Kent he was appalled. He paced up and down her drawing room: "But, dear lady," he warned her, ". . . but, dear lady . . . he has lived his life at sea—dear lady . . . he has never met a civilised woman. . . . No, dear lady, he has lived a rough life and is not used to talking to. . . ."[32] And he raised his arms to indicate the sort of woman he imagined Ottoline to be. She also told Desmond MacCarthy of her intended visit and he advised her that, as Conrad saw few ladies of fashion, she should wear something unusual for the occasion. This was not difficult for Ottoline. But on arrival at Ashford she found Conrad to be a perfect gentleman and she returned to London full of his praises, which she proceeded to sing to Russell, who was still feeling morose. On her recommendation he later went to see Conrad and they became lifelong friends.

Back in London Ottoline found the Russian Ballet had returned and that Lytton had fallen in love with Nijinsky. He persuaded her to arrange an introduction and bought for the occasion a new dark purple suit and an orange stock, though he was terrified of uttering a single word in French. Delighted at finding "Nij" no eunuch, he sent him basketfuls of flowers at his performance of *Le Sacré du Printemps*. But before long his bedazzlement faded and he began calling him "that cretinous lackey."[33] He spread mischievous stories about Ottoline's worship, describing her as "gaping and gurgling" over Nijinsky "like a hooked fish."

Russell's stay in Cornwall had done little to sort out his feelings about Ottoline, and in August he went to Italy, sending back bitter letters. On August 10 he told her:

> I can't help feeling that what makes you less useful than you might be is a kind of selfishness. . . . I am very sorry you miss my letters so much. I have felt the need of not thinking too constantly about you . . . when I care for people I like to be with them; yet you would rather ruin my life and work than be very much with me.[34]

He became more and more desperate. He told her he had been flirting with a German woman. While he was in this mood Ottoline took the opportunity to break the news about his breath, and he replied that he would get his teeth cleaned and see a doctor about his breath as soon as possible.

In August, before going to spend a few weeks at Black Hall, Ottoline held a reception at Bedford Square for a group of African chiefs who were visiting London. One of them, Chief Odunta Labinjo, was particularly impressed with Ottoline and later wrote from Nigeria sending her a parcel of native cloth and his photograph (taken at Harrods and copied by a native photographer in Lagos). He and Ottoline continued to correspond for several years.

In September Ottoline and Philip had to go up to Burnley for a month and there, to help relieve the boredom, Ottoline would spend Saturday afternoons watching the local soccer team. Her favourite player was a little red-haired youth named Moscrop, who was later one of the few conscientious objectors in Burnley. Another diversion was Gladstone League rambles on which Ottoline made friends with the girl millworkers, one of whom wrote to her:

> It is with great pleasure that I forward the [bed] cover I promised. . . . Dear Lady Ottoline you must excuse me for being so long as I have had to do it in my spare time in the evenings and it has taken me rather a long time as work in the mill occupies all my time during the day; hoping it will give you much pleasure in receiving, as it does me in sending, I Remain "Yours and earnest Gladstone League Worker." Signed Bessie Burrows.[35]

After Burnley Ottoline left for Switzerland to join Julian who was recovering from tuberculosis at a sanatorium there. When she arrived she wrote to Norton asking him to join her, but he declined. Meanwhile Lytton had taken a country cottage near Marlborough from where he wrote asking how she was getting on: "An escapade with John? Or an amorous adventure with an ice-cream boy?"[36] He declined to spend Christmas, 1913, with her because he had a prior engagement with Lamb. Instead he sent her a spoon dated 1759: "The year *Candide* came out."[37]

For Ottoline the year 1913 ended on an uneasy plateau. Lamb was gone and Russell was beginning to stray. Where was she to go from here? London beckoned, but she felt she couldn't respond with all her heart; the country beckoned, but she feared it wouldn't be the answer to her problems. In February, 1914, she wrote in her diary: "For many months I have felt a dire loneliness that nothing will ever relieve. I seem to have tried everyone and found them all wanting. . . . At one time I seem to have plunged into others' lives—Roger Fry, Lamb, Lytton, Bertie, but from some cause they all seem to have come to an end."[38] That month the most severe crisis so far in her friendship with Russell occurred. It was over Bertie's continued flirtations with the German woman and some harsh words were exchanged, after which Russell and Ottoline agreed to part. But on February 5 he wrote her:

> My dearest I can't bear that we should part with bitterness on both sides it is too dreadful after what we have been to each other. . . . The longing for children has grown & grown in me, & the pain of not having a child by you has been terrible. . . . When you spoke the other day, the bitterness of all the pain & hunger I have suffered became just too much & I couldn't bear it any more. . . . I must break with you, or I shall be broken—& I must not be broken yet. . . . You think I no longer love you & that is why I break. That is an *ABSOLUTE MISTAKE.* I have no wish of any sort or kind to have anything to do with any other woman, that was only an attempt to bear the pain.[39]

For several weeks letters between them were almost formal, then she sent him a telegram and went to see him in his flat. Within days they were back on the best of terms—just in time for Russell's departure to the United States. On February 25 he wrote: "It is quite extraordinary how deep and strong the tie is between us—such storms one would have thought would destroy any tie—yet it always emerged as living as ever."[40] On March 19 he wrote from Harvard: "America produces a type of bore

more virulent, I think, than the bore of any other country—they all give
one exactly the same information, slowly, inexorably, undeterred by all
one's efforts to stop them."[41] Also, the large number of spittoons he observed everywhere surprised him. He was unimpressed with his fellow
academics: "They were all barbarians, but some, who had been to Oxford, accentuated their barbarism by a Common Room veneer. Ygh!"[42]
The only consolations were a bright young student named T. S. Eliot, the
money, and a young lady named Helen Dudley who had written to him on
his arrival in America inviting him to stay at her parents' home. Russell
fell in love with her and she agreed to return to England to live with him.
Russell broke the news to Ottoline:

> My Darling,
>   This is the last letter before I sail—thank heaven. I am *longing* to be with
> you again my Dearest. When I started I assured you I should not have any
> adventure here but I have had one, a rather important one.[43]

He went on to tell her of Miss Dudley, including the information that they
had spent at least one night together and that she was following him to
England in a few months. He added: "I do not want you to think this will
make the *smallest* difference in my feeling towards you, beyond removing the irritation of unsatisfied instinct." What Ottoline would think
of this he would have to wait to discover on his return.

When Ottoline came back from another trip to Lausanne she began to
enjoy London with newfound zest. That spring the capital seemed more
gay and interesting than ever. Nijinsky was back—with his own troupe,
having quarrelled with Diaghilev, who had opposed his recent marriage.
She stood at the door of Nijinsky's suite at the Savoy, her arms full of
flowers, waiting to greet him and his young bride. Ottoline's entertainments at Bedford Square that year surpassed even those of the previous
two. She was also growing more interested in Vanessa Bell's husband
Clive, a development Lytton wasn't very happy about. "Your new intimacy with the Lady O. alarms me."[44] Later Ottoline looked back on her
activities during that summer with a certain awe. She had begun to live
her own legend—the extraordinary Lady Ottoline Morrell, the *grande
dame* who caused crowds to form around her in the streets, the Scarlet
Woman whom the gossips liked to tear to shreds, the woman who knew
everyone *intimately*. One entertainment followed another with bewilder-

ing speed. She held luncheons and dinners and soirees, spent weeks up in Burnley helping Philip, and still found time to go to the ballet and opera and meet everyone of interest in the capital. She wrote: "What fun it all was that summer. Everything seemed easy and light, as if the atmosphere had something electric and gay in it, imbuing anything that was done with a lovely gay easy quality absorbing from it the worry and care and fret."[45]

Ottoline had been appointed buyer for the Contemporary Art Society for six months and with the money entrusted to her she bought a large farmyard scene by a young artist named Gilbert Spencer, whom Henry Lamb had introduced to her along with Gilbert's brother Stanley. Ottoline and Philip went to the Spencers' home:

> One lovely hot Saturday afternoon we went down to Cookham to see them, and found the old father and mother in their little house. A disused bedroom upstairs was used by the two artist brothers as a studio. They had more the appearance of two healthy red-faced farm labourers with their rough shocks of hair and teeth protruding in all directions. . . . Stanley, the elder one, who was smaller in stature, was the more remarkable of the two, more of a genius, more intense, and slightly crazy.[46]

There were several other brothers, one who became professor of music at Cologne and another a lion tamer. When Ottoline and Philip left they hailed a passing London taxi—a gesture that so astonished the whole Spencer family that, according to Ottoline, they "nearly fell backwards with their canvas shoes in the air."

In May Ottoline held her most ambitious entertainment yet. Some whispered it was her last bid to secure an undersecretaryship for Philip— and, if subsequent events hadn't ruined all chances of such an appointment, she might have been successful. That evening she surpassed herself. Lytton told his brother James of some of the people he saw there: Asquith, Lady Howard de Walden, Henry James, the Walter Raleighs, Sir Matthew Nathan. . . . Lytton himself was scooped up by his hostess and planted on a sofa with the Prime Minister, who talked about the increasingly worrying Ulster problem. "My head spun round and round at finding itself cheek by jowl with so many eminent persons," Lytton told Ottoline.[47] But such occasions were very exhausting, as Ottoline told E.M. Forster, who sympathised: "Yes those evenings must be nervous work, I wouldn't even entertain white mice, were two or three of them gathered together.''[48] Around June 10 Russell arrived back in London and Ottoline immediately set about reclaiming him. Before he went away she had told him their relationship would have to be entirely platonic. She now saw that this had been the root of all the trouble and reestablished normal physical relations with him—an easier proposition now his bad breath, the result of pyorrhoea, had been cured by American dentists. Russell says in his autobiography: ''Ottoline could still, when she chose, be a lover so delightful that to leave her seemed impossible.''[49] She had just over six weeks before Helen Dudley's arrival. She told Russell she quite understood what had happened, and he in turn told her that already he was growing less fond of Miss Dudley; he said it was partly the American's ardour and partly the quality of her writing that had enamoured him. Ottoline invited him to a party at Bedford Square and went for long walks in their old haunt, Richmond Park. Ottoline found Bertie less possessive, and in July wrote in her diary: ''I feel tremendously alive, and very happy.''[50] Russell was delighted by Ottoline's new attitude and told her:

> MY DARLING LOVE,
> I cannot tell you how full of happiness I feel or what complete joy it is now when we are together. It all seems so easy and natural—there is not a trace of the constraint which had grown up . . . . I thought at first it was due to H. D. but I don't think so now. I think it is much more due to my teeth being all right.[51]

Ottoline had won round 1 and was in a good position for round 2 when Helen Dudley arrived. But, as it turned out, she had no need to worry: events elsewhere were beginning to overtake questions of personal happiness. Late in July Ottoline was at an afternoon party at Asquith's country home where the main topic of conversation was the assassination of Archduke Ferdinand. Afterwards she and Asquith went for a stroll by the river and she asked him what he thought might happen. He replied: ''This will take their attention away from Ulster, which is a good thing.''[52]

Chapter 10

Part i
1914

ON July 28, three days after the Asquiths' party, Austria declared war on Serbia. Two days later France's ally Russia mobilised and on August 1 Germany declared war on Russia. If France went to war Britain was committed to go to war too, and in London military fever swept the capital. Yet within the Liberal Party there was still substantial opposition to intervention in Europe, and one of the leaders of this opposition was Philip Morrell. On Saturday August 1 Philip and Ottoline went down to Black Hall intending to spend the weekend there, but the news from Europe was so grim that the following morning Philip decided to hurry back to try to rally antiwar feeling.

Though it was Sunday Bedford Square was crowded and groups of young men were marching up and down singing patriotic songs. On Monday Germany declared war on France and Russell came down from Cambridge to lunch with Ottoline and discuss the madness descending around them. Why people wanted war was a mystery to them both, but Russell thought hatred of Germany was the main reason. "And yet," he explained to her, "for once Germany is wholly disinterested and guided by honour."[1] Later Ottoline went to the House where Philip was waiting to make his protest. She heard the Foreign Secretary, Sir Edward Grey, warn Germany that Britain would not stand neutral if France or Belgium were invaded. Grey sat down to shouts of approval.

When Philip stood up there were hostile murmurs and cries of "Sit down" from all sides.[2] England was being asked, he told them, to go to war merely because Germany had insisted on its rights (angry Tory shouts of "Rights?"); they were being asked to go to war because a few German regiments might be marching across a corner of Belgian territory (hostile jeers); the real reason, he believed, was not honour but fear and jealousy of supposed German ambitions. If Britain went to war it would be just as much to preserve Russian despotism, and little love as he had for Germany he had less for Russia ("Hear, hear"). Other radical Liberals voiced

140

similar sentiments and the Labour member for Merthyr Tydfil, Keir Hardie, said honour was always the excuse used to wage war—and a flimsy one it was too. Philip's friend Arthur Ponsonby told the House that the previous night he had seen a band of half-drunken youths outside a great club in St. James's Street being egged on by members from the balcony. Such speeches, however, went unheeded. Philip and Ottoline walked away from the House in despair.

That night, like bedraggled seagulls in a storm, a small group of anti-war MP's came to Bedford Square to wait for Grey's ultimatum to Germany to expire; at midnight it did and the country was at war. Over the next day or so Philip and Ottoline's home became a rallying point for the pacifist cause. All who gathered there were bewildered at the way their world—that civilised world for which Leonard Woolf and others had held out such high hopes—was collapsing. It was as if some highly contagious disease were sweeping the world, and Ottoline and Philip and a handful of others were the only ones immune. A week or so earlier Russell, aghast at the way Europe was heading towards war, had begun collecting signatures around Cambridge to a statement against English involvement and on August 1 he told Ottoline he had not found a single person of any party or class who was in favour of the war: "*All* think it folly and very unpopular."[3] But four days later things had suddenly changed. Bertie had a letter from Mrs. Whitehead in favour of war and he discovered that most of the dons who had signed his petition had had abrupt changes of heart. "We are terribly alone," he told Ottoline.[4] She herself detested the drumbeating and rabble-rousing of the warmongers and was horrified that Europe could throw aside the moral and human code that had taken centuries to build. War was an ugly, evil force that would destroy everything fine in civilisation and she opposed it as a Liberal, as a woman, and as a Christian. Above all she was repulsed at the glorification of brutality. "Why is it," she asked, "that yesterday we called death by another man's hand murder or manslaughter, now it is called glorious bravery and valour?"[5]

Philip's August 4 speech in the Commons had been brave. He knew it might end his political career and all that that meant to him, yet still he spoke. And ruin his career it did. From now on most of his parliamentary colleagues treated him as a pariah. But up in Burnley his stand was at first welcomed and the day after his speech the local Liberal branch met and the secretary said he thought Philip's speech was perfectly correct and patriotic. Philip had offered to come up and explain his views, but the secretary wrote him not to bother because they were sure that in the end his view would be justified. Indeed, several committee members confessed they now thought more of Philip than before. The meeting passed a vote of confidence in him. However, their letter telling him of this asked him to keep the vote secret. It was an augury of what was to come.

Of the many sordid aspects of the war, one which particularly affronted Ottoline and Philip was a rabid campaign, fomented by the press, to stir up anti-German feeling. As a result, the Royal family changed its surname Saxe-Coburg to Windsor, kindergartens became "infant schools," and German nationals were hounded and harassed. Philip and Ottoline did what they could to help in individual cases of persecution brought to their notice and also joined a society which supplied money to wives of interned aliens. One German wrote to thank Ottoline:

> I beg to thank you very much indeed for your great kindness in helping us as you did and for the great interest you took in my family and myself.
>
> I have been trying hard to get some work or other, but impossible—they even refused to let me address envelopes in the big banking concern I used to be in. . . .
>
> I am afraid I have lost my brother. He was officer on one of the ships in Chinese waters. . . .
>
> Dear Madam will you please accept the kindest regards from my family and the heartiest thanks from
>
> yours very respectfully,
MAX GIELAND [6]

The war caused deep rifts between Ottoline and some of her friends. Hilda Douglas-Pennant was only one of the many who no longer called at Bedford Square. Ottoline's relations with Asquith were strained and a friendship with his daughter Violet nipped in the bud. In May, 1914, Violet had written to Ottoline: "I long . . . to be with you beyond all people. Goodbye dearest."[7] But on August 29 Violet wrote: "I haven't been because I heard you didn't want to see anyone who was in favour of the war—including me."[8] Philip and Ottoline were now even more at odds with their families. Portland's son went off to join the cavalry while Portland and his wife themselves did all they could to aid the war effort. Philip's relations were equally patriotic and hard words were exchanged whenever Ottoline and Philip visited Black Hall. Of Ottoline's men friends Henry Lamb was most influenced by the call of King and Country—he threw up painting to return to his medical studies and become an army doctor. A bad knee prevented Augustus John from joining up but he eventually did his bit in Lord Beaverbrook's band of war artists while E. M. Forster volunteered as a Red Cross observer in Egypt. As a whole, however, most of Ottoline's circle shared her convictions. The Bloomsbury Group was fervently antiwar and over the next two or three years Ottoline and Bloomsbury were closer than at any other time.*

The war also brought Ottoline and Russell closer. For the moment Bertie had no thought for anyone else—certainly not Helen Dudley, who turned up in London with her father in mid-August. Ottoline wrote: "She came, poor girl, panting with high hopes and ardour, expecting B to welcome her with passionate love, and unfortunately the war had intervened." Or rather the war and Ottoline had intervened. She handled this latest peccadillo of Bertie's with consumate skill. Miss Dudley and her father thought that Russell was intending to put them up prior to a speedy divorce from Alys and a marriage ceremony soon after. But the Russell who greeted them was not the Russell they had said good-bye to in America a few months earlier. Bluntly he told Miss Dudley that his attitude had changed and plans of marriage would have to be dropped. He enlisted Ottoline's help to explain to the Dudleys that the war had so devastated him that all previous plans were void; but he cautioned her: "I don't think she realises *quite* what you and I are to each other, and now there is no reason why she should. It would be very unfortunate if she thought you had anything to do with my change toward her."[9]

Ottoline agreed to do what she could and went to see the Dudleys, reporting back to Russell that she liked Miss Dudley. She recalled later: "She was an odd girl of about 27, rather creeping and sinuous in her movements; she had a large head, a fringe cut across her forehead, a very long chin, rather underhung, and thick lips."[10] Ottoline felt sorry for the way Miss Dudley, through no fault of her own, was being treated, and once she discovered the girl was no threat she went out of her way to be sympathetic. After Mr. Dudley returned to America she invited Miss

---

*Later in August Ottoline's young friend Norton wrote to her: "I find this war horrible—horrible in fact, horrible in imagination; in retrospect & anticipation, past present & future, hateful & hateful." (Norton–OM, August 23, 1914, HRC)

Dudley to stay at Bedford Square. But no sooner had she moved in than the two women began exchanging stories about Russell, and Miss Dudley brought out some of Bertie's love letters which, to Ottoline's dismay, were couched in terms familiar to her—he'd actually repeated the same phrases he had used in letters to her! At first this upset her and she told Russell so. He replied: "My Darling Love—I am very very sorry that H. D. goes on telling things that bother you—*do* try to stop her—there is no use in her telling them and you really know all about it now."[11] Next Ottoline complained (rather petulantly) that his letters to Miss Dudley were more passionate. He replied by showing her a letter he wrote to her in March, 1912, when he was feeling particularly passionate. Yet it still rankled. "Why should one mind?" Ottoline asked herself, "but one does. . . . I feel somehow it is *too* indiscriminating. The same form, the special offering, to be used to two people as unlike as Helen and myself."[12] But Ottoline's anger did not last long; she recognized it was partially her own fault: "*Après tout,* I have never given him enough, and so I cannot complain."

Despite the less than enthusiastic welcome she had received in London Helen Dudley did not surrender Russell without a fight. One day Ottoline and Russell were in his flat when she knocked at the door, though Russell assured Ottoline he had forbidden her to visit him there. Ottoline recalled: "We heard knock, knock, knock, and hands banging on the door. B refused to open, as he was sure it was she, and I imagined I heard her panting outside."[13] The following day Miss Dudley told Russell she had heard breathing sounds when she knocked and he had to admit he had been in. Gradually, however, Miss Dudley realised Russell was a lost cause and began turning her attentions elsewhere. Unfortunately she happened to choose men whom Ottoline regarded as her preserve—Gilbert Cannan, for one. Worse, she conducted her operations in Ottoline's own drawing room, amidst clouds of cigarette smoke. Very soon Miss Dudley was packed off to stay with some relatives of Philip's in the country. There Russell would sometimes visit her (later she contracted a spinal disease and returned to America where she died insane).

Meanwhile the war news from France was so painful for Ottoline she could hardly bear to read it. It hurt both ways: the fighting revolted her pacifist beliefs, yet each German victory made her feel guilty that she could not bring herself to join in the patriotic fervour.* Other things upset her too; in particular the sight of young women throwing themselves into war work. Against them she felt a sharp resentment in that they should be gaining freedom by freeing men to be sent out to the front as cannon fodder. Ottoline tried to assuage some of her conscience by taking in Belgian and French refugees. Among these was a young Belgian girl, Maria Nys, who soon became almost one of the family at Bedford Square. A plump, pretty girl, Maria developed an adolescent crush on Ottoline, following her around like a young calf.

In November, 1914, Ottoline started up her Thursday at homes again. These gatherings had always been somewhat out of tune with what the rest of the world was doing; now the difference became almost grotesque. While the battle of Ypres raged in northern France, Ottoline and her friends dressed up, played charades, and danced abandonedly to noisy tunes pumped out by Philip on his pianola.† Later Ottoline asked herself why they had all been so gay when they should have been sad. It wasn't that they were heartless about the death and suffering across the Channel, rather their unhappiness was so great that any diversion was welcome, especially in the company of those who were sympathetic. That company included some recent additions. Several came from the Bloomsbury sphere: Gerald Shove, Francis Birrell (Augustine's son), and David Garnett. Another three came from the Slade School and were brought to Bedford Square—wearing masks—by Mark Gertler, a young Jewish painter Ottoline had taken under her wing. The trio trooped into Ottoline's drawing room, unmasked, and were identified as Dora Carrington, Barbara Hiles, and the Hon. Dorothy Brett. Carrington was Gertler's great love, and Brett, who was almost deaf, was the daughter of Lord Esher. All

*But she was not deaf to appeals to relieve the suffering in Flanders. John Masefield wrote to her asking for a gift towards £3,500 to equip a field hospital in France. Ottoline complied and Masefield wrote back: "Thank you very much indeed for your most kind generous help. It is most good of you to have got me all this money." (Masefield–OM, May 11, 1915, HRC)

†This pianola, bought by Ottoline and Philip in October, 1913, became famous. As the guests gathered round to sing and dance Philip treadled out such tunes as "If You Were the Only Girl in the World" and other popular songs of the day. One evening Hilaire Belloc came round to Bedford Square to see Ottoline but could not make his knocks heard because of the noise of the pianola and had to go away.

three wore corduroy trousers and had their hair cut short in the Slade style, which was why Virginia Woolf called them cropheads. They were a liberated trio and Carrington and Brett (they preferred to be addressed that way) were to become close friends of Ottoline's.

Meanwhile the war had at least one happy consequence: it forged a bond of friendship between Russell and Philip, and now Bertie could come and go at Bedford Square as he pleased. The gay goings-on there were for Russell a blessed relief from the tragic events in France. He even joined in the dancing. While Philip provided the accompaniment, the various guests would step out as the spirit moved them: Duncan Grant bounded around like Nijinsky; Russell pumped his legs up and down "with an expression," noted Ottoline, "of surprised delight at finding himself doing such an ordinary human thing as dancing"; and Lytton stepped out in a courtly minuet with his brother James and sister Marjorie.[14] Ottoline herself liked putting on her lace mantilla and doing wild gypsy dances with Augustus John. On other occasions Ottoline would give over her drawing rooms to concerts by two talented Hungarian sisters, the D'Aranyis, who played the violin.

And so, 1914 drew to a close. It had not been a happy year; Ottoline had suffered intense anguish and lost many friends. But there were some gains. She and Philip were happier together and her friendship with Bertie was on a firmer basis. Russell felt this too. "I *do* feel the difference in you," he told her. "And in me there is a *great* difference. I have a really firm resolve to avoid philandering in future."[15] In October he had returned to Cambridge for the new academic year but found lecturing on mathematical logic a futile occupation and devoted most of his time to nonwar or antiwar causes. At Christmas he visited destitute German aliens with Ottoline. On December 26 he told her he was still firmly resisting the temptation to philander. He had had a visit from the D'Aranyi sisters, who invited themselves to dinner and only left at ten thirty, when he put them out; he said Titi D'Aranyi had been particularly flirtatious and it had taken all his firmness to deflect her resolute assault. But Ottoline suspected it was only a matter of time before he would succumb to someone. She was now almost forty-two and beginning to feel, if not old, certainly weary. The move to Garsington was drawing near and the future seemed uncertain. Yet just around the corner was a meeting with a man who was to assume an importance in her life second only to that of Russell.

Part ii
1914–1915

———

Ottoline first heard the name D. H. Lawrence in October or November, 1914, when Gilbert Cannan lent her Lawrence's novels *The White Peacock* and *Sons and Lovers*. These books, with their vivid descriptions of the Nottinghamshire countryside and mining villages, made a deep and startling impression on her, reviving memories of her own childhood at Welbeck. But not just nostalgia attracted her to Lawrence's work: she discerned in him a sensitivity that excited and intrigued her. Lawrence in 1914 was twenty-nine and had recently married Frieda, Baroness von Richthofen, a German aristocrat who had deserted her English husband (who was Lawrence's professor of French at Nottingham) and their three children to run off with this penniless miner's son. They were living at Chesham in Buckinghamshire and Lawrence was just becoming known as a writer. He was already friendly with Cannan, David Garnett, and Mark Gertler and in August, 1914, he had made his first essay into "the dress-suit world" at a dinner party at the H. G. Wells'.

It was almost inevitable he and Ottoline should meet. The actual introduction was made by Cannan, who brought Lawrence and Frieda to Bedford Square one evening late in December. Ottoline's first impression was of "a slight man, lithe and delicately built, his pale face rather overshadowed by his beard and his red hair falling over his forehead, his eyes blue and his hands delicate and very competent. He gave one the impression of someone who had been undernourished in youth, making his body fragile and his mind too active."[16] They liked each other immediately. Ottoline was just the type of woman who fascinated Lawrence. He had all his life an obsession with the idea of a relationship between a man of the people and a woman of rank—the Lady Chatterley theme. His marriage to Frieda had fed this obsession without satisfying it; now here was an aristocrat on a much grander scale: the sister of a duke—and a patroness as well. Lawrence was dazzled. And Ottoline was equally dazzled by him. For many years she had been searching for someone who had the sort of intuitive feel of life she had always hoped existed—a prophet, a messiah in direct touch with the true essence of the universe. For a time she believed that Bertie might have been such a prophet; instead he seemed more interested in sex, and his god—reason—just a graven image. Lawrence was more promising material. Moreover he was a man of the people, a mind in the mold of Burns and Blake, a mind with fresh, virile ideas—better ideas perhaps than those of her class. After their first meeting Ottoline wrote to Lawrence inviting him to come and see her when next he was in London. He should like to come, he replied, but poverty precluded regular trips to the capital: "I shake down the thermometer of my wealth and find it just nearly at zero."[17] She told him how much she enjoyed his stories and he replied that the appreciation of people like her meant a lot to him. He couldn't come to lunch on January 14 but he managed dinner on the twenty-fifth when he turned up with Frieda and was seated next to E. M. Forster. After dinner more people arrived and there was dancing. Ottoline, wearing her lace mantilla, pranced around with Duncan Grant until he caught his toe in her train and both crashed to the floor; undeterred, she left the bruised and shaken Duncan to recover and took Gertler as her next partner. Later she talked to Lawrence about Grant's paintings and he expressed a wish to see some, at which Grant invited Lawrence, Frieda, Gertler, and Forster to tea in his studio the following afternoon. There Lawrence took it upon himself to lecture Grant on what was wrong with his work—the first intimation that Lawrence and Bloomsbury were not going to get on. Lawrence told Ottoline about the afternoon: "We liked Duncan Grant very much. I really liked him. Tell him not to make silly experiments in the futuristic line with bits of colour on a moving paper. Other Johnnies can do that."[18]

The Lawrences had now moved to Greatham in Sussex from where he wrote to enlist Ottoline's aid in persuading Frieda's ex-husband to bring her children to Bedford Square to see their mother: "I wish you could tell him you are Lady Ottoline—the sister of the Duke of Portland."[19] The Bentinck name continued to fascinate Lawrence ("Bentincks were always looked up to as being disinterested")[20] and he returned again and again to this theme: "It *is* rather splendid that you are a great lady. Don't abrogate one jot or tittle of your high birth: it is too valuable in this commercially-minded mean world. . . . I really do honour your birth. Let us do justice to its nobility: it is not mere accident. I would have given a great deal to have been born an aristocrat."[21] Lawrence had invited Ottoline down to Sussex to see his new home and on January 27 she arrived and sat at the long refectory table while he cooked lunch and poured out a torrent of talk. "It was impossible not to feel expanded and stimulated by the companionship of anyone so alive," Ottoline wrote later. "Indeed he seemed to possess a magnetic gift of quickening those he talked to and of making them blossom with new ideas, new enthusiasm, new hopes." In spite of his vehemence she found him gentle and tender. "I felt when I was with him as if I had really at last found a friend." Each of them saw in the other possibilities of a new and better world. Lawrence's intuitive philosophy appealed to Ottoline: "He seemed to open up the way into a Holy Land."[22] He told her he wanted her to be the hub of this new world: "I want you to form the nucleus of a new community which shall start a new life amongst us—a life in which the only riches is integrity of character. . . . We can all come croppers, but what does it matter?"[23] He hoped his utopia, his Rananim,* would be the new hope of the common people; it would be based "not on poverty, but on riches, not on humility, but on pride, not on sacrifice but upon complete fulfillment in the flesh of all strong desire." This sort of talk struck a familiar chord in Ottoline: it was just the sort of thing that Russell seemed to be looking for, so she decided to take the first opportunity to bring the two of them together.

Russell had been a worry to her lately. The war was eating into his soul and he was extremely melancholy. In addition he had fallen from his high resolve not to philander and had embarked on a half-hearted affair with his new secretary, Irene Cooper-Willis. When Ottoline discovered what he was up to she confronted him and he tried to explain the situation: "I think I may easily come to have a *very* great affection for Irene—not a very passionate feeling, but one which might give happiness and be free from pain of passion."[24] At first she encouraged him in this dalliance, but in the end she couldn't bear to see him slip away to a rival and decided to rein him in. As usual he responded immediately and they spent several

*The name was derived from a Russian lullaby sung by his friend Koteliansky (Kot).

happy days together, after which he wrote to her: "Last night had *everything*—there was a note of wildness of Hey nonny no, men are fools that wish to die."[25] By now Russell probably realised that the one certain way to ignite Ottoline was to make her jealous, and, unconsciously or not, this was the ploy he often adopted over the next year or so.

Towards the end of February Ottoline took him down to Sussex to meet Lawrence and her hopes that they would get on well together were quickly confirmed. He was awestruck by Lawrence and as they drove away he exclaimed to her: "He is amazing, he sees through and through one. . . . He is infallible. . . . He sees everything and is always right."[26] The friendship that flared between these two passionate, rebellious men was like a firework, intense and bright, but liable to burn out suddenly. Yet while it lasted it provided Russell with an outlet for his excess passion and mental frustration. "He can give me a vivifying dose of unreason," he said.[27] At first, Lawrence was a little scared of "Mr. Russell": "I feel as if I should stutter," he told Ottoline.[28] But once they got talking and arguing it was Lawrence who had the upper hand. He had the convictions, Russell was rudderless. Soon Lawrence began to feel that in Russell he might have found the perfect male friend he always sought. Early in March he wrote to Ottoline confessing a hastening of love for Russell; he told her he felt they were all young and a great cause lay ahead.

Frieda was nowhere near as keen on these new friendships as her husband. She went along with the relationship with Ottoline only because she thought the contact would be useful. In February she wrote Koteliansky: "The Ottoline is a nice simple person."[29] This misjudgement was indicative of Frieda's general lack of perception about the whole business. Ottoline too tended to dismiss Frieda as unworthy of a mind such as Lawrence's; to her she seemed a rather blousy hausfrau. Meanwhile Ottoline and Lawrence exchanged gifts: she sent him an opal pin and he gave her a box he had painted himself and adorned with a phoenix, the symbol of his new society which was to arise from the ashes of the old world.

Ottoline had said that when she and Philip took over Garsington in a month or so one of the outbuildings could be set aside as a cottage for Lawrence and Frieda. Lawrence accepted readily. Garsington would be the site of Rananim: there each member of the new utopia would live a communal life and fulfil their own natural and deep desires. On February

22 he wrote telling her he wanted to hear about "the cottage, the cottage, the cottage."[30] On March 6 Russell took Lawrence up to Cambridge to show him off to the other dons, but the visit was not a success. Russell reported to Ottoline: "He hates everybody here, as was to be expected."[31] He took Lawrence along to see Keynes, whom Russell regarded as the finest mind in Cambridge. But although it was eleven A.M. Keynes was still in pyjamas, which, Lawrence thought, was corrupt and unclean. "Lawrence has quick, sensitive impressions which I don't understand, tho' they would seem quite natural to you," Russell told Ottoline. "I love him more and more."[32] Lawrence was particularly put off by the atmosphere of sodomy he discerned among some of the dons. In this Russell agreed with him: "Lawrence has the same feeling against sodomy as I have; you had nearly made me believe there is no great harm in it, but I have reverted; and all the examples I know confirm me in thinking it is sterilizing."[33] Keynes, however, thought Lawrence's antipathy was due to his jealousy of Bloomsbury— Ottoline's "other world"—and the hold it had on David Garnett, Lawrence's young friend. Lawrence wrote to Ottoline about his visit: "To hear these young people talk really fills me with black fury. . . . There is never for one second any outgoing of feeling and no reverence. . . . I will not have people like this—I had rather be alone. They made me dream of a beetle that bites like a scorpion. But I killed it—a very large beetle."[34] These instinctive reactions of Lawrence's were a mixed bag; much of what he said was nonsense, yet more often than not it did contain a kernel of truth. Russell agreed with him about Bloomsbury, there was something slightly creepy about them. However Lawrence's sensitivity could cut both ways, and when he took his knife and began to dissect Ottoline, she didn't know quite how to take it. He wrote to her:

Why don't you have the pride in your own intrinsic self? Why must you tamper with the idea of being an ordinary physical woman—wife, mother, mistress? Primarily you belong to a special type, a special race of women: like Cassandra, and some of the great women saints. They were the great media of truth, of the deepest truth: through them . . . the truth came —as through a fissure from the depths and the burning darkness that lies out of the depth of time. It is necessary for this great type to re-assert itself on the face of the earth. It is not the salon lady and the bluestocking . . . but the priestess, the medium, the prophetess. Do you know Cassandra in Aeschylus and Homer? She is one of the world's great figures, and what the Greeks and Agamemnon did to her is symbolic of what mankind has done to her since—raped and despoiled and mocked her, to their own ruin.[35]

All through March Lawrence could hardly wait to move to Garsington—"And we cuckoos, we shall plume ourselves, in such a nest of a fine bird"—and he protested that the rent Philip had suggested for the cottage was far too low.[36] Lawrence and Ottoline exchanged letters regularly and he told her she shouldn't be afraid of writing dull things: "They are not dull. The feeling that comes out of your letters is like the scent of flowers, so generous and reassuring."[37] Frieda by now was beginning to get annoyed at the amount of time Lawrence was spending visiting and writing to Ottoline; nor was she very excited about the idea of being Ottoline's tenant at Garsington; to Frieda this smacked of serfdom. She and Lawrence were poor, Ottoline was rich—and to a woman with as fiery a temper as Frieda, and a fellow aristocrat to boot, this rankled. Ottoline's attitude towards her didn't help. Lawrence began to suggest he should come to see Ottoline without Frieda: "There is no reason why we should always be a triangle."[38] Soon Ottoline and Philip began to have second thoughts about the cottage idea. This change of heart led to Philip writing to Lawrence in mid-April to tell him that the cost of converting the suggested cottage would be very high. Shocked, Lawrence replied: "Of course the costs . . . are impossible beyond all consideration."[39] The same day he wrote to Kot: "Probably we shall not have the Lady Ottoline cottage. In my soul I shall be glad. I would rather take some little place and be by myself. We will look out for some tiny place on the sea."[40]

The preparations for moving to Garsington had exhausted Ottoline and in May she decided to take a few days' holiday at Buxton in Derbyshire. Before leaving Bedford Square a disturbing incident occurred. Returning one day from a walk she was sitting at her dressing table when the Belgian refugee girl Maria walked into the bedroom, looked at Ottoline reproachfully, and murmured: *"J'ai pris du sublime."*[41] Then she started to sway alarmingly. Apparently she had been looking forward to going to Garsington, but Ottoline, feeling oppressed by the girl's devotion, had grasped the opportunity to deposit her with some friends in London. Maria had reacted by swallowing some mercuric poison. Ottoline ran to the door and called her maids, Millie and Edith, who tickled Maria's throat while Ottoline telephoned for a doctor. After Maria recovered it was agreed that she should go to Garsington after all. When Lawrence heard of the suicide attempt he placed the blame on Ottoline:

> We were shocked about Maria: it really is rather horrible. I'm not sure whether you aren't really more wicked than I had at first thought you. I think you can't help torturing a bit. But I think it has shown something—as if you, with a strong, old-developed *will* had enveloped the girl, in this will, so that she lived under the dominance of your will: and then you want to put her away from you, eject her from your will. So that was why she says it was because she couldn't bear being left, that she took the poison, and it is a great deal true.

He concluded: "Why must you always use your *will* so much, why can't you let things be, without always grasping and trying to know and to dominate."[42] This upset Ottoline very much and was an event that was to echo later. She told Russell about Lawrence's outburst and he tried to soothe her, saying that of course she had a terrific will, but she didn't use it tyrannously. He assured her Lawrence himself had plenty of will: "It is only that his theory doesn't recognise will, because like most tyrants, he dislikes will in others."[43] So Ottoline departed for Buxton in a sad mood, mulling over the changes in her life and the uncertainties before her at Garsington. Lawrence, realising he had hurt her, tried to patch things up: "Don't take any notice of my extravagant talk—one must say something." He upbraided both her and Russell for being unhappy:

> Why, then are you both so downcast, both you and Russell? . . . What ails Russell is, in matters of life and emotion, the inexperience of youth. He is, vitally, emotionally, much too inexperienced in personal contact and conflict for a man of his age and calibre. . . . Tell him he is not to write lachrymose letters to me of disillusion and disappointment and age: that sounds like 19, almost like David Garnett. Tell him he is to get up and clench his fist in the face of the world.[44]

Lawrence was looking forward to a council of war with Russell and the Cannans at Garsington soon. "Don't be melancholy," he told Ottoline, "there isn't time."

GARSINGTON

Chapter 11

1915–1916

IN spite of Lawrence's pep talk Ottoline was still feeling melancholy as she travelled down from Buxton on May 17, 1915, to begin a new era in her life. Philip had been living at Garsington for several months managing the farm and overseeing the renovations to the manor house, which was in disrepair. He met Ottoline at the local station, Wheatley, and as they drove the few miles to Garsington Ottoline looked around at the countryside that was to be her home for the next fourteen years. It could almost have been a Constable landscape—tall elms, drowsy cows munching the spring grass, fields dotted with wildflowers, and a hill around which a small village and a church clusters. As they neared the house the church broke out into a peal of bells. The high-gabled manor, two storeys plus attics, was built of grey Cotswold stone with mullioned windows and surrounded by 200 acres of garden and farmland. Double wrought-iron gates opened straight off the road into a small gravelled courtyard leading to the front door; but the real front of the house was around the other side, overlooking the Berkshire Downs. There a large garden sloped away through a group of ponds to an orchard, beyond which were open fields and an unobstructed view to Wittenham Clumps. It was one of the most beautiful houses in Oxfordshire, built originally, it was said, for some monastic order; it was also said that the ponds were mentioned in the Doomsday Book. After tea Ottoline and the gardener wandered around in the warm twilight discussing what trees they would plant and where new terraces would be made. The church bells were still carolling and she asked him if they practised every day at this time. He looked at her curiously, then said: "Why, they're ringing to welcome you and Mr. Morrell, My Lady."[1]

The first few weeks slipped by as if in a dream. Each morning Ottoline got up early, donned overalls, breakfasted off toast and coffee, then set to work around the house. A team of builders under the direction of a Mr. Davis arrived, and while Philip made himself useful on the farm, Ottoline, Mr. Davis, the workmen, and Ottoline's maids transformed the old house into something at once comfortable and exotic. Ottoline's vision now flew beyond the unorthodox decor of Bedford Square into a new realm of Bakst and Beardsley. The centrepieces were to be the two large drawing rooms on the ground floor. Though the rooms were beautifully panelled in oak, Ottoline decided to defy tradition and paint one a vivid Venetian red and the other sea-green. For the hall she devised a colour scheme of dove grey overlaid with varnish that reflected the red curtains in imitation of a winter sunset. Then the furniture arrived—Chinese boxes and cabinets, blue china and Chelsea porcelain, Samarkand rugs, silk hangings, lacquered screens—and was distributed round the house while Ottoline decided where to hang her Gertlers, Johns, Conders, Lambs, and Duncan Grants. By far her most ambitious plans were reserved for the grounds, which were to be like an Italian garden. Ottoline had the biggest of the ponds enlarged into a small, rectangular lake round which hedges were planted. Classical statues lined its perimeter and a larger statue was erected on an artificial island in the centre. When the hedges grew Gothic arches were cut through so people swimming or punting or strolling could look out and see the blossoming trees in the orchard beyond. Into this arcadian setting Ottoline, with a final flourish, introduced some peacocks to strut and preen, much as Lawrence imagined he and Frieda might have done.*

As May lengthened into June Ottoline found herself drifting languidly through her rooms, trailing her long fingers through the bowls of potpourri, swirling her taffeta skirts across the stone floor, merging into dappled shadows, then walking out into the sudden sunlight of the lawn over which a huge ilex tree leaned and a latch gate in a stone wall led to a large flower and vegetable garden. Though most of the work had been done and all her friends were clamouring to visit her and see her new home she was strangely paralysed.† She felt Garsington wasn't ready to have guests . . . there was only one bathroom—and what would Lytton's critical

---

*Soon after Ottoline moved to Garsington, Julian, aged nine, joined her parents. She had a governess now, a young Swiss girl named Juliette Baillot (called Mademoiselle), who was later to marry Julian Huxley, whose brother Aldous was to marry Ottoline's other helpmeet, Maria.

†Desmond MacCarthy wrote: "I passed your home in Bedford Square the other day & plumbed the hole your absence makes in London." (MacCarthy to OM, July 1, 1915, HRC)

eye make of the house? Would anyone want to come all the way from London to see her? And what was she creating at Garsington—a home for Philip, herself and Julian? Or something more . . . an oasis perhaps, isolated not only from war but from all material values, a place where artists, writers and other sensitive people might relax and express themselves in a congenial atmosphere. This was what she hoped for, what she had been striving for. Yet still she was assailed by doubts and uncertainties.

It was Lawrence who shook her out of her lethargy. He was still bubbling over with plans for the utopia that he and Ottoline and their friends would inaugurate at Garsington. He wrote to her impatiently, demanding to know when he could come down and see the house for himself. Though he had turned down the offer of the cottage, he still had hopes of some other, cheaper accommodation, as Ottoline had dropped vague hints that there might be a gardener's cottage or something similar for them. Russell was also anxious to come—it had been almost a month since he had seen her, and he was feeling lonely.

To satisfy them both, Ottoline decided that her first function at Garsington would be a housewarming to coincide with her forty-second birthday on June 16, and she invited not only Bertie and the Lawrences but Mark Gertler and the Cannans too. At first everything went smoothly. Lawrence was charming and sympathetic and Frieda behaved herself; everybody put on overalls and helped put the finishing touches to the red drawing room, Russell being sent up a ladder to paint the ceiling beams while Lawrence, who had a talent for manual work, outlined the red panels with the straightest and finest of gilt lines. But while everyone else worked Frieda sat on a table swinging her legs, laughing and mocking the others' efforts and offering advice on what curtains Ottoline should hang. "She has a terrible irritant quality," Ottoline said later, "and enjoys tormenting, and she liked to torment me because I was taking trouble to make the house nice."[2] Little wonder Frieda was jealous. She had no home, Ottoline's was magnificent. And Frieda harboured an active fear that Lawrence, for whom she had thrown up everything, might yet leave her, perhaps for Ottoline. After all, Ottoline had attracted a man like Russell, and Lawrence seemed a much weaker reed. Also Ottoline felt Frieda was envious of the admiration Lawrence attracted. She once overheard Frieda say, "I am just as remarkable as Lorenzo."[3] On the last night of the Lawrences' stay Frieda's insecurity boiled over, she and Lawrence had a violent quarrel in their room and objects were heard being thrown around. In the morning Lawrence came downstairs looking whipped and Frieda stomped off in a temper back to London. After she had gone Lawrence stood in the hall, pathetic and cowed, his thin frame stooped, unable to decide whether to follow or not. Ottoline and Philip advised him not to, but in the end he capitulated and went off to Hampstead where he and Frieda had recently taken a flat. Frieda told everyone she was "having ructions'' with "the old Ottoline" and to one friend she wrote: "She will say such *vile* things about me—and I think it's so mean, when she is rich and I am poor and people will take such a mean advantage of one's poverty." She said that at Garsington she had felt an outsider —"a Hun and a nobody."[4] But such outbursts from Frieda were not uncommon, and Ottoline had not seen the last of them. Lawrence himself had no wish to terminate the friendship and the day after his return from Garsington he wrote to Cynthia Asquith: "I want you to know Lady Ottoline. So few women—or men—have any real sense of absolute truth."[5]

Meanwhile Lawrence and Russell were still cooperating despite the fact that Frieda believed—quite rightly—that Russell's opinion of her was not high. While Lawrence worked at the final draft of *The Rainbow* he and Russell argued over their personal philosophies and tried to agree on some mutual plan for helping mankind. One day in July Lawrence took Russell to Holborn to meet some of his closest friends— Koteliansky, John Middleton Murry, and Katherine Mansfield. But Russell's reaction to Lawrence's friends was almost identical to Lawrence's reaction on meeting Russell's Cambridge friends. "I thought Murry *beastly*," he reported to Ottoline, "and the whole atmosphere dead and putrefying."[6] Later the same day Russell and Lawrence went to the zoo then on to Hampstead where they argued into the night, Russell doing his best to hammer some logic into Lawrence's wild theories about blood consciousness. At last superior debating technique prevailed and Lawrence became discouraged and said he would go off to the South Seas to bask in the sun with six native wives. When next Russell called, Lawrence was writing a long letter to Ottoline and when Frieda saw what he was doing she snatched it from him and ripped it up. Undeterred, Lawrence sat down again and wrote another, and this one he managed to get safely to the postbox. Russell told Ottoline that Lawrence had been *very* angry and had said to Frieda: "Come off that, lass, or I'll hit thee in the mouth."[7]

Throughout the summer Russell and Lawrence held regular conferences to thrash out a series of lectures on human relations. Full of enthusiasm, Lawrence wrote to Ottoline asking her to preside at their joint lectures: "You must be the centre-pin that holds us together, and the needle which keeps our direction constant."[8] Garsington would be their headquarters; there they could meet—himself, Ottoline, Russell, Katherine Mansfield, Middleton Murry, the Cannans—and knit themselves together. It would be like something out of Boccaccio. "That wonderful lawn, under the ilex trees, with the old house and its exquisite old front— it is so remote, so perfectly a small world to itself."[9]

As yet Lytton hadn't been invited to Garsington, an intimation perhaps that he had slipped slightly in Ottoline's order of precedence. Throughout May and June she put him off, pleading the renovations were incomplete. All the while Lytton was agog with her descriptions of the new house. On June 8 he wrote: "I imagine wonder—ponds, statues, yew hedges, gold paint."[10] At last, in the second week in July, he arrived to see for himself, accompanied by Duncan Grant and Vanessa Bell.* Lytton seemed to be impressed and afterwards sent Ottoline an enthusiastic letter telling her how much he had enjoyed his stay and inviting himself back a fortnight later. But in another letter posted the same day, this one to David Garnett, he was less enthusiastic: "The house is a regular galanty-show . . . very like Ottoline herself, in fact—very remarkable, very impressive, patched, gilded and preposterous."[11] The contrast between the two reactions was an indication that Lytton's attitude to Ottoline was changing. That he liked Garsington there is no doubt, yet he felt he should be more cynical about it to others, particularly his Bloomsbury friends. On Lytton's second visit later in July he found more things to complain about. Ottoline was fond of lapdogs and these apparently made a special point of harassing Lytton. This time he had come with Clive Bell and Mary Hutchinson, together with two of the Slade cropheads, Barbara Hiles and Faith Bagenal. While the cropheads joined Maria, Juliette, and Julian scampering around the lawn, Lytton, Clive, Mary Hutchinson, and Ottoline sat

*There had been some marital changes in Bloomsbury: Vanessa and Clive had split up and Vanessa (though still friendly with Roger Fry) was living with Duncan Grant. Clive meanwhile had struck up a friendship with Mary Hutchinson.

under the ilex tree discussing life and art. To Lytton's mind it was like a scene from Watteau or Fragonard. But the cursed pugs spoilt it. In a letter to David Garnett he wrote: "Since beginning this [letter] I've already had three visitations from the pug world."[12] He felt horribly lonely, he told Garnett, and usually sat apart from the rest, dozing over Swift's correspondence. But his thank-you letter to Ottoline was in a different vein: he didn't know if it had been the air, or the vegetables, or her conversation, but his visit had done wonders. "I find even my vigorous health taking on new forces so that I am seen bounding along the glades of Hampstead like a gazelle or a Special Constable."[13] In September, he returned again, spending a pleasant week—though, as he reported to his sister Pippa, there were still too many pugs for comfort, plus the added hazard of being waylaid by some budding poetess and forced to listen to her verse. But to Ottoline he wrote saying that not even angels were equal to the task of describing how much he had enjoyed himself; should she hear a faint sigh among the bushes she would know it was his departed spirit, still fluttering about.

Later that summer, Lawrence, anxious to reestablish friendly relations, invited Ottoline up to London to see the Hampstead flat. Frieda was still a little aggressive but was obviously regretting her outburst at Garsington and trying to make amends. Lawrence was as friendly as ever, if rather depressed. He walked with Ottoline on Hampstead Heath and told her he needed to escape, to get out of England and go somewhere clean and new. He had decided to travel to the United States to write for Americans. He would go to Florida where his health would improve and where he could set up his utopia. He begged Ottoline to go with him; if she didn't fancy Florida, then to some Pacific isle, where he would be king and she could be queen. Ottoline didn't warm to this proposal. "He rushes about with one idea after another like an excited dog, barking and barking at an imaginary enemy," she wrote.[14] So she returned to Garsington, thankful her own utopia was nearer at hand.

Throughout 1915 the war seeped more and more into Ottoline's life. In April, 1915, a combined British and French force landed in the Dardanelles and with it were two of Ottoline's brothers, Lord Charles Bentinck and Lord Henry Bentinck. Their presence there gave Ottoline's antiwar feelings a personal edge, for although she had drifted away somewhat from her family she nevertheless felt anxious about them, particularly fifty-two-year-old Henry who, unlike Charlie, was not a professional sol-

dier and had only joined up in a fit of quixotic patriotism. Henry contracted dysentery and, after almost dying, was invalided back to England.
Charlie was also returned wounded to England but later went back to continue fighting; he was wounded again and sent home to recuperate in a
nursing home where he and Ottoline met accidentally in 1917.

Most of the latter half of 1915 Ottoline spent relatively quietly at Garsington, mainly overseeing the final renovations and getting the garden
into order. Visitors came only occasionally and then they were mostly old
friends like Lytton and Augustine Birrell. Maynard Keynes came to convalesce after an appendix operation, and the Sangers, now devoted pacifists, also came. Meanwhile relations between Lawrence and Russell
were showing signs of strain. Mainly to blame was Lawrence's habit of
telling truths that were too close to home. Like Ottoline, Russell felt guilty about his lack of patriotism, and Lawrence concentrated his arguments
on this weak spot. In midsummer Russell wrote to Ottoline: "I am depressed partly by Lawrence's criticisms. I feel a worm, a useless
creature."[15] Lawrence continued to bore in. The plan for a series of joint
lectures foundered for want of an agreed prospectus, then there was an argument over a book Russell planned to publish in conjunction with his
own social reconstruction lectures. Finally, in September, Lawrence
wrote Russell a scorching letter that broke the spell. Ottoline reported that
after reading it Russell was stunned and sat without moving for a whole
day. In the letter Lawrence accused Russell of being a super-war-spirit.
"What you want," he wrote, "is to jab and strike, like the soldier with
the bayonet, only you are sublimated into words." He also alleged that
Russell "was full of repressed desires which paraded themselves in the
sheep's clothing of peace propaganda." He told him:

> I would rather have the German soldiers with rapine and cruelty, than
> with your words of goodness. . . . The enemy of all mankind, you are,
> full of the lust of enmity. It is *not* the hatred of falsehood which inspires
> you. It is the hatred of people, of flesh and blood. It is a perverted mental
> blood-lust. Why don't you own to it.

He concluded: "Let us become strangers again, I think it is better."[16]
Russell recalled later that for some time after receiving the letter he contemplated suicide. He recovered, however, and though he and Lawrence
resumed their correspondence their friendship was virtually over.

One reason for Lawrence's rabid attack was his own insecurity. In October *The Rainbow* was published and instead of meeting with acclaim it was universally reviled. Ottoline was almost the only person to write to him praising it. A Sunday newspaper critic named James Douglas took it into his head that it was obscene and urged its suppression. Within days of publication a magistrate had banned it and copies were seized by the police and burned. Philip Morrell tried to get the ban lifted and asked several questions in Parliament about the matter, but to no effect. This blow reinforced Lawrence's desire to quit England, and while he made his travel arrangements he worked with Middleton Murry on a new magazine which he pressed on Ottoline at 2/6 a copy.

That autumn she asked him to Garsington and he came several times, at least once accompanied by Frieda. On one visit he helped Ottoline plant iris bulbs around the pond. He also built a small summerhouse for the garden, cutting and nailing the wood with his deft fingers and planting climbing roses around it; when it was finished he stood back and exhorted the roses to grow with their "essential and primitive rose-force."[17] Later some of Ottoline's guests mocked the rustic structure, calling it "suburban," but she always saw that it was propped up and preserved, long after her friendship with Lawrence had faded. In the evenings at Garsington Lawrence read poetry by the fire and told stories about his early life. Once he decided they would all act in a version of *Othello* he adapted for the occasion. Inspired by his enthusiam, Ottoline, the Cannans, Julian, and Maria all dressed up and once more played out Lawrence's obsession of the affair between a noble lady and an outcast male; Lawrence, decked out in an Arabian coat and large straw hat, took the part of the Moor. In mid-November Lawrence was still planning to go to Florida on a cotton boat and he repeated his invitation to Ottoline to join him. Again she declined, sending him instead £30 to help with expenses; she also wrote to George Bernard Shaw asking him for £5 for the same purpose.* The week before Lawrence was due to depart he went to a farewell party given by Dorothy Brett and several more of his disciples. Ottoline wasn't pres-

---

*Shaw complied, though reluctantly. "I suppose I cannot refuse," he said, "but as the love of money grows on me you cannot imagine what a pang it costs me." (GBS–OM, nd, HRC) Ottoline also wrote to Eddie Marsh saying: "I wonder if you would help me in an effort I am making to collect a sum of money for Lawrence—to enable him to go to Florida. Poor fellow, he is miserably depressed and hopeless and he feels that there is *no* opening for his work here and that he must go forth to new fields. It seems an awful pity that we should lose him as he is a real genius—isn't he?—but I don't think he would live through the winter if he remained." (OM–Marsh, November 12, 1915, HRC)

ent but she did crop up as a topic of conversation. They pulled her to pieces, Brett recorded—so much so that she cried out, "Stop! We must leave her just one feather!" But Lawrence, again according to Brett, was more malicious, saying: "We will leave her just one draggled feather in her tail, the poor plucked hen!"[18] The next day Lawrence wrote to Ottoline: "Don't trust Brett very much: I think she doesn't quite tell the truth about you."[19]

But Lawrence didn't go to America—the British authorities denied him the necessary clearance—and late in November he was at Garsington again. Two other guests were a tall young man from Oxford, Aldous Huxley, and a young musician, Philip Heseltine. Ottoline was busy getting the house ready for a big Christmas party for the village children and Lawrence found piles of "exquisite rags" heaped everywhere waiting to be transformed into party outfits; it was like some Eastern bazaar.[20] Lawrence had bought a new suit and Frieda had on a new coat and a hat Lawrence had created from bits of fur. Both Ottoline and Lawrence enjoyed these visits and even Frieda was feeling less out of things now. Ottoline still fascinated Lawrence. "She is a big woman," he told Cynthia Asquith, ". . . her whole effort has been spent in getting away from her tradition, etc. Now she is exhausted."[21] He felt Ottoline was like an old tragic queen.

Some odd people were to be found at Garsington in 1915—usually as a result of a casually dropped invitation from Ottoline. A Japanese dancer called Itow came for a week in summer and spent his time fishing in the pond while Maria stood nearby watching him with big eyes. Later a Chilean painter named Guevara, a friend of Duncan Grant, came, but all he could be induced to talk about was boxing—not one of Ottoline's favourite subjects. A more interesting guest was Charles Gore, the Anglican Bishop of Oxford. Ottoline had a way with prelates, and Gore, who was a trifle fey, began to make regular calls. He even helped bring in the harvest, and the sight of Ottoline, clad in a large hat and flowing skirts, and the local bishop, plus England's greatest philosopher (Bertie also helped) bringing in the sheaves caused some amusement among the local villagers. An old lady, a regular churchgoer, felt it her duty to warn Gore of the company he was keeping; wasn't he in danger of compromising himself being seen with such controversial people? "Oh, but I like her so much," the bishop replied.[22]

During most of autumn Russell was almost a permanent guest. Ottoline prepared a small flat for him in Home Close, a large cottage across the road from the manor house, furnishing it for him and filling it with flowers. Between lecturing commitments he would travel up to Garsington and spend several days, or several weeks, resting and writing his latest book. It was a restful existence, but one still fraught with traumas. The Lawrence business still disturbed him, the war was a constant nagging worry, and his relationship with Ottoline remained unsatisfactory. He still hungered after her, but mostly she was cool. With him in permanent residence she didn't need to rouse herself to keep his interest. He, on the other hand, felt frustrated having Ottoline so close and yet so distant. But at least he could talk to her and get some of his troubles out of his system. Ordinary mortals he couldn't talk to, he told her, because "I feel I am talking baby language, and it makes me very lonely."[23] Before Christmas he left to return to Cambridge where his antiwar views were causing increasing disquiet.

Ottoline was almost glad of Bertie's absence at her Christmas festivities. She invited her biggest party yet, and almost every bedroom was full. There was Clive Bell, Lytton, Keynes, the philosopher George Santayana, Middleton Murry, Lord Henry Bentinck, Vanessa Bell and two of her children, plus Marjorie and James Strachey. Ottoline was determined to make this Christmas the brightest and best ever and the entertainments included games of backgammon, a charade entitled Life and Death of Lytton, and a large tree hung with gifts. The crowning event was a party in the large barn for the villagers and their children. Ottoline conducted proceedings with effortless style. To break the ice she grabbed a kitchen maid and twirled spiritedly round the floor with her. Then everyone joined in the dancing and games. "I suppose it's her aristocratic tradition that makes her able to do it," Vanessa Bell commented in a letter to Roger Fry, adding that in contrast Philip had made a rather stingy spectacle of himself by dividing up one and a quarter chickens among nine adults and three children.[24] Lytton was also impressed with Ottoline's performance: "It takes a daughter of a thousand earls to carry things off in that manner," he told his mother.[25]

The Lawrences were also absent from Garsington that Christmas; instead they invited Ottoline to Cornwall where they had taken a cottage in the village of Porthcothan. She was planning to go in January when another row with Frieda intervened. What happened this time isn't very clear, but it seems the young musician Heseltine was to blame. He had been at Garsington on an occasion when Frieda and Lawrence were not, and, as at the Brett party, the topic of absent friends came up with Ottoline apparently airing her views about Frieda. Heseltine later went to visit Lawrence at Porthcothan and let something drop, and Frieda dragged the rest out of him. She was livid and wrote a most abusive letter to Ottoline. Ottoline in turn complained to Heseltine who replied ingenuously that he had merely been truthful: "After living with the Lawrences for several weeks, I have come to the very definite conclusion that Mrs. Lawrence has been most unjustly maligned behind her back. She has known this for some time past and, very naturally, she is unhappy about it. Am I, therefore, to blame for trying to help her mend matters?"[26]

Ottoline thought he was; at any rate the visit to Cornwall was off and the atmosphere was cool for several weeks. Before long relations were restored and Ottoline resumed her flow of gifts to Lawrence—books, a counterpane she herself embroidered, and cheques. Lawrence's financial problems were getting worse and he was also suffering recurrent ill-health, the early symptoms of the tuberculosis that would eventually kill him. Ottoline renewed her offer of accommodation and sent him boxes of food. In return he gave her a green bowl and a copy of part of his new philosophical treatise. He told her he particularly liked the embroidered counterpane, though, unable to decipher her handwriting, he called it "the countrypair," and said Frieda and he would often lie on it and discuss its colourful design.[27] Little did Ottoline realise that as Lawrence lay on her counterpane what in fact he and Frieda were discussing was his new novel, in which Ottoline would feature as a hideous caricature of herself—the bitter snake-goddess, Hermione Roddice.

Chapter 12

Part i
1916

R USSELL's love for Ottoline cooled during the winter of 1915–1916. He hadn't enjoyed his stay at Garsington in the autumn and his absence at Christmas was not surprising. At an unhappy meeting in November bitter words were exchanged, mainly about faults each saw in the other's character. The real trouble was that Russell was not prepared to be a kept poodle at Garsington, while Ottoline would not agree to come and see him regularly in London. On November 10 he wrote: "It will be some time before I can make myself believe that you do not hate me—*please* don't be *froissée* if I am a little shy for some time."[1] Later in the month he threatened suicide again. Russell also had other emotional problems on his mind. His former student, T. S. Eliot, had recently arrived in London and Russell had put him up in his flat. Eliot was married now and scratching a meagre living teaching. His young wife Vivienne was a rather flighty creature with a tendency towards instability, and already the marriage was showing signs of strain. An inveterate fisher in other people's troubled waters, Russell decided to look after them, providing both accommodation and financial support. He told Ottoline: "I am every day getting things more right between them."[2] But, almost inevitably, he became emotionally involved with Mrs. Eliot and in January he broke the news that the two of them would be going away for a week's holiday together, although he assured Ottoline his motives were entirely honourable—he was merely giving the woman a holiday away from her husband, who had been ill; it would all be "quite proper." What Ottoline thought of this idea isn't recorded, but she was probably quite pleased: It would keep Bertie occupied. But Russell's conscience continued to nag and from the holiday resort he wrote to explain further: it was merely a question of health—he himself detested the place—she appealed to him as a child in pain would, and so on. The holiday had even helped him understand why he was oppressive and tiring: "It is really a clash between artistic and inartistic," he said; Mrs. Eliot, like Ottoline, was artistic—and

168

she found him oppressive too.[3] For the next few months matters drifted along. Russell spent quite a lot of time with Mrs. Eliot and wrote Ottoline only a few scrappy notes. In March he refused an invitation to Garsington, pleading a previous engagement. He also tried to tell Ottoline what attracted him to Vivienne: it wasn't lust, she merely brought out his latent paternalism; there had been moments when he had been tempted to make love to her, but these had passed; in any case, Vivienne would not want it. He told Ottoline it was she whom he really wanted: "My whole soul cries out for you, but I must not listen."[4] Ottoline wrote back sympathising. She knew these moods of Bertie's very well by now. She told him she loved him and he could be confident of that; she wasn't perfect either. He replied: "You are nearer to perfect goodness than anyone I have ever known."[5]

But the problem of Mrs. Eliot was not in the forefront of either Ottoline's or Russell's thoughts in the early months of 1916. That place was reserved for the question of conscription. If Ottoline, Philip, and Russell had been opposed to events in 1914, they were even more averse to the thought of forcing people against their will to go out to France to be thrown against German machine guns. Philip and Russell actively opposed conscription, as did most of Bloomsbury, many of whom would be liable for call-up. But it was no use. Under the threat of another khaki election Asquith was compelled in January, 1916, to put through the first Conscription Bill, making all unmarried men liable for compulsory service. No sooner was the Bill enacted than the militarists were demanding universal conscription and, a few months later, Asquith caved in again and a second Bill was passed conscripting married men too. From then on opposition to conscription by Ottoline and her friends took the form of aiding conscientious objectors. Philip, still a solicitor, offered to appear at the tribunals set up to hear their cases. Russell became a leading member of an anticonscription organisation called the No-Conscription Fellowship (NCF) and Lytton, Clive Bell, and several others of the Bloomsbury Group were also active in it. Ironically it was Philip—safely above call-up age—who was first to suffer for his stand. His vote against the January Bill landed him in serious trouble with his supporters in Burnley and on February 8 he went up to defend himself. At a meeting of the Liberal Association he began on a personal note: he could have wished for a happier circumstance to remind him the date was his fourteenth wedding anniversary. He said he understood the political problems in Burnley, but he could not put party before principle; conscription was what you would expect of the Prussians, not Liberal Englishmen. The Association decided to do nothing at present, but Philip was warned that if feeling in Burnley hardened further his position would be precarious.

Ottoline felt helpless in all this. She gave moral support to Philip and Russell and anyone she knew to be in trouble and she used her friendship with Asquith to try to influence him. She also took any opportunity that came her way to seek out and foster examples of that sensitivity and culture which had gone by the board with the declaration of war. One morning in January, 1916, she found in an unlikely place—among the war news and propaganda in *The Times*—a small poem entitled "To Victory (By a Private Soldier at the Front)." It began:

> Return to greet me, colours that were my joy
>   not in the woeful crimson of men slain,
> But shining as a garden. . . .

In these lines, signed S. S., Ottoline found an echo of her own feelings and she decided to discover who this young poet might be. She wrote to *The Times* asking who S. S. was. Edmund Gosse, a literary critic and erstwhile dinner guest of Ottoline's, replied that S. S. was a charming, simple, and enthusiastic young man named Siegfried Sassoon, who was not a private soldier but a lieutenant in the 1st Battalion Royal Welsh Fusiliers, and who had sent Gosse several poems composed in the trenches in Flanders. Gosse urged Ottoline to write directly to Sassoon, which she did. Several weeks later Sassoon wrote back thanking her for her letter. He told her the battlefield was not the harsh landscape she and others imagined and that it could be beautiful if one had the eyes to see it. He spoke also of the English countryside he loved and where he used to ride and hunt. He promised to send her a book of his verses and in due course she received the small volume together with a photograph of a handsome young officer. She wondered if she would ever see him in person or whether he too would be blown to pieces.

At the beginning of March Ottoline travelled up to London to attend one of Bertie's lectures and give Lytton moral support at his forthcoming tribunal appearance. She stayed with Philip at Bedford Square, part of which they had sublet and part retained for their occasional visits. Lytton was delighted that his chief patron and confidante was back in residence. "I shall fall on the green door's neck like a long-lost friend," he told her. On March 7 he appeared at a pretribunal hearing, which recommended to the full tribunal that he be conscripted. While waiting for the final verdict Lytton accompanied Ottoline to a range of functions. "Yesterday," he wrote, "there was a curious little party at Maynard's, consisting of her ladyship, Duncan with a cold, Sheppard with a beard, James and me. There she sat, thickly encrusted with pearls and diamonds, crocheting a pseudo-Omega* quilt and murmuring on buggery."[6] Many of Ottoline's friends came to visit her in her improvised boudoir at Bedford Square and Lytton observed with awe the constant stream of visitors received by Ottoline in "exactly-timed tête-à-têtes—like a dentist." The principal event of the week was Bertie's antiwar lecture, which was attended by an odd assortment of people: Ottoline and Philip, the Sangers, Clive Bell, Gertler, Vernon Lee, various other pacifists, and—to everyone's surprise—Ottoline's brother Lord Henry, who turned up in military uniform.† The speeches were equally odd—Vernon Lee gave a discourse about a cigarette case and someone else talked about arts and crafts being a cure for war. Eventually Russell had to call a halt and deliver his own speech, after which he joined Ottoline and Philip at Clive Bell's for dinner. The next evening Ottoline and Philip dined at a Soho restaurant with Russell and the Eliots: it was Ottoline's first meeting with Mrs. Eliot and she was not impressed. As they walked away from the restaurant Mrs. Eliot headed Bertie off, linked arms with him, and generally made a display of their intimacy.

Ottoline didn't wait for Lytton's tribunal appearance—it was thought its unfavourable verdict was a foregone conclusion—but returned to Garsington, taking Bertie and Lord Henry with her. Philip stayed up in London to attend the hearing as chief character witness for Lytton and there heard Lytton deliver his celebrated reply to the question of what he

---

*Roger Fry and several others including Vanessa Bell and Duncan Grant founded the Omega Workshops at 33 Fitzroy Square. It was mainly devoted to craft work.

†This is not so surprising. Despite Lord Henry's valour in going off to fight, his views on many things were similar to Ottoline's. He was the brother most close to her and he enjoyed visiting her, especially from 1916 onwards. Usually he had to confine his visits to occasions when his wife was away, for she was hostile to Ottoline—perhaps she still resented Ottoline's "stealing" Axel Munthe away from her back at Grosvenor Place.

would do if he saw a German soldier trying to rape his sister ("I should try and come between them").[7] The case was adjourned for a medical examination held a few days later and which rejected Lytton as medically unfit for any sort of war activity. The whole thing had been a grave strain and Lytton hastened down to Garsington to recover. Ottoline was most solicitous and Lytton reported to Virginia: "I lie about in a limp state, reading the *Republic,* which I find a surprisingly interesting work. I should like to have a chat with the author."[8]

On Sunday, March 20, Henry Lamb's friend Anrep turned up at Garsington, dressed in the uniform of a Russian army captain and accompanied by two fellow officers. The once gentle and naïve Anrep had turned into a great red-faced, brutish fellow, puffed up with pride over his glittering uniform. He had left his wife Junia, who had returned to Russia, and now he was fancy-free. He spent most of the day strutting around Garsington trying to impress Maria and jumping over stiles to show off his legs. As Anrep left, Sir John Simon and two of his daughters arrived. Simon was a lawyer and a leading Liberal minister who had recently spoken out against conscription. Despite the views they shared, Ottoline considered him insincere and consequently she failed to turn her full charm on him, a failure made more acute by the fact that she was suffering from temporary loss of hearing. Throughout tea Maynard Keynes had to keep poking her in the ribs and saying: "Sir John is talking to you Ottoline."[9]

At Easter Ottoline invited a large number of people to Garsington, and several more dropped in uninvited. Bloomsbury was particularly well represented with Molly MacCarthy, Clive Bell, Mary Hutchinson, Norton and—of all people—Roger Fry. Obviously Ottoline's friendship with the rest of Bloomsbury was helping to thaw old feuds. The weather was lovely and there were picnics in the wood, long walks in the countryside, and prolonged conversations under the ilex tree. On Easter Monday a large car arrived and Ottoline suddenly realised the Prime Minister had descended on them. While Philip showed Asquith's wife Margot and daughter Violet over the house, Ottoline took the opportunity to buttonhole Asquith in her boudoir and talk to him about conscientious objectors. She described the scene in her memoirs:

> I started by saying, "You know I am a rebel! I am passionately in sympathy with the conscientious objectors." . . . He asked many questions

and seemed impressed and sympathetic. I was very frank and "explic-it" . . . . He on his side abused Military People. After this rather nerve-racking conversation was over, we relapsed into sentimentality, and talking over old days, when he used to come and see me in what he called "My Tower" in Grosvenor Place.[10]

But in a letter to Lytton (who had spent Easter with the Woolfs) Otto-line gave a slightly different account of the interview: "It was indeed a hurly burly I made prostitute love with P. M. after having made *a hard clear* serious concise statement of my C. O. case."[11] An even more lurid version came from Vanessa Bell: "According to Mary [Hutchinson] there was love-making everywhere from the pugs and the peacocks to Ott and the Prime-minister—everyone except Philip."[12] Roger Fry reported to Vanessa that the weekend had been amusing and Ottoline had been very nice to him. "There was no chance for me to do any lovemaking, so I had to listen all night long to doors opening and shutting in the long passage, though in common decency I suppose I ought to have gone out to the WC once or twice to keep up appearances."[13]

Part ii
1916

After Easter life at Garsington began to quicken—so much so that the house that summer seemed at times more like a popular guesthouse than a private home. Indeed, Ottoline needn't have feared that in removing her-self to the country she was isolating herself from her friends or from meeting new people: now her problem had become one of trying to man-age the almost ceaseless flow of visitors. Lytton remarked: *"Mon Dieu! There are now no intervals between week-ends—the flux and reflux is endless—and I sit quivering among a surging mesh of pugs, peacocks, pianolas, and humans—if human they can be called—inhabitants of this Circe's cave."*[14] Of these inhabitants there were three categories: the per-manent, the floating, and the casual. Permanent residents, apart from Circe herself, were Philip, Julian, Juliette, Maria, the maids, cook, and other staff, together with long-term guests like Mark Gertler and Dorothy Brett (who had studios in the Monk's building adjacent to the house), and, from August onwards, Aldous Huxley. The floating population—those constantly toing and froing, staying a weekend here and a fortnight there—included Lytton, Russell, Slade girls such as Carrington and Barbara Hiles, elements of Bloomsbury such as Maynard Keynes and Desmond MacCarthy, and other regular guests such as Ottoline's brother Henry and Carrington's friend Alix Sargant-Florence. Heterogeneous as these inhabitants were, the casual callers were even more diverse. So wide had Ottoline spread her circle that literally anyone could turn up at Garsington—from the Prime Minister down.

In addition there was another group connected with but set apart from Garsington. These were the conscientous objectors, a detachment of whom lived across the road at Home Close. Their presence was due to the habit of tribunals of exempting pacifists from military duty on condition they did noncombatant work. Of such work farm labouring was probably the most congenial, so Philip and Ottoline took in a number of CO's as part-workers, part-guests. The first was the young Cambridge economist Gerald Shove, who moved into Home Close around the middle of 1916 and was later joined by his wife Fredegond, Virginia Woolf's cousin. Soon there was quite a little colony of these agricultural dilettantes. They were of various ages and included for a time Clive Bell who, naturally enough, tended to spend more time chatting with Ottoline and her guests than toiling in the fields. Some of the CO's worked hard, but others, especially the younger ones, were less industrious, attracting unflattering comment from the villagers and the attentions of reporters who lurked about trying to spot signs of "slacking."

Ottoline and Philip themselves had some cause to regret their generosity to these pacifists, not the least because of the numerous friends the CO's would invite to Garsington. At weekends crowds of young people would descend on the house, arriving by motorcycle, taxi, bicycle, and on foot, their footsteps crunching on the gravel, their voices clamouring for towels, bathing costumes, and food. Ottoline, observing a particularly frenetic group, remarked to Gilbert Cannan, himself not an infrequent guest: "They regard me merely as a kind manageress of a hotel." To which Cannan replied: "Of course we do."[15]

Putting up—and putting up with—all these guests and visitors was no easy task, and inevitably there were strains. Also, Ottoline was still enough of an aristocrat not to care particularly if she appeared at a disadvantage occasionally before her guests. Soon stories began to circulate, especially around Bloomsbury and its rural retreats, about odd goings-on at Garsington. Ottoline, it was said, was stingy with the food. At breakfast she would get up dreamily from the table and go over to a cupboard and spoon out a mouthful of jam for herself without offering her guests any. Lytton, it was said, complained of the spartan nature of his breakfast and Ottoline had retaliated by each morning sending up to his bedroom trays groaning with eggs, toast, and sausages, which, to her chagrin, he demolished. Another story concerned Ottoline's habit of dropping into bedrooms clad in an enormously long nightgown that trailed several feet behind her to chat with her female guests as they brushed their hair. Other stories were about her matchmaking and meddling in her guests' love lives, others about the insufficiency of bathrooms at Garsington. Carrington heard some of the gossip and complained to Mark Gertler: "What traitors all these people are! They ridicule Ottoline! . . . I think it's beastly of them to enjoy Ottoline's kindness and then laugh at her."[16]

Undoubtedly there was an element of truth in some of these stories. Ottoline was often vague and sometimes eccentric. It is true she tried to economise at times. But with so many mouths to feed, who could blame her? And she *was* an inveterate gossip and an incorrigible matchmaker—Carrington recorded that Ottoline once sent Russell and Brett out to walk together on the downs three times in the one morning. Also she did make a habit of summoning her guests up to her boudoir where she would pump them for details of their private lives, much to the embarrassment of some of them.

Often, however, the tales people spread about Ottoline were cruelly exaggerated or even completely fabricated. It is here, it seems, the legend—or rather the myth—of Ottoline originates, and the more the myth develops and is embellished the greater it diverges from the truth. Why this distortion should have occurred is not difficult to see. Many of the people who came to Garsington had reason to be grateful to Ottoline, and, human nature being what it is, they couldn't bear to be beholden to her. The spreading of malicious stories which pulled her down helped them reassert their independence. Another factor that encouraged gossip was Ottoline's reluctance to talk about herself. To the younger generation she was, at forty-three, very much a mystery woman and it was inevitable this mystery would inspire rumours about her past life and loves.

Probably the person most to blame for propagating a false picture of Ottoline was her most favoured friend, Lytton. Virginia Woolf said she couldn't understand why Lytton continued to spend so much time at Garsington if he found Ottoline and the house so annoying. To those unused to Lytton's mode of writing, the double standard of his behaviour—accepting Ottoline's hospitality and denigrating her behind her back—might seem mean and petty. But the fact is that Lytton was incurably addicted to exaggeration—about everything and everyone, and particularly about those he was fond of. He was just as mischievous about people even closer to him than Ottoline, and once described Clive Bell as "a corpse puffed up with worms and gasses" and Virginia as "some strange amphibious monster."[17] Nor was Lytton the only one in Bloomsbury prone to hyperbole. Virginia, Clive, Vanessa—in fact all of them—indulged in amusing exaggeration. This tendency was also copied by the younger people in the Bloomsbury sphere like David Garnett and Dora Carrington. In fact at this very moment it was said that Garnett was writing a play lampooning Ottoline and her friends, entitled *The Hue and Cry After Genius*.

Today it is hard to visualise what life was actually like at Garsington in 1916. But some idea can be gained from snapshots taken at the time. Ottoline was a keen photographer and took hundreds of pictures, which she preserved in albums. These faded snapshots record still moments, vignettes on the Garsington lawn. There is Lytton, his long frame lounging in a deckchair on the lawn, a straw hat shading his glasses. He leans over occasionally to instruct Maria, who is learning Latin at his knee. . . . There is Bertie, smiling a little primly, on a rug with T. S. Eliot. The tea bell has rung, but one group is still on the pond in the punt . . . Asquith, white-haired, strolls on the terrace. . . . Augustine Birrell, in a canvas hat, wanders under the ilex tree. Now and then somebody else clicks the shutter and Ottoline joins the group in her flowing garments, buckled shoes, and large hat tied under her chin or a scarf knotted gypsy style around her head. Also Philip is there, a somewhat lonely and misunderstood figure. Many of Ottoline's friends tended to dismiss him as inferior and scoff at what they regarded as his pomposity. David Garnett remembered Philip clad in riding boots, jodhpurs, double-breasted waistcoats, and high stiff collars that caused his nose to incline parallel to his forehead. "He was awfully nice to one," Garnett said, "but instead of handing information to the younger men, which is what one would have expected, it was more the other way round—he seemed to be looking for something from them. He was profoundly uneasy, always."[18] Philip tried to join in the fun. He treadled out ragtime on the pianola, cut the girls' hair into Slade bobs, did his utmost to be a good host. But he suffered failure after failure in his dealings with the clever, sharp-tongued guests of his wife. He meant well, and he undoubtedly worked hard—attending the tribunals of CO's all around the country—but there was, it seemed, a bumbling quality about him.

An example of his good intentions was his attempt at persuading Carrington to give up her notorious virginity. One evening after dinner he invited her to go for a walk with him around the pond, and without any preface he launched into the subject, saying how disappointed he had been to hear she was a virgin and how wrong she was in her attitude to Mark Gertler, whom everyone presumed she was destined to marry. He lectured her for a quarter of an hour, ending up with a gloomy story about his brother Hugh, who committed suicide. When Carrington escaped back to the house Ottoline took over, lecturing her for another hour and a half in the asparagus patch on the same subject. Carrington said later she preferred Ottoline's approach. "And also she suddenly forgot herself, and told me truthfully about herself and Bertie. But this attack on the virgins is like the worst Verdun onslaught and really I do not see why it matters so much to them all."[19]

Actually, had Ottoline and Philip had their ears to the ground they would not have been so concerned. For unbeknown to them Carrington was developing an affection for—of all men—Lytton Strachey! Ottoline can be excused for not suspecting anything in this direction, as she had long ago given up hope that Lytton might be rescued for the female sex. In November, 1915, Carrington—who admittedly was rather boyish—and Lytton were out walking when Lytton suddenly stopped and kissed her. Later the same day, as Michael Holroyd describes in his biography of Lytton, Carrington sought to pay back "that horrid old man with a beard" by snipping off his whiskers while he lay dozing. However, just as the scissors were poised Lytton awoke and looked into her eyes. "The effect was instantaneous," says Holroyd. "She seemed to become hypnotised, and fell, there and then for the rest of her life, violently in love with him."[20] Carrington's "great love," Mark Gertler, was equally ignorant of this volte-face. He was conducting what he thought were the final stages in his campaign to induce Carrington to come to bed with him and believed his cause would be advanced if she were to have a higher opinion of him and his art. Lytton, who had made unsuccessful homosexual advances to Gertler and apparently appreciated his painting, seemed to Gertler to be just the person to influence Carrington in this regard, so he took every opportunity to bring Lytton and Carrington together, even encouraging Ottoline to invite them both to Garsington that they might be left alone to discuss his (Gertler's) work. Instead the unlikely twosome spent most of the summer going off for long walks and holding cosy tête-à-têtes, falling, in their own ways, in love with each other.

Another couple who were to be seen quite often at Garsington in 1916 were the New Zealand writer Katherine Mansfield and her lover, later husband, John Middleton Murry. Ottoline, who had first met them in February, 1915, when Lawrence brought them to Bedford Square, had not taken immediately to Katherine; this may have been because on that occasion Lawrence had made a violent political speech which so embarrassed Katherine that she froze into silence. Ottoline described her at the time as "very silent and Buddha-like on the big sofa—she might almost have held in her hand a lotus-flower!"[21] Later Ottoline read some of Katherine's short stories and revised her opinion, starting up a correspondence with her. And when, around Christmas, 1915, Katherine was in France convalescing from an attack of lung trouble, Ottoline insisted on contributing towards Murry's fare so he could go and join her.

The fact that puzzled many of Ottoline's pacifist friends was why Asquith was made so welcome at Garsington. If Ottoline so despised the war and all its works, why did she entertain not only its chief architect but all his family as well? They did not realise how deep the friendship between Ottoline and the Prime Minister had once been, nor the fact that Ottoline and Violet Asquith had once been friends. And there was also the consideration that while Asquith continued to come freely to Garsington, Ottoline and Philip and their friends at least had some access to government thinking. Even so there were occasional embarrassing moments. One weekend Ottoline invited Violet to join a house party at Garsington, but almost as soon as she issued the invitation she regretted it and wrote to

Maynard Keynes: "I beg and entreat you to come then. Only you can save me!—what shall we do for a bath for them—could we hire one—you must bring bath salts—brilliant talk . . . pâté de foie gras—caviare."[22] Keynes turned up and joined Lytton and Desmond MacCarthy in trying to keep conversation in safe channels, for Violet was much more a militarist than her father. But on Sunday afternoon, while Ottoline was saying good-bye to her brother Henry at the door, an uncomfortable incident occurred. Ottoline returned to the tea table to find Violet had vanished. Jokingly she looked under the table and asked Lytton: "Where have you hidden Violet?" In a high, strangled voice he whispered: "She has fled upstairs to her room."[23] While Ottoline was absent Violet had abused Lytton about conscientious objection, saying the CO's had disgraced England and ought to be deported to a desert island. Lytton retorted that if this was the government's view he didn't see much difference between them and the Prussians. Violet, red-faced, had picked up her hat and bag and stamped up to her room and it took the combined efforts of Ottoline and Desmond MacCarthy to get her into a good temper again.

The following Sunday another embarrassing—though more amusing—Asquith incident occurred. As it was a lovely hot day Ottoline took Lytton, Carrington, Clive Bell, and some others for a walk, and while they were having tea in the wood a maid ran up and mumbled breathlessly: "The Prime Minister arriving . . . Lucy drowning . . . and a gentleman plunging into the pond."[24] Ottoline ran back to the house to find the Prime Minister and his party had already left and was told by another maid what had happened. Several girls from the house had been bathing in the pond when they saw Asquith arriving with some friends. Either as a joke or to avoid reprimand, one of them, named Lucy, called out that she was drowning, whereupon one of Asquith's party, Robbie Ross, dived fully clothed into the pond to rescue her—only to discover the water was just four feet deep.* Everyone except Ottoline enjoyed the joke and within days the story of how the Prime Minister had saved a girl's life at Garsington was spreading round London. Asquith took it with characteristic good grace and for years afterwards his first question when he met Ottoline was "How's Lucy?" Another pond incident involved Asquith and Russell. One day, imagining no one was about, Russell decided to take a

---

*He divested himself only of a pocket watch that had been presented to him by Lord Alfred Douglas after Oscar Wilde's trial.

dip in the pond. He dived in and surfaced to find Asquith standing on the edge looking at him. As Russell was naked at the time, he felt that the quality of dignity which should have characterised a meeting between the Prime Minister and a leading pacifist was lacking.

Russell had recently written a pamphlet about a young man called Everett who had been gaoled for refusing military orders. Several people were arrested for distributing this pamphlet and Russell wrote to *The Times* demanding that if anyone were to be arrested, it should be he. Nothing happened for several weeks and Russell filled in this time by lunching regularly with Mrs. Eliot. Finally, at the end of May, two detectives served a summons on him and in June he appeared before the chief magistrate in London. Ottoline and Lytton went to the hearing and made a dramatic entrance together, Lytton's storklike figure and red beard providing a foil for Ottoline's spectacular hat and cashmere coat of many colours. Russell was convicted and fined £110, but he refused to pay. Instead of gaoling him the authorities seized his books and put them up for auction. Russell, determined to be a martyr, refused to save them, even though they included several valuable editions. Finally Ottoline and some of his friends clubbed together to buy them back—which rather incensed Ottoline as she disliked having to pay out money for Russell when he himself was spending money for Mrs. Eliot's dancing lessons.

Ottoline in fact was becoming annoyed with Russell. She realised she should not mind his leading a double life with his lady friends (after all she had led a double life in the past), nevertheless she did. And despite the still-intimate tone of his letters to her, he was obviously beginning to move away from her. In June he forgot her birthday, a sure sign his mind was on other things. Ottoline warned him he was being a fool over Mrs. Eliot who, Ottoline thought, was frivolous to the point of stupidity. Russell retorted that his interest in Mrs. Eliot was superficial and waning. Besides, he had other matters on his mind. His NCF work was attracting a lot of publicity and a proposed lecturing trip to America had to be cancelled because of it. Next his fellowship at his beloved Trinity was withdrawn because his colleagues there disapproved of his "unpatriotic" activities. At the beginning of August he came up to Garsington to stay a few days and Ottoline took the opportunity to discuss his philandering. She told him he was being ingenuous in giving Mrs. Eliot money, as consciously or unconsciously he was in fact buying her affection and forcing her to rely on him more and more. Russell told Ottoline he wanted to put an end to the relationship but was afraid of what might happen. What he didn't reveal, however, was that he had already found another woman friend in whom he took a deep interest. Her name was Lady Constance Malleson. She was married to the actor Miles Malleson and was herself an actress, appearing under the stage name of Colette O'Niel. The Mallesons had been helping the NCF cause and it was through this that Russell met Colette, who was young, very beautiful, and dedicated. Throughout the rest of 1916 he gradually transferred to her much of his affection.

Part iii
1916

The picture many people have of Ottoline is of a rare and beautifully marked butterfly flitting from one genius to the next. But behind the flightiness was concealed a considerable strength of will and profound concern for humanity, as both Russell and Crompton Davies had discovered. When Ottoline was up in London attending one of Bertie's court hearings she met Eva Gore-Booth, the sister of Constance Markiewicz, who had been one of the leaders of the Easter Uprising in Dublin. Eva was trying to get up a petition to save the life of Sir Roger Casement, sentenced to death for treason for his part in the uprising, and Ottoline agreed to help. She was outraged that Casement, who had helped fight slavery in the Congo, could be put to death by the British for trying to obtain Home Rule for Ireland—a cause which Gladstone had espoused. Besides, Ottoline always looked on Ireland with special sympathy, partly because of the Irish blood on her mother's side.* She soon discovered, however, that many of her friends were not as passionate about Casement as she was. Russell offered little more than sympathy and Lytton was quite cold, telling her: "Casement I don't take much stock of . . . . Of course, I

---

*Philip too was active on Casement's behalf and even tried to see the King to plead for him, but was thwarted by the king's private secretary, Lord Stamfordham.

should be very glad if they didn't hang him, but I can't believe there's much chance of that.''[25] Ottoline also pleaded with Keynes, who worked in the Treasury: "I know you are awfully reasonable and Anti Irish—but if you can say anything to McKenna or Morgan? or anyone of influence I *beg* of you to do so. It would be beastly to hang him. After all, he *has done* good work and is fine—and it is silly as regards Ireland to kill him. I have written to P. M.''[26] But Keynes could do nothing. She also wrote to Conrad, who had known Casement in the Congo, but he replied that he did not agree with Casement, adding that he wished he himself could get on to a minesweeper.

Any hope that Casement might be saved was dashed when someone in the government "leaked" Casement's diary which exposed him as a homosexual. In a letter marked "strictly private" Asquith told Ottoline that Casement was "a depraved and perverted man" and he refused to intervene. Casement was hanged on August 3.[27]

Towards the end of August Ottoline was back at Garsington and sitting—or rather standing—for a portrait by Dorothy Brett. It was an early venture into portraiture for Brett and she was having trouble fitting all of Ottoline onto the canvas. So, rather than start the portrait again, she tacked on a few feet of extra canvas, making the picture over nine feet high and necessitating the use of a stepladder, which Brett climbed up and down murmuring "Marmelade." On this particular day Ottoline was posing in Brett's studio in a loft of the Monks' building when one of the maids knocked on the trapdoor and announced that Robbie Ross, the hero of the pond incident, had arrived with a friend. As Ottoline climbed down the ladder she saw that standing next to Ross in the doorway was a young man in khaki. "This," said Ross, "is Siegfried Sassoon."[28]

For months Ottoline had been looking forward to this meeting, as indeed had Siegfried. For almost a year he had been in the front line, becoming more disillusioned with war (though he had won a military cross for bravery) and for much of that time he had been building up a mental picture of the titled lady who wrote such nice letters to him. He imagined her some overintense aristocratic maiden; now, as he looked up at the long pair of legs encased in voluminous pale pink Turkish trousers descending backwards down the ladder, his illusions were shattered. After introductions the three of them climbed back up the ladder to view Brett's painting, and Ross, a colleague of Ottoline's in the Contemporary Art Society, pointed to the tacked-on canvas and remarked that it wasn't every portrait that went into a second edition. Siegfried didn't think much of the picture—and wasn't much more impressed by Ottoline. He felt she had dignity and was charming and gay but thought her appearance ludicrous. After tea Siegfried and Ross drove off in a taxi each clutching a peacock feather Ottoline had presented to them. Ross urged Siegfried to be nice to Ottoline as she could help when his poems were published. "But you really must not try and look so much like a shy and offended deerhound next time you are talking to her," he told him. Siegfried replied that it had been those Turkish trousers—they were too much.[29]

A few days later Ottoline and Brett cycled into Oxford to meet Siegfried and show him around the Ashmolean Museum, but he didn't turn up. The two of them wandered around dejectedly and were just about to leave when they heard footsteps behind them. It was Siegfried. Fearing Ottoline would turn up in her Turkish trousers, he had hidden behind a column to check on her outfit before revealing himself. Ottoline returned to Garsington feeling that in Siegfried she had found an almost perfect example of that romantic and sensitive spirit she had been searching for all her life and that in John, Lamb, Lytton, Bertie, and Lawrence she had found only in imperfect proportions. Actually she was beginning to fall in love with Siegfried and she invited him to come and stay at Garsington as often as he liked before he returned to France.

Before the end of August Ottoline went off to spend a weekend at Wisset, Vanessa Bell's and Duncan Grant's Suffolk cottage where David Garnett and Duncan cultivated vegetables as their contribution to the war effort. Vanessa had invited Ottoline in a moment of weakness and as the date of her arrival approached she was having doubts. She told Roger Fry: "Next week I rather fear we shall have Ottoline on us, which I dread," adding that she was worried her young son Quentin might pinch Ottoline's bottom.[30] Ottoline duly arrived and Garnett wrote this account of how it went off:

> The weather was wet. The low-ceilinged little rooms would scarcely contain our magnificent visitor, who I think was uncomfortable. Duncan and I went out most of the day—working, and Heaven knows how Vanessa kept her entertained. Blanche reported that when she went into Ottoline's bedroom with a tray of tea in the morning, Ottoline was lying in bed with her face already completely made up. I remember the feeling of relief when

Monday morning came and Cutts drove his dogcart up to the door. Ottoline, who retired after breakfast, suddenly appeared in a dress which she had not worn before during her visit. It might have been designed by Bakst for a Russian ballet on a Circassian folktale theme. Russian boots of red morocco were revealed under a full, light-blue silk tunic, over which she wore a white kaftan with embroidered cartridge pouches on the chest, on which fell the ropes of Portland pearls. On her head was a tall Astrakhan fez. As we gathered around, with Julian [Vanessa's elder son] and Quentin there to say goodbye. . . . She went down to kiss Quentin, [and] the little boy flinched and asked: 'Why have you got all that on?' There was a moment's silence after this unanswerable question; then a deep gurgle . . . from Ottoline, which passed itself off as a laugh—a rush of farewells from Vanessa, Duncan handed Ottoline up beside Cutts, she seated herself and waved and off they drove looking exactly like the advertisement for a circus.[31]

Vanessa told Roger Fry she didn't think the visit had been a success. She had decided she really couldn't stand Ottoline for very long—she couldn't relax in her presence. Ottoline, however, enjoyed the weekend, though she thought the house damp and exceedingly untidy. She wrote: "It is difficult to get one's eye used to untidiness if it has been trained to care for order, but with practice I expect one could probably do it."[32] It also upset her that Duncan, who should be painting lovely pictures, was forced to do hard manual work to save himself from being sent to France.

Back at Garsington, Carrington, in spite of her growing interest in Lytton and reluctance to break away from Gertler, was conducting a mild flirtation with Aldous Huxley, who had recently finished at Oxford and accepted Ottoline's invitation to stay at Garsington. One night when the weather was hot Carrington and Huxley took their mattresses up on to the roof and slept under the stars, to be awakened in the morning by the swish of trailing peacock tails on their faces. Carrington reported the incident to Lytton: "Strange adventures with birds and peacocks & hoards of bees. Shooting stars, other things."[33] Carrington at this time was still well-disposed to Ottoline, though she did feel a little guilty about having to hide Lytton's letters to her.* She complained: "She makes me steeped in

---

*Fairly well disposed. To Lytton, however, she affected a more cynical attitude. In September, 1916, she wrote to him from Garsington: "A concert is in preparation for this evening. Great confusion. Like Clapham Junction, chairs and tables being shunted about everywhere . . . and Pipsey at the Pianola! What an evening last night. Philip reading

debt by giving me *all* her letters to read. And then has long jabberfications about people deceiving her . . . !'' Carrington asked Lytton to contribute something to a journal she and Ottoline were thinking of getting out for the amusement of the inhabitants of Garsington and its regular visitors. To be called *The Garsington Chronicle,* it was heralded by a prospectus that Carrington got out in a parody of Ottoline's literary style:

> In this dark and monotonous land these days at Garsington seem to the humble inhabitants precious and varied and perhaps they may have a thread of eternity in them. To test this we the dwellers in this small island of freedom wish to weave a chronicle of the days as they pass. We ask you to stretch forth your skill and coloured fantasy to aid us weave this tapestry which will hang we hope before us in the future.[34]

But Lytton declined.

In the autumn Philip's troubles at Burnley flared up again. His opposition to the two conscription bills had hardened feelings against him and he realised that his support had been so eroded that he would have to announce he would not stand again at the next election. He wrote a long letter late in September telling the local Liberals of this decision and the reasons for it. "I have been guided always by the same principles—mainly, that it is our sacred duty even in time of war to preserve the liberties that have come down to us, so far as they are not incompatible with military efficiency."[35] The Burnley Liberals accepted his decision with obvious relief.

In October Ottoline fell ill and went off to a spa at Harrogate to take one of her periodic cures. It was while undergoing a starvation cure at the spa that she met her brother Charles, whom she had not seen for several years. Writing to Maynard Keynes, Ottoline reported that she found she had little in common with her brother, apart from their childhood at Welbeck. His views on the war were even further to the right of those of the *Morning Post;* conversation, consequently, was limited to the subject of fox hunting. "What he would think of me if he knew what I really

---

Boswell's life of Johnson with his own remarks freely strewn between the passages 'That's good excellent,' . . . 'all this part is very dull I'll leave it out,' Clive cackling in the comfortable chair, your chair, pugs snoring, Ottoline yawning, Maria, Mademoiselle and even Katherine knitting woolen counterpanes. What a scene!" (Carrington's *Letters* p. 39)

thought I tremble to think,'' Ottoline told Keynes. "I feel sure he would hurry me off to the nearest asylum.''[36] This letter sparked a rumour which swept Bloomsbury that Ottoline's brothers were trying to get her certified. Clive Bell, himself ill at Garsington, wrote to Ottoline asking if there was any substance to the rumour. Aldous Huxley also wrote telling her the house was made miserable by her absence. "Everything crumbles, footsteps echo hollowly,'' he wrote. "It is like walking through the deserted palaces of Nineveh.''[37] He spent his days discussing Life with Juliette and pining for Maria, who had gone to London to stay with Brett.

Ottoline returned to Garsington in November to discover that one of the workmen on the farm, an aged cowman, had drowned in the pond. This melancholy news was lightened by the prospect of another visit from Siegfried, on whom Ottoline was beginning to pin more and more hopes. She set aside a room for him in which she placed a copy of the *Oxford Book of English Verse* next to his four-poster bed. The book was covered in pale green vellum—"so civilised but so vulnerable,'' thought Siegfried. He had come to the conclusion that Ottoline was an idealist with a deficient understanding of how to deal with the problems she contemplated with such intensity. He wrote: "She had yet to learn that the writers and artists whom she befriended were capable of proving ungrateful.''[38]

Chapter 13

1916–1917

WHAT had become of Lawrence since last we saw him lying along-side Frieda on Ottoline's embroidered counterpane? After Lawrence went off to live at Porthcothan in December, 1915, he and Ottoline wrote each other regularly for the next two or three months. The trouble over Heseltine that had caused Ottoline to cancel her trip to Cornwall seems to have blown over fairly quickly and on February 3 Lawrence told her: "Let the trouble between you and Frieda be forgotten now."[1] Throughout February Lawrence received regular parcels of books, medicines, knicknacks, and anything else that might make his stay more comfortable. He was grateful and told her he was dedicating his new book of poems, *Amores* to her. Following this flurry of letters there was a hiatus until the next letter, dated March 9, from the Tinners Arms, Zennor, St. Ives, in which Lawrence said they were moving to a smaller and cheaper cottage at nearby Higher Tregarthen.* He asked about Bertie and told Ottoline there was a farm near their new cottage where she could stay if she came down to see them. Lawrence's next letter, over a month later, was still friendly, though he was rather sour about the prospect of general conscription. Katherine Mansfield and Middleton Murry had joined them at Higher Tregarthen, taking a nearby cottage, and all four were settling down to a simple rural life in their pocket-sized Rananim. All along the Bristol Channel the gorse was coming out, but, said Lawrence sadly: "It will never be springtime in the world, for us."[2] Then there is another gap to the next letter (dated May 24) in which Lawrence told Ottoline about his recent reading and said he had altered the dedication in *Amores* to read simply "To Ottoline Morrell" as he thought she would prefer that. After this letter there is an ominous silence. A little earlier, however,

*However, around the end of February Lawrence sent Ottoline a completed copy of his "philosophy" *(The Signal)* and Ottoline reported to Russell: "It is dreadful stuff—bad in *every* way. I feel so sorry & miserable about it. It is rubbish. A child of Frieda's." (OM-BR, March, 1916, McMaster)

there was a short exchange of letters between Ottoline and Frieda. The
two apparently quarrelled again around April and although what the argument was about isn't known, the upshot was that Frieda sent off an angry
letter accusing Ottoline of being arrogant and vulgar. Frieda told Cynthia
Asquith:

> I had a great "rumpus" with dear Lady Ottoline, finally; I told her what
> I thought of her. All her "spirituality" is false, her democracy is an auto-
> crat turned sour, inside those wonderful shawls there is cheapness and
> vulgarity.[3]

A little later, in an undated later, Frieda changes abruptly and is all sweetness and light. She said she hoped Ottoline had forgiven her nasty letter
of the spring. "Few people I have met have moved me so deeply," she
said and begged Ottoline to come and visit them.[4] This was followed by
another undated letter in which Frieda said she wanted to "start afresh"
and added: "My quarrel with you was never that you were fond of Lawrence but that you seemed to underrate *me*. And what you wanted
Lawrence to be, and his work to represent, was not my idea of him."[5]

Ottoline was well aware that Lawrence was working on a new novel;
he had started to rewrite an earlier draft of it, called *The Sisters,* in late
1915. In his May 24 letter he told Ottoline: "I have got a long way with
my novel. It comes rapidly, and is very good." Though Lawrence no
longer figured prominently in her life, Ottoline was nevertheless interested to see what her errant genius would come up with next. Lawrence
finished the main draft of the new novel, which was retitled *Women in
Love,* in November, 1916. What happened next isn't certain. On November 7 he wrote Koteliansky saying: "I have done with the Murries, both,
for ever—so help me God. So I have with Lady Ottoline and all the rest.
And now I am glad and free."[6] Lawrence had quarrelled with "the Murries" earlier in the year and Katherine had stalked off to a more congenial
cottage in southern Cornwall, taking Murry with her. But there is no direct evidence that Lawrence quarrelled with Ottoline. Yet around this
time she found out he had portrayed her in the new novel in a poor light,
for on November 27 Lawrence wrote from Cornwall to his friend Catherine Carswell, whose husband Donald was checking through the MS,
saying:

I heard from Ottoline Morrell this morning, saying she hears she is the villainess of the new book. It is very strange, how rumours go round—So I have offered to send her the MS—so don't send it to Pinker [Lawrence's literary agent] until I let you know. . . . Don't talk much about my novel, will you? And above all, don't give it to anybody to read, but Don. I feel it won't be published yet, so I would rather nobody read it. I hope Ottoline Morrell won't want the MS. [7]

But Ottoline was not to be put off and around Christmas, 1916, Lawrence sent her a copy of the novel which she began reading either the last week of 1916 or the first week of 1917.

As she turned the pages she was on the lookout for a character that might resemble her. She did not have far to look. Early in the first chapter Lawrence describes a wedding at which the two main female characters in the book, Ursula and Gudrun, watch a bridal procession. The text reads: "The chief bridesmaids had arrived. Ursula watched them come up the steps. One of them she knew, a tall, slow, reluctant woman with a weight of fair hair and a pale, long, face. This was Hermione Roddice."[8] Lawrence's description of Hermione shows how closely he had observed Ottoline. Hermione "drifted forward as if scarcely conscious, her long blanched face lifted up, not to see the world . . . she drifted along with a peculiar fixity of the hips, a strange unwilling motion."[9] Physically there were differences—Hermione's hair was not red, but fair, and she was in her twenties not her forties—nevertheless Ottoline could hardly have avoided seeing herself in Lawrence's portrait. He wrote: "People were silent when she passed, impressed, roused, wanting to jeer, yet for some reason silenced."[10] Hermione was a woman of the "new school," full of intellectuality, passionately interested in reform, the daughter of a Derbyshire baronet. She moved in the world of culture and of intellect; she was a medium for the culture of ideas. She speaks in long slow murmurings full of emphasis and pregnant pauses:

"Well—" rumbled Hermione.
"I don't know. To me the pleasure of knowing is *so* great, so *wonderful*—nothing has meant so much to me in all life, as certain knowledge—no, I am sure—nothing."
"What knowledge, for example, Hermione?" asked Alexander.
Hermione lifted her face and rumbled—"M—m—m—I don't know

. . . But one thing was the stars, when I really understood something about the stars. One feels *uplifted,* so *unbounded.* . . ."[11]

Lawrence gave Hermione Ottoline's bizarre taste in clothes. Hermione wears ostrich feather hats, cloaks of greenish cloth lined with fur, dresses of prune-coloured silk, and shawls "blotched with great embroidered flowers. . . ."[12] Few people who knew Ottoline would have been in much doubt where Lawrence got the inspiration for the physical shell of Hermione. Yet, if this were all Lawrence did, Ottoline might not have minded so much. What roused her to a fever of indignation was the character Lawrence put into that shell.

In the paragraph where Hermione is introduced Lawrence set the tone, describing her as "macabre . . . repulsive"; she "seemed almost drugged, as if a strange mass of thoughts coiled in the darkness within her, and she was never allowed to escape."[13] With what seemed to Ottoline almost fiendish relish, Lawrence proceeded to build up Hermione's tormented, twisted character. She was a demonic woman, possessed by hatred and envy, a thwarted high priestess over whom a mantle of death and poison hung. And to cap this evil portrait Lawrence portrayed Hermione as being crazed with lust for Birkin, the chief character in the book, who forsakes Hermione to fall in love with the heroine, Ursula.* And just as it seemed obvious to Ottoline that she was Hermione, it appeared equally clear that Birkin was a self-portrait—Lawrence—and Ursula was Frieda.

As Ottoline sat in her boudoir at Garsington reading the manuscript it seemed to her the full weight of Lawrence's vituperation was being heaped upon her. Her dresses were described as "shabby and soiled, even rather dirty"; another outfit made her look "tall and rather terrible, ghastly"; she was incapable of decent passion and instincts.[14] And if for a moment she attempted to seek refuge from the terrible caricature in some dissimilarity, Lawrence rudely dragged her back. In one particularly telling scene he harkened back to the letter he wrote her after Maria took poison at Bedford Square in 1915. Birkin is arguing with Hermione:

"You want a life of pure sensation and 'passion.' " He quoted the last word satirically against her. She sat convulsed with fury and violation,

*Evil, that is, in Ottoline's eyes. Other people have found Lawrence's portrait almost flattering. See Frieda's comments in Chapter 18.

speechless, like a stricken pythoness of the Greek oracle. "But your passion is a lie," he went on violently. "It isn't passion at all, it is your *will*. It's your bullying will. You want to clutch things and have them in your power. You want to have things in your power, and why? Because you haven't got any real body, any dark sensual body of life. You have no sensuality. You have only your will and your conceit of consciousness, and your lust for power, to *know*."[15]

The words of Lawrence's letter must have echoed in Ottoline's ears: "Why must you always use your *will* so much, why can't you let things be, without always grasping and trying to know and to dominate?"[16]

Early in January, 1917, Clive Bell, who was still living at Garsington, mentions in a letter that Ottoline had "calmed down a little now."[17] Indeed, she must have been extremely angry. In her memoirs she recalled her feelings at the time: "I read it and found myself going pale with horror, for nothing could have been more vile and obviously spiteful and contemptuous. . . . I was called every name from an 'old hag' obsessed with sex mania, to a corrupt Sapphist. . . . In another scene I had attempted to make indecent advances to the Heroine, who was a glorified Frieda. My dresses were dirty; I was rude and insolent to my guests."[18] What particularly upset her was that Lawrence had satirised not only her but Philip, Julian, Juliette, Maria, Bertie Russell, her house and garden, and many more of her friends as well. "Oh, I read, chapter after chapter, scene after scene all written, as far as I could tell, in order to humiliate me."[19] She said she showed the manuscript to Aldous Huxley, who was also at Garsington at the time and said that he was "equally horrified" and thought it "very very bad."[20] She added: "for many months the ghastly portrait of myself written by someone whom I had trusted and liked haunted my thoughts and horrified me."[21]

Why did Lawrence turn on his first major patron and benefactor, twisting her into a character apparently so venomously drawn that even people with little sympathy for Ottoline feel sorry for her? The short answer is that Lawrence probably had no intention of doing anything of the sort. He simply did not realise that Ottoline would take Hermione as a violent personal attack on her. It seems that—on the surface at least—all he intended to do was to use certain aspects of Ottoline's appearance and character to make a point about a certain type of woman: the civilised, unspontaneous, "sex-in-the-head" priestess archetype which Lawrence regarded as the opposite to the earthy, intuitive, "mother goddess" archetype. In *Women in Love* and other of his works he argues that it would be better for everyone if the goddess should prevail. When he began rewriting *The Sisters* in late 1915 the representative of the "priestess" archetype is called Ethel and was probably based on Jessie Chambers, Lawrence's first love, whom he portrayed as Miriam in *Sons and Lovers.* In his first rewrite of *The Sisters* Ethel becomes Hermione but this early Hermione still bears more relation to Jessie Chambers than to Ottoline. It is only when Lawrence starts his third rewrite, around March, 1916, that Hermione becomes based on Ottoline. Perhaps Lawrence decided Ottoline was a far more vivid example of this type of woman.

When Ottoline read *Women in Love,* however, she had no way of knowing how Hermione had evolved and could not make the distinction that Lawrence probably retained in his own mind between the earlier character-type based on Jessie Chambers and the new physical shell of Ottoline.

Oddly it was Frieda whom Ottoline mostly blamed for the Hermione caricature. After finishing the MS Ottoline said: "The only assuagement to the shock was that all the worst parts were written in Frieda's handwriting." She seems to be implying here that Frieda either composed these sections or inspired them. (When later Ottoline read a published copy of *Women in Love* she wrote in the margin against those sections such comments as: "Frieda!" "Surely Frieda," and "Frieda again!"[22]) But most scholars reject the idea that Frieda wrote any part of Lawrence's work. It seems the most likely explanation for Ottoline's misapprehension is that Frieda helped transcribe and correct the MS that Lawrence sent Ottoline to read.

To Ottoline this portrait seemed nothing but cruel and vicious. Yet, in Hermione, Lawrence created a memorable character; Ottoline, admittedly unwillingly, had participated in the creation of a major work of art. And though Lawrence was creating a figure of fiction, in choosing Ottoline for his inspiration he was saying something important about her. The portrait contains some truth: Hermione is possessive, so to some extent was Ottoline; Hermione is not earthy, nor was Ottoline; Hermione overflows with almost electrical energy, so did Ottoline. Above all, Hermione disdained the vulgarity of sex and regarded it as a weapon to be used to ensnare Birkin. Ottoline's view of sex was similar to this—and

Lawrence was perceptive to discern it. In fact, in *Women in Love,* Lawrence, for reasons of his own, was talking about subjects that went to the very heart of Ottoline's philosophy of life. In the novel—as in Ottoline— there is a tension between sensuous, intuitive experience on the one hand and cerebral, conscious knowledge on the other; Lawrence instinctively latches onto that aspect of Ottoline's personality which was one of the main causes of her unhappiness in her relations with other people. Lawrence describes Hermione as

> knowing perfectly that her appearance was complete and perfect, according to the first standards, yet she suffered torture, under her confidence and her pride, feeling herself exposed to wounds and to mockery and to spite. She always felt vulnerable, vulnerable, there was always a secret chink in her armour. She did not know herself what it was. It was a lack of robust self, she had no natural sufficiency, there was a terrible void, a lack, a deficiency of being within her.
>
> And she wanted someone to close up this deficiency. To close it up forever.[23]

It is a constant lament in Ottoline's memoirs that she, like Hermione, can never find anyone to close up this ''deficiency of being'' within her. Perhaps this is why she reacted so violently to *Women in Love*— overreacted in fact—Lawrence had discerned her Achilles' heel.

How did Ottoline find out about Hermione Roddice? This is an interesting question. In her memoirs she says: ''Lawrence had mentioned in a letter, which now I cannot find, that he was writing about me in his new novel, but I didn't trouble myself about it until the MS arrived.''[24] If Lawrence did write that letter it has been mislaid. Even so, it seems odd he should have volunteered the information that he was writing about her. It is much more likely she found out about it from some other source— possibly Katherine Mansfield. While staying at Higher Tregarthen she almost certainly would have learned about Hermione, and following the split with Lawrence she might well have told Ottoline. There is also another interesting possibility. In his May 24 letter to Ottoline, Lawrence mentioned having read several of J. A. Cramb's novels. (Strangely, this reference is not in the published version; it was crossed out on the original letter, possibly by Ottoline.) Probably Ottoline sent Lawrence these novels—otherwise he would not have realised that J. A. Revermort, the name on the books, was Cramb's pseudonym. In the deleted part of the May 24 letter Lawrence remarks that one of Cramb's novels; *Hester Rainsbrook,* was rather good. He makes no mention of the other novels, nor the fact— which must have been obvious to him—that one of them featured a thinly disguised character who was Ottoline. Why did Ottoline send Cramb's novel to Lawrence? Was she showing him how she had been portrayed before? Or even was she giving him a subtle go-ahead to portray her? It seems there is at least a possibility that Ottoline knew or suspected all along that she was to figure in *Women in Love.*

Whatever the truth, there is no mystery about Ottoline's reaction after she read Lawrence's novel. She acted like a scalded cat. First of all she showed it round the Garsington household where, it appears, no one, apart from possibly Philip, got anywhere near as angry as she did. A day or so after Clive Bell read the MS he wrote to Ottoline playfully, chiding her for not turning up at Home Farm where she had been asked to tea: " 'No you don't Hermione' as I dare say you remember Lawrence's hero says when he has had a smart clip with a lapis-lazuli ball over one ear and looks for no less over the other. No, my dear Ottoline, you don't put the blame off onto me. I remembered quite well that I had asked you to tea and I still hoped at four o'clock that you would still come.''[25] But Ottoline was so beside herself with anger that forgotten tea appointments were as nothing. The next thing she did was to despatch a furious letter to Lawrence. Precisely what she said is not known, as Lawrence seldom kept his correspondence, but Clive Bell knew something of its contents, for he reported to Vanessa:

> Ottoline returned Lawrence his MS with an incredibly foolish reply, in spite of excellent counsel from me, and some desperate admonitions from Philip against falling into the depths of folly. Every line of her letter that I was allowed to hear revealed a wound: Lawrence must have rejoiced. She, also, it seems, commanded him to return a rather expensive pearl pin that she had given him. But he, very sensibly, having sold it or pawned it, declined to do anything of the sort.[26]

Bell is slightly wrong here: it wasn't a pearl pin but the opal one Ottoline had given Lawrence in happier times. Ottoline herself says in her memoirs that she wrote to Lawrence to protest about Hermione but his only answer was that Hermione was a "very fine woman."[27] She goes on to say that Desmond MacCarthy was later asked his opinion about whether the book should be published and that he had replied that it was a very poor book and advised against it. Ottoline then says that Philip took up the matter of the libellous aspects of the portrait with Lawrence's literary agents. She says Philip told them that if the novel were published he would sue for libel. Lawrence did not find anyone to publish it for several years, though whether this was due to Ottoline's threatened writs, or because it was unmarketable anyway until the war was over is an open question. Ottoline claims that when *Women in Love* was eventually published Lawrence had expunged from it—presumably because of her threats—"some of the worst scenes."[28] But evidence that Lawrence did alter the manuscript in this way has yet to be found.

Ottoline's reaction to *Women in Love* killed her friendship with Lawrence. For several months her efforts to have the book suppressed were the main talking-point of Lawrence's friends. On February 6, 1917, Frieda wrote Koteliansky: "Campbell will tell you about L's quarrel with the Ott. She played Salome to L's John the Baptist!" Frieda also wrote to Campbell (Gordon Campbell, Lord Glenavy, a friend of Lawrence's) telling him about the book: "You must read the novel, it will be sardonic enough for you even—the 'Ott' read it—was furious, wrote as a vulgar cook who writes to her young man. She asked for an opal pin back she had given him!! Lawrence wrote and said that he had given it to me, I keep it, be more careful another time to whom you give your friendship so freely!"[29] Frieda added that Ottoline was just a flapper full of cheap spirituality and adoration of young geniuses. Anyway, Frieda concluded smugly, she and Lawrence were really happy now.

Lawrence's own primary reaction was anger. After his agents told him about Ottoline's libel threat he wrote back to them on February 20:

Really, the world has gone completely dotty! Hermione is not much more like Ottoline Morrell than Queen Victoria, the house they claim as theirs is a Georgian house in Derbyshire I know very well—etc. Ottoline flatters herself. There *is* a hint of her in the character of Hermione: but so there is a hint of a million women, if it comes to that. Anyway, they could make libel cases for ever, they haven't half a leg to stand on.

But it doesn't matter. It is no use trying to publish the novel in England in this state of affairs. There must come a change first. So it can all lie by. The world is mad, and has got a violent rabies that makes it turn on anything true, with frenzy. The novel can lie by till there is an end of the war and a change of feeling over the world.[30]

After this a feeling of bewilderment came over him and he wrote Mark Gertler, who was close to Ottoline, asking him for his opinion: ". . . *please* tell me how much likeness you can see between Hermione and the Ott."[31] To Cynthia Asquith Lawrence denied that Hermione was meant to be a portrait of Ottoline—Hermione, he insisted, was infinitely superior. Cynthia alleges that Philip wrote to Lawrence's publisher asking him to come down to Garsington and compare the fiction of Hermione to the reality of his wife. "Fancy calling in that worm of a publisher as detective," Cynthia commented.[32]

Over the next eighteen months Lawrence and Frieda, after being expelled from Cornwall, went from friend to friend and house to house virtually living on charity. By February, 1918, Lawrence was reduced to such a state that Koteliansky suggested some of his troubles might be relieved if he tried to make up with Ottoline. Lawrence replied: "I got your letter. Yes, I know the Ot. is very nice, somewhere. I once was *very* fond of her—and I am still, in a way. But she is like someone who has died: and I cannot wish to call her from the grave."[33] And a few days later he warned Mark Gertler: "I should beware of Garsington. I believe there is something exhaustive in the air there, not so very restful."[34]

On March 5 Cynthia Asquith recorded in her diary that Lawrence had "*said* Ottoline no longer minded about the book (I wonder if this can be true) and that she was anxious to see him again, but that he was unwilling."[35] Whatever the truth about who was approaching whom, rapprochement failed and later that month Lawrence wrote Gertler again: "As for the Ott—why should I bother about the old carrion?"[36] A day or so later he wrote Koteliansky asking him to get some of his poem manuscripts back from Ottoline. She obviously obliged, and Lawrence wrote to thank her:

My Dear Ottoline

　　Thank you for the two bundles of MS. which came this morning. I am sorry to have troubled you—but I wanted to hunt up a few old things that might possibly meet a publisher in these days of leanness.

　　I am awfully sick of the world that is. I wish to heaven there would be an end of it. Meanwhile one persists in one's way against it all.

Perhaps we shall meet in some sort of Afterwards when the laugh is on a new side.

D. H. LAWRENCE[37]

A few months later Lawrence was begging Gertler to see if Ottoline would accept him and Frieda back at Garsington but Gertler wasn't enthusiastic. Six months later Lawrence was still sour and wrote to Kot complaining about the injustice of it all.

Lawrence had deeply offended Ottoline. She says in her memoirs: "The hurt that he had done me made a very great mark in my life."[38] The wound took many years to heal and even as late as 1932 she was describing *Women in Love* as "that wicked, spiteful book." She had opened her heart and mind to Lawrence as she had to no other person apart from Bertie and Philip and she vowed that never again would she leave herself so vulnerable.

Chapter 14

1917

WITH the discovery of Lawrence's caricature of her, 1917 had started badly for Ottoline. But worse was to follow. At her party at Christmas she had detected certain undercurrents that did not please her. From Carrington's behaviour it was obvious she had gained some hold over Lytton, confirming the rumours about them. Also other rumours eddying around London for some time began lapping at Ottoline's doorstep. In Chelsea, it was said, a group was putting on a play featuring an eccentric character called Lady Omega Muddle. Slowly it began to dawn on Ottoline that many people—some of them her close friends—regarded her as a figure of fun. Another disturbing undercurrent was the interest Russell was taking in Katherine Mansfield.

For more than a year now Ottoline's relationship with Russell had been growing more casual. At first he had resented this, but as he found other women friends it turned into a blessing. Ottoline suspected something of what was going on and, as we have seen, was not too unhappy—it saved her from having to take the brunt of his affections, and allowed her to keep things to the more spiritual level she preferred. All the same, she didn't like to see Bertie drift too far. It had been the inelegance rather than the seriousness of his affair with Mrs. Eliot that had annoyed her, and she had been content to let it run its course without too much interference. Now that Mrs. Eliot was out of the way she waited to see where his fancy would settle next. But she had underestimated Bertie. Almost as soon as he had decided to disengage himself from Mrs. Eliot he had embarked on a far more serious liaison with Constance Malleson (whom he called Colette). Writing in his autobiography of this period, Russell says: "I used to go down to Garsington fairly frequently but found [Ottoline] comparatively indifferent to me. I sought about for some other woman to relieve my unhappiness, but without success until I met Colette."[1] He says that what most impressed him about Colette was that, like Ottoline, she was very courageous.

After their first meeting in mid-1916 they saw each other casually several times until one evening when Russell escorted her back to her house after one of his lectures. It was a similar situation to that evening in Ottoline's Bedford Square drawing room back in March, 1911. "We talked half the night," Russell says, "and in the middle of the talk became lovers."[2] He did not go to bed with Colette that night, as there was too much to say, but from that moment it was Colette, not Ottoline, who was central to his life. It took him some time, however, to break this news to Ottoline. In September, 1916, he was still writing affectionately: "I yearn for you terribly. The rest of the world fades away in comparison. Dearest I hardly knew before how profoundly I love you."[3] He told her that he was trying to disentangle himself from Mrs. Eliot, and as soon as he had he would come to Garsington. However he did add that unless he could overcome his feeling that he had failed with her, he would go on looking for stimulus elsewhere. Ottoline had recognised this as a danger signal and early in November invited him to visit her at Harrogate where they had a happy reunion. Russell wrote to her afterwards: "Yes, it was a very very happy time. I felt we were *very* much one—I loved it."[4] It was not until December 3 that he first let slip some hint of his involvement with Colette. Breaking the news in between professions of devotion, he said: "In a gay boyish mood I got intimate with Constance Malleson, but she doesn't suit serious moods." He ended this letter by reiterating how much he was longing to see Ottoline: "I want your spirit, my dearest."[5] Perhaps because she didn't attach enough significance to this hint, or perhaps because she was genuinely occupied with other matters, Ottoline told Russell she couldn't see him until Christmas. Russell wrote her: "I am sorry to lose the time with you and sorry you have so many worries."

When Russell did come to Garsington for Christmas, 1916, he spent most of his time talking to Katherine Mansfield. For some time he had been showing an interest in her and had dined with her at least once. At meetings such as this the two of them discussed Ottoline to her detriment. During the Christmas festivities Katherine and Bertie sat up one night in the room beneath Ottoline's bedroom talking about their hostess into the early hours. Next morning Ottoline—for a joke—said she had heard what they had said about her and the guilty look on their faces showed her remark had struck home. A little later Russell told Ottoline to beware of Katherine as she had a vicious tongue. In his autobiography he says: "It had become clear to me that I must get over the feeling that I had had for Ottoline, as she no longer returned it sufficiently to give me any happiness. I listened to all that Katherine Mansfield had to say against her.''[6] Although much of this tittle-tattle he later rejected, at the time it helped him to rationalise his desire to free himself from Ottoline, and by January, 1917, he had made up his mind to do to Ottoline what he had done to Alys: kill her love.

He decided a clean break, a quick amputation, was the best and possibly the kindest method. Precisely how he set about this is not known as his letters to Ottoline of this period have been mostly lost or destroyed; in their absence we have to rely on what Ottoline says in her memoirs, plus passing references in letters from other people. In her memoirs Ottoline says that about a month after Christmas Russell wrote to her saying he must ''shake her off.''[7] She said:

> It is a sort of garden party parting, polite and formal, unexpected and casual. . . . He has hurt me so much by this way of parting that I feel I can never get over it or be frank with him again. . . . My rapier is out. I will elude him in future and defend myself from him and be free; free for my own flights, unimpeded by him. Cut all that binds me to him, my soul must be free, and rise above it all, free to embrace trees, clouds, sunsets, and far distances, to brush away all these dead thoughts and grievances.[8]

She refers to long walks with Russell in April during which he told her some ''truths'' about herself. Here Ottoline's dating seems incorrect and it seems certain (from cross-referencing with Brett's letters) that these conversations belong to a period of about a month beginning around January 15. What probably happened is that around this date Russell wrote saying he had decided to break with her. As he had said this several times before over the past four or more years she didn't take his words too seriously. Almost certainly he disguised the real reason for his wanting to break—Colette—nor did he reveal that in fact he had either spent or planned to spend a three-day ''honeymoon'' with Colette at a hotel near Buxton. Ottoline was not prepared for Russell's defection and she reacted testily and unsympathetically. Harsh letters must have been exchanged and a meeting followed at which harsher things were said. Neither was in a concilliatory mood and Ottoline, still recoiling from Lawrence, was at a low ebb. Her account of the meeting is bleak: Russell told her she was uninstinctive and lacking in the qualities that would make her a comfortable compaion; she was too like Blake and not enough like Shakespeare; she was too fastidious and aloof, always wanting the transcendental and not content with ordinary companionship. Ottoline says she was stunned by his words and had no wish to argue or retaliate. A day or so later they had another meeting at which Russell told of his deep involvement with Colette. Now Ottoline knew the real reason for his hurtful words. As they parted he delivered an exceptionally cruel thrust, saying to her: "What a pity your hair is going grey."[9]

That Ottoline was upset by Russell's onslaught is shown by her erratic behaviour over the next few weeks. She took to making pathetic efforts to hide her years and in a letter in January Brett refers to Ottoline dyeing her hair bright orange. Russell and Ottoline continued to exchange letters full of accusations and recriminations. On one of his envelopes Ottoline jotted distractedly: "Don't let me go. . . . The end of intimacy. . . . All is in the past. . . . You have lost me. . . . Don't you see I can never be friends with you again. . . . I am *gone* [underlined three times]."[10] Brett, for one, warned Ottoline not to do anything irrevocable. "Don't be hard on Bertie," she told her, "I mean don't misinterpret him. Be awfully sure you are right in what you think. I am not very sure myself that you are."[11] Bertie's cry for freedom, said Brett, was the cry of help creative people gave to keep from losing their individuality—it was the same sort of thing that had caused Henry Lamb to "turn on you & stamp on you," she added.

In February Ottoline's gloom lifted slightly when a telegram arrived from Siegfried Sassoon asking her up to London to lunch with him. She took a room in a Bloomsbury hotel and waited for him to arrive but he was late and when he did come her pleasure at seeing him was marred by the news that he had been ordered to return to France and was to leave the next day. He told her he wanted to take her to the Ritz for lunch, but the thought of trying to converse accompanied by a jazz band put Ottoline off, and instead she suggested a quieter restaurant in Percy Street after which they went on to the National Gallery. Lytton also happened to be at the gallery that day and extracted some amusement from the sight of Ottoline gliding through the rooms, her long dress sweeping the floor, followed by the pale and worried-looking Siegfried. Afterwards Ottoline and Siegfried walked to Tower Bridge where they stood looking at the grey river and Ottoline murmured that there was "something so moving about it—so mysterious and immense."[12] Siegfried agreed, but wished she wouldn't go about looking quite so extraordinary. Then they went back to Ottoline's rooms for tea and sat by the fire while he told her he was afraid he would be killed. She tried to lift his depression and said he must stay alive to write poetry. As he left she gave him a piece of opal.

Feeling lower than ever, Ottoline returned to Garsington and to a discovery that relegated all her earlier blows to comparative insignificance. The discovery was all the more devastating because of its total unexpectedness. Philip—that rock on which her whole life was built, the cornerstone of her sanity—had been unfaithful to her. The full story of what happened cannot be told here as it affects people who are still alive, but it can be said that the details of the discovery dealt Ottoline a blow from which she did not fully recover—ever. For weeks after the initial shock she was reduced to a state of partial sanity. She would wander off into the woods, totally distraught, talking aloud to the trees in her black despair. The entries in her diary are wild and chaotic . . . she envisaged Furies coming down to mock her, she felt she was at the bottom of a deep pit and that light and sunshine had left her. Her life had become a mockery; all her foolish dreams and ideals were in tatters. The whole fantastic edifice had collapsed.

Lytton came down to Garsington at the end of February and was genuinely shocked by Ottoline's condition. Disguising his concern in flippancy, he told Virginia Woolf: "Lady Omega Muddle is now I think almost at the last gasp—infinitely old, ill, depressed, and bad-tempered—she is soon to sink into a nursing-home, where she will be fed on nuts, and allowed to receive visitors (in bed)."[13] Lytton, of course, didn't guess the reason for Ottoline's sudden decline. Early in March she did go into a nursing home in London and Lytton visited her there.

Only gradually did Ottoline recover from this breakdown. Looking back from 1936 she says that the anguished things she wrote in her diary were but faint cries compared to her real feelings: "The potter's thumb-marks are still there," she wrote, "but as life has baked me and made me firm, and age has made me wiser and experience has helped me to lose more of self, so I hope I may never feel again those agonies."[14] She added that after this time she formed the habit of pulling down a safety curtain between herself and the outside world.

While Ottoline was in the nursing home, back at Garsington Philip was going through his own hell. For years he had played second fiddle to Ottoline and her frenzied guests. He had been derided and ignored. His efforts to mix in and to help people met with constant rebuffs. So over the years he had retired behind his own stolid façade and led a private life of his own. The ingratitude of the conscientious objectors, together with what happened in Burnley and the way his colleagues in the Liberal Party had treated him had left him little to feel proud of; now there was the additional burden of Ottoline's discovery of his infidelity and her subsequent breakdown. It was too much and he too collapsed.

After leaving the nursing-home Ottoline returned to Garsington and spent several weeks attempting to recover her equilibrium. Much of her time was spent sitting for the portrait that Brett was still labouring over and Clive Bell gleefully spread a rumour that Brett's "Colossus" had turned out to be a cruel caricature "au Lawrence." And though Brett strove long and hard it soon became clear to everyone that the picture was not a success. Julian told her: "It's no good your painting Mummy, you can't ever make her as beautiful as she is."[15] When Ottoline viewed the completed work she accused Brett of making her look like a prostitute, an accusation Brett denied vehemently.

Like Maria, Brett had a sort of schoolgirl crush on Ottoline. Early in 1917 someone must have cast doubts on the nature of Brett's affection, for around this time Brett wrote to assure Ottoline that her love was "entirely pure." She had no physical feeling for her, she said, beyond the "intense enjoyment a beautifully shaped head and beautiful form give to anyone who loves forms and shapes. I have no real perversion. My love for you is as clean and clear as Crystal & fresh as the Wind."[16] Yet sometimes Ottoline found Brett's adoration cloying, just as her deafness was irritating. At other times Brett's sympathy was helpful and they would spend hours closeted together discussing Ottoline's emotional problems. Especially worrying for Ottoline was Siegfried's attitude towards her. Did his aloofness mean he rejected her friendship? Or was it just shyness and diffidence? Brett was doubtful and advised that Ottoline would be wise to give up any idea of having a close emotional relationship with Siegfried and concentrate on helping him as a poet.

By May Ottoline had recovered sufficiently to venture up to London where she stayed at 3 Gower Street where Brett had rooms. The city

seemed to her lonely, arid, and empty. She saw few soldiers—only wom-
en, children, and old men. The only pleasant memory was of an afternoon
with Virginia Woolf, who was herself recovering from a mental breakdown and was about to launch into the printing business. Virginia accepted an invitation to come to Garsington later in the year. Ottoline also
spent an evening with Katherine Mansfield and they went to a balalaika
concert at the Grafton Galleries. For an hour or so the music swept them
both away from the drabness of London and the depression of war, but afterwards, as they walked away arm in arm to the tube station, Katherine
turned to Ottoline and said: "My corns are hurting, I must go to my old
corn cutter tomorrow. Good night darling."[17]

Meanwhile Ottoline's relations with Russell had recovered a little.
With Siegfried absent and Philip a doubtful quantity Ottoline turned back
to Bertie for comfort and reassurance. He welcomed the reconciliation, as
he was finding he could not let Ottoline go as easily as he had thought: If
he were to break away the process would have to be more gradual. By
Easter 1917 their letters had resumed an affectionate tone and during the
summer he was a frequent guest at Garsington. Early in May he told her
he was tired and depressed and couldn't prove to her how much he wanted her. But the thought of him seeing Colette continued to annoy Ottoline, and she told him so. He replied: "You mustn't imagine that I see
C. M. constantly—only now and then when I happen to have nothing to
do."[18] Ottoline replied in friendly terms and he wrote back gratefully:
"My Darling, Thank you, thank you for your letter—it gave me very
great happiness."[19] He said he was looking forward to coming to Garsington and saying lots more things to her—"all nice things."

Lytton was another visitor in May. He noted that Ottoline had improved greatly and had returned to her old self.* He sat out on the terrace
in a deck chair listening to Russell, "Old Birrell," and Clive Bell—and
observing in a bemused fashion Ottoline's "new love," Siegfried, who
had returned from France. Ottoline was overjoyed to have him safely

---

*Lytton wrote to Carrington: "Her ladyship is more fevered, jumpy and neurasthenic
than ever, though as usual there have been moments (especially at first) when my heart
melted towards her. She seems to me to be steadily progressing down to the depths of
ruin. Perhaps the whole thing is simply the result of physical causes, perhaps if she could
really rest and eat and be alone for a month or two we should see wonders, but I can hardly
believe that now she ever will." (May 28, 1917, Strachey Trust)

back—the more so because he was now totally opposed to the war: his months in the trenches had shattered his nerves and he had written no more poetry. Siegfried felt he should make some public statement protesting the slaughter and was encouraged in this by Ottoline. Philip was less keen, pointing out the absurdity of a solitary second lieutenant raising his voice. Siegfried thought Philip's attitude was weak-kneed. He remembered one talk he had had with Philip: "Staring at the sunset he leant on a farm gate, he himself—in his wide-brimmed hat—had looked somehow defeated and ineffective, a compromising pacifist who had lost hope of dissuading mankind from its madness."[20] But Philip had been fighting for his beliefs far longer than Siegfried. Soon the poet had to return to his camp near Liverpool and a constant stream of gifts followed him there, including a large rug Ottoline had crocheted and doused with scent, the smell of which caused much ribaldry among his fellow officers. Finally in July he sent to a newspaper his "Soldier's Declaration" against the war and waited for the storm to burst. When nothing happened he flung his MC ribbon into the Mersey. Two of his friends, Robert Graves and Eddie Marsh, fearing Siegfried might do something to get himself into even deeper trouble, mounted a campaign to have him declared mentally overwrought, and soon afterwards Siegfried was sent to a convalescent hospital near Edinburgh.*

Ottoline's infatuation for Siegfried was a topic of much amusement, and even Philip was guilty of a little wry humour, remarking one day when an airman flew over Garsington and dropped a billet-doux to one of the lady guests: "Siegfried is Ottoline's airman."[21]

Despite her unhappiness Ottoline did her best to keep up appearances that summer and more than ever before Garsington seemed like some tableau transplanted out of the France of Louis XV, with Ottoline playing the part of Madame du Deffand. No wonder Lytton relished it so. Brittle though it was, Ottoline clutched at the outward gaiety, to prevent her inward doubts from rising up and overwhelming her. Things continued to turn sour on her. Even Siegfried was proving a disappointment. One day Middleton Murry, who had helped Siegfried draft his Soldier's Declaration, showed Ottoline a letter in which Siegfried thanked him warmly for

---

*Graves in particular thought that Ottoline and her fellow pacifists were a disruptive influence on Sassoon and one reason he wanted to get him certified was to rescue him from their clutches.

his help and support. Ottoline wrote bitterly: "He has never once said a word of thanks to me, and after all I have done a good deal for him."[22] In June she went up to London where she met Russell and they had another quarrel over Colette, whom Ottoline had conceived a dislike for, describing her as "beautiful in rather a vulgar, stagy manner . . . too assured and self-confident, too much the attitude of the duchess."[23] She had made no secret of this opinion and this was why—as Russell explained to her—he had been so cruel to her in January. "It was practically the first time I had deliberately disagreed with your judgment of anyone," he told her.[24] He admitted that his relationship with Colette was not as casual as he had earlier implied, but, he assured her, this made not the shadow of a difference to what he felt for her. "Nearly a year and a half ago now I realized once and for all that I must detach my instinct from you because otherwise life was too painful to be borne.* That left me with a feeling of grudge, unless I could let my instinct go to someone else."[25] For a while this satisfied Ottoline and she and Russell were back on pre-January terms. "I got your dear letter yesterday," he wrote later in June, "I *will* hold on to you. . . . My Darling, I love you always, always. I mustn't look to you for a sort of mundane every-day happiness, but you hold my inmost being . . . my love, my dear one."[26] But it was a reconciliation on shaky ground and a month later the more usual on-again, off-again pattern was resumed. "There are times when I am *absolutely* in tune with you," he wrote in July, "but they would not be quite genuine unless they were interspersed with moods of a different kind."[27]

Early in the same month Ottoline caught the measles from Julian and was laid low for several weeks, afterwards going off to convalesce on the Isle of Wight, accompanied by Philip. In the train down they sat opposite each other and Ottoline saw Philip's lips moving in silent conversation. *How inaccessible we all are,* she thought, *so apart and alone.* On the Isle of Wight they joined Julian, who was already holidaying there with several young friends. Ottoline swam and sunbathed and, although she got sunburned, her strength began to return. When she got back to Garsington, she found a letter from Middleton Murry asking her to take in as a boarder his brother Arthur, who was about fifteen. "Dear Ottoline," Murry wrote, "shape my brother. I would have him in no other

---

*"Instinct" is Russell's euphemism for sexual relations.

hands.''[28] After her experiences of the past twelve months Ottoline doubted her ability to shape anyone, but she agreed to take Arthur, who was put to work on the farm. Around the middle of August Katherine Mansfield came to stay for a few weeks. The weather was warm and she and Ottoline spent many happy hours pottering around the garden cutting lavender and other aromatic plants. She told Ottoline: ''I positively lead another life with you there, bending over the flowers, sitting under the trees, feeling the delights of the heat and the shade.''[29] It was on a late summer's evening that Garsington was at its most magical. Katherine would watch Ottoline come out on to the lawn swinging a Chinese lantern while the moon shone down illuminating the grey stone house and the silver pond in the distance. On one particularly balmy evening Mark Gertler, Bunny Garnett, Carrington, Murry, and several others dressed up in fancy costume and danced an improvised ballet on the lawn as Katherine wandered the paths, her senses alive to the sights and smells of the night. She wrote a poem about that scene, entitled ''Night-scented Stocks,'' the first two verses of which went:

> White, white in the milky night
> The moon danced over a tree.
> ''Wouldn't it be lovely to swim in the lake!''
> Somebody whispered to me.

> ''Oh, do-do-do!'' cooed someone else,
> And clasped her hands to her chin.
> ''I should so love to see the white bodies—
> All the white bodies jump in!''

A little later Katherine returned to London leaving Murry behind to spend hours talking with Ottoline about life and literature. Ottoline thought the relationship between Murry and Katherine was rather curious. When Katherine was around Murry acted like a devoted spaniel, but Katherine sometimes treated him very offhandedly, once calling him ''a little mole hung out on a string to dry.''[30] Ottoline herself liked Murry and regarded him as just as poetical and idealistic as Katherine. One evening, after a long discussion about Lawrence, Murry and Ottoline were standing alone in the red room when Murry suddenly asked her if ''he might come into her heart.''[31] He went on to say how wonderful it was that he and Katherine had found someone whom they could love and trust and he implied, according to Ottoline, that he wanted to demonstrate his love in a more concrete way. "My answer," wrote Ottoline, "was rather vague, as I was quite unprepared for any emotional intimacy with him." After they had retired to their respective rooms Ottoline found she couldn't sleep and went out into the garden to think over what had happened. "After wandering about for some time," she recalled later, "I couldn't resist calling up to Murry in his room, as I saw his light was still burning. 'You must come down, Murry. It is wicked to miss this lovely night.'" They walked together round the garden talking "very openly, very intimately, not of love but of life."[32] Later Ottoline went to bed happy in the belief that in Murry and Katherine she had found two close friends. Murry returned to London next morning to rejoin Katherine and Ottoline was surprised not to hear from either of them for some time. At last came a polite letter from Murry refusing Ottoline's offer of a cottage at Garsington. This abrupt change of tone hurt Ottoline and she wrote in her diary: "Why did he ask to come into my life and push against the door as he did, and then run away?"[33] Ottoline's account of this incident, however, could be suspect. It may be that she read into Murry's behaviour more than was actually there. She wrote in her diary: "Why am I tormented by the desire of companionship? . . . I am too easily hurt, too fastidious and proud, too sensitive. But now I must put all these desires away and be happy alone."[34] Yet a letter Murry wrote Ottoline a little before this implies that there was some reciprocal affection between them. He wrote: "But when I try to find a name for my feeling towards you, then it is that I begin to suspect that I am in love with you."[35] After Murry returned to London, Katherine's letters to Ottoline became distinctly cooler, and Brett, who met Katherine in London, said Katherine told her she was bitter and angry about Ottoline.

The next time Ottoline was in London she went to see Katherine. At first Katherine was "formal and haughty" but at last she told Ottoline why she had changed: Murry had come back from Garsington "exceedingly distraught" and had collapsed on a sofa groaning and sighing, and when Katherine asked him what was wrong he told her a "dreadful thing had happened"—Ottoline had fallen deeply and passionately in love with him![36] Katherine then accused Ottoline of treachery and said she was trying to take Murry away from her. Ottoline laughed, but to Katherine it was no laughing matter, and it brought to a premature end the budding intimacy between her and Ottoline. It did not, however, end Murry's friendship with Ottoline, though this resumed a strict platonic tone. (This last adds a little weight to Katherine's interpretation of what happened between Ottoline and Murry at Garsington—for if Ottoline's version were correct it would be unlikely that Murry would have dared show his face there again.)

More disillusioned than ever, Ottoline pinned her hopes for finding the sympathetic soul she had always been searching for entirely on Siegfried. Even though he too had disappointed her he still remained her symbol of how the Moloch of war was devouring England's youth and creativity. Long intimate letters, interspersed with gifts of books and quilts, continued to follow him to his military hospital in Scotland. In November he told her that now his protest had failed the only way he could help his fellow soldiers was to go back to France. Horrified, Ottoline wrote urging him to change his mind and even offering to send Bertie up to dissuade him. Siegfried responded: "I don't think there is any doubt about my going back to the war as I've dreamt that something burst and it smashed me up. But it doesn't matter does it?" [37] Ottoline decided she should go up to see Siegfried in person. She had expected him to meet her train, but he wasn't there: he had been playing golf and couldn't get to the station on time. So she hired a cab and went off to wait for him at her hotel. Finally he arrived and they had dinner together; he poured out his problems and doubts, interspersing them with remarks about some of the other female guests in the dining room whom he criticised for wearing furs "like primitive savages."[38] (For a former fox-hunter this was indeed strong talk.) Next morning she waited for him to come and pick her up but he was late again. In the afternoon they went for a walk and Siegfried told her he found her very complicated and artificial. That night Ottoline went back to her room feeling chilled and rejected. The next day she left. Siegfried didn't see her off—he was playing golf again. In the train she broke down and wept. In her memoirs, Ottoline, describing this visit, says: "It is exhausting to give and give . . . without any return. One deludes oneself with the belief that by giving one will receive something, but it isn't true."[39] Back at Garsington she didn't parade her disappointment and in fact her friends thought she and Siegfried were still on the best of terms. Hearing about her visit to Edinburgh, Mark Gertler wrote her saying: "I wonder. . . . 'Not a word, Ah! Hah! Hem! Hem!' as George Robey would say.'' [40] On February 12, 1918, Siegfried, now recovered, was ordered out to Egypt to continue his war service.

Throughout the autumn of 1917 Ottoline's relations with Russell went from crisis to crisis. One Friday she returned from seeing a film in Oxford to find that a very unhappy Bertie had arrived to stay the weekend. "He flattened me out at once and extinguished all my sparkle," Ottoline wrote. "He is always depressed when I have had a happy time that he hasn't shared in."[41] On the Sunday they had a long talk in Ottoline's boudoir and Ottoline recorded in her journal that Russell had said "his usual unkind things" about her, accusing her of living in a state of high tension and of tiring everyone.[42] But the real point of disagreement was Colette. Ottoline wrote: "He isn't able to manage a friendship. I thought now that he is happy, in love with someone else, it would be easier and that we could be good friends; but he is so very reserved about that side of his life, which makes it awkward and then my pride is hurt and I am reserved too, so the residue is small."[43] She believed that Russell's protestations of unhappiness were a sham and she suspected that he spent most of his time gallivanting around London with Colette. On one of his sad September letters she had noted: "He was really very happy at this time with C. M.!" She accused him of "enjoying life up to the hilt" and told him she would have no further truck with him and that they would have to end their friendship.[44] Russell replied: "I can only accept what you say—but I am profoundly unhappy that things should end in such a spirit." He finished his letter with a curt "Goodbye."[45] Yet within a week both were regretting what they had said and on September 20 he wrote saying he wanted "to start afresh." They should put aside mutual criticism, he said: "I *do* want to get back to a sense of union, not division."[46] Ottoline, too, was tired of bickering and from now on things between them began to improve.

Her fingers by now well and truly singed, Ottoline began to turn for companionship and sympathy to the younger people who came to Garsington. To them Bedford Square meant nothing. Most came not from Cambridge but Oxford and did not bring with them the background of gossip and intrigue that Bloomsbury implied. One of the first of these Oxford youngsters was Aldous Huxley. For over a year now he had been a permanent guest at Garsington and Ottoline was beginning to regard him

as one of her dwindling band of intimate friends. Lytton didn't like him—
"too Oxfordy" he said[47]—but Aldous was the shape of things to come in
Ottoline's life: the forerunner of a new generation which tended not to
talk with Ottoline on equal terms but to sit instead at her feet—or at the
feet of her illustrious guests—and listen. At Garsington Aldous worked at
what odd jobs he could manage around the farm (he was almost blind)
and spent the rest of his time peering through a magnifying glass at a
book, or just sitting in a chair, his long body coiled up, observing the
crazy and fascinating things that went on around him.* Many people, including Ottoline at first, took his long silences as aloofness, but it was
only a device he used to disconcert people. Aldous found it easy to talk
with Ottoline, for though she often disclaimed any conversational or intellectual ability she was nevertheless able to sustain the interest of people
with minds of the quality of Huxley's and Russell's for long periods and
over many years. Sometimes Aldous and Ottoline talked most of the day
and late into the night. Then he would follow her up the stairs, pausing on
each step to continue the discussion, talking all the way down the corridor
and into her bedroom where Ottoline would undress unselfconsciously
while he sat on the floor talking on and on past midnight. In letters he was
always telling her how much he appreciated her and Garsington. "After
all, Ottoline," he wrote once, "you and I are some of the few people who
feel life is real, life is earnest."[48]

In September, 1917, Aldous left Garsington to take up a teaching post
at Eton but he returned regularly for visits, particularly to hear news of
Maria, of whom he had grown very fond. She had been packed off first to
stay with Brett in London, then to her family's villa in Florence where Ottoline hoped she would settle down happily and lose some of her childish
ways. Ottoline felt Aldous' friendship with Maria to be ill-starred: "He
so intellectual and so highly cultivated and self-absorbed; she so very passive and yet like all foreign girls, expecting so much attention."[49]

In November, 1917, in response to the invitation Ottoline had issued
earlier in the year, Virginia and Leonard Woolf paid a visit to Garsington.
There Virginia observed people strewn about in a "sealingwax coloured
room" and Aldous Huxley toying with great discs of ivory and marble—

---

*Huxley's father did not approve of his son visiting Garsington. "Where (he said) all
the cranks are." (AH-OM, February, 1916, HRC)

"the Garsington draughts." Brett was there, and Gertler. Lytton was "semi-recumbent in a vast chair," Philip "tremendously encased in the best leather," and Ottoline in velvet and pearls.[50] Droves of guests moved from room to room and up to Ottoline's boudoir for private chats. The day drifted on. Fredegond Shove was admitted to the inner sanctum in the morning and after tea Virginia herself was admitted for an hour or so's chat over a log fire. Virginia found Ottoline more likable than she had expected: "Her vitality seemed to be a credit to her and in private talk her vapours give way to some quite clear bursts of shrewdness." Virginia felt that as an artist she ought really to quarrel with Ottoline because of her aristocracy—she was sure that was why so many of Ottoline's artist friends were so disagreeable—however she felt Garsington was quite enough of a work of art to justify Ottoline casting her and them off as she wished. She told Ottoline that when she wrote her great Garsington novel there would be a streak of white lightning—and that would be Ottoline. Virginia saw Garsington not as a house but a caravan, a floating palace, and she noted in her diary:

> The horror of the Garsington situation is great of course, but to the outsider the obvious view is that O. and P. and the house provide a good deal, which isn't accepted very graciously. However to deal blame rightly in such a situation is beyond the wit of a human being: they've brought themselves to such a pass of intrigue and general intricacy of relationship that they're hardly sane about each other. In such conditions I think Ott. deserves some credit for keeping her ship in full sail, as she certainly does.*[51]

Ottoline's ship might have appeared to be in full sail in November but, for her, it was still an unhappy vessel. "I feel as if some black evil cloud has descended onto this place, and has blackened all the happiness and joy, eclipsing colour and sunshine."[52] She wrote Vanessa Bell saying

---

*Lytton described the "horrors" in slightly different terms: "Virginia was in high feather & dominated the assembly: very different from her demeanour about 10 years ago at Peppard, when she crouched before Ottoline like a suppliant kitten. [Ottoline] was worm-eaten with envy & malevolence, one hardly knows where to tread—very unfortunate. I thought, too, (after 24 hours of tête-à-tête) that I detected something like a sense of guilt, and perhaps if one got hold of her, isolated from Philip and the rest of the horrors, she might take on a new lease of life. The worst of it is that she shows no symptoms of *liking* anybody—it is all either underhand cat's-clawing or vague romantic flummery: decidedly most unfortunate." (LS-Carrington, November 21, 1917, Strachey Trust)

that Keats was the only soul she could commune with and feel sure of, at which Vanessa commented to Roger Fry: "Did you ever hear such twaddle? Think of poor Keats as Ottoline's latest poet at Garsington!"[53] Ottoline even considered going off and leaving Garsington, of escaping somewhere and becoming purged and renewed. She discussed the idea with Brett, who offered to go with her. Finally she decided to stay and keep going through the motions. "Everything I lived for seems to be knocked over," she wrote in her diary. "Everyone that I thought was a friend has shrivelled up, faded away . . . I have a feeling that I am in a long dark tunnel—calling, calling for help—but no answer comes."[54]

And so 1917, the worst year in Ottoline's life, drew to a close. It had begun badly and it finished badly. Christmas that year at Garsington was a pale spectre of the festivities of the two previous years, and Mark Gertler hardly improved the day by recounting the gossip which was currently circulating about Ottoline. Then matters were made even worse when a turkey served up proved to be suspect. There are several accounts of this incident. David Garnett says it was one of the peacocks, called Argos, whose feathers had fallen out and whose skin had broken out in green carbuncles. Clive Bell was horrified to see the bird served up for dinner and refused to take a helping, but the rest of the guests tucked in and almost immediately were stricken with violent stomach pains. Ottoline, says Garnett, insisted it was a mass outbreak of appendicitis, but this unlikely explanation was rendered even more suspect by the fact that Brett, one of the worst stricken, had had her appendix removed years before. Clive wrote an amusing letter about the disaster and left it on the hall table ready for the post the next day. Someone, possibly Gertler, suggested it ought to be opened and read. Ottoline probably had no part in this but she certainly got to hear its contents. She was not amused.

Chapter 15

1917–1918

ACTUALLY the incident of the carbuncular turkey (or peacock) could have been an echo of another event at Garsington around the end of 1917. This was the famous workers' revolt. The Wat Tyler of this insurrection was the economist Gerald Shove, who had assumed moral leadership of the CO's who worked on the farm. ("Worked" is perhaps overstating it: according to Ottoline almost all of them were bone lazy, and Shove the laziest of the lot.) A practising socialist, he believed it was his duty to expose injustice wherever he found it—even in the house where he was a guest—and one of the first things he did at Garsington was form a union. Most of his fellow CO's signed up but the farmworkers from the village weren't so enthusiastic and the idea lapsed. Next Shove decided to reorganise the fowlhouse and convinced Philip egg production could be boosted if a special feed were purchased. But, instead of improving, the egg yield dropped; moreover, the hens became increasingly prone to sickness. Meanwhile Shove's socialistic ambitions were still simmering and, so one story goes, he decided on a grand stroke. At the head of a group of CO's he stormed the manor house shouting: "Down with capitalist exploitation!" The revolution was short-lived and soon afterwards its leader decamped in a taxi, taking with him a number of the Garsington hens. When Philip went down to the fowlhouse to count the loss he discovered why the hens had been so poorly lately: Shove had failed entirely to attend to their material well-being; the roosts hadn't been cleaned and the unfortunate occupants were sitting on mounds of accumulated droppings and rancid grain. So the presence of a sick fowl at the Christmas dinner table would not have been altogether surprising. From this it might be thought that Philip was not a competent farmer, but this isn't so. His personnel policy may have been faulty—though there were reasons for this—but in other respects he was both conscientious and knowledgeable in agricultural matters. Farming had interested him long before he bought Garsington and in Parliament he was a frequent speaker on land reform

214

and help for agricultural workers. During the war he made Garsington virtually self-sufficient in food and he was always going off to sales to buy new equipment and stock. In every way he was the epitome of the gentleman farmer—a career he was to concentrate on more and more as his political star waned.

By early 1918 Ottoline had begun to recover. In January she wrote: "I think I am emerging . . . as I look back on the past year it seems as if I had traversed a land of swamps and mire and jungle and fever and horrors. Now I am in a canoe alone, pushing off from that unhappy country."[1] She was much more cynical than before, yet she still needed people—they were as essential to her as light and oxygen—so she had to force herself to overlook the insults and gossip. Thus in January when Katherine Mansfield asked if Murry, who was ill, could come to convalesce at Garsington, Ottoline welcomed him. But Murry spent most of his time with Brett, and Ottoline suspected they were talking about her behind her back. Katherine also came for a weekend and her attitude filled Ottoline with distrust. "She is too dreadfully lacking in human kindness," she wrote in her memoirs; "I was relieved when they left."[2] But if it was so unpleasant to have Katherine, why did Ottoline encourage her to come? And why did she invite her back later in 1918? The answer is that Ottoline was not always consistent. At times she liked Katherine, at others she didn't; and this applied to other friends too. In fact Ottoline's memoirs cannot be taken as always reflecting her considered opinion. Compiled from her diaries, from which she transferred large hunks without much revision, they were, as Ottoline herself says, her "only outlet," and into them she poured all her private moans, grievances, and fears.* Moreover, these she usually expressed in a style that today is regarded as sentimental and Victorian—what Vanessa Bell called twaddle. But behind this "twaddle" was a lively mind and keen perception, as Virginia Woolf recognised when she said that once Ottoline banished her vapours she could be sensible and acute.

In February, 1918, Ottoline spent several days in London, staying at the Kenilworth Hotel in Bloomsbury (Bedford Square was now fully let

---

*She never intended her diaries to be made public and had only the vaguest ideas about publishing her memoirs, the first much-edited volume of which appeared in 1963 and the second in 1974. It appears that the MS of Ottoline's diaries was destroyed during the 1939–1945 war.

and soon to be sold) where she witnessed an air raid. She also went for a long walk to Waterloo Bridge and observed on her way how much London had changed since August, 1914. When she returned to Garsington she composed a short sketch which she called "Shadows" describing her visit. She recounted how she met several old friends whom she expected would help lift her depression, but their self-centered conversation merely increased her loneliness, and when the air-raid siren sounded they scuttled off without saying good-bye.

The next day she went out into the streets searching for real human beings. In Whitehall she saw office girls flowing out of the War Office "fluttering off like a flight of birds, shaking their feathers in the air."[3] Where did they come from? she asked herself. Did they realise as they tripped from one office to another that they were frail little shuttles in a vast machinery of destruction? She was swept along with them into the Strand where she saw group after group of men in uniform, mainly from overseas. On the corner of Waterloo Bridge, standing on the edge of the pavement, she saw a young soldier, mud-stained, weather-beaten, and just back from the front. It began to dawn on her it was these young soldiers— not her cynical London acquaintances—who were the real, substantial people she sought. With this discovery Ottoline's pacifist attitude began to change. The hatred she felt for the war and all its works slowly evaporated and was replaced by a sense of helpless compassion for those caught up in its machinery. To her this suffering seemed all the more real because her young poet Siegfried had returned to face the guns again. From the Middle East he wrote her: "The whole thing is too mad. Why should I be in *Palestine,* and being paid 15/- a day, to *kill Turks*?"[4] She sent him books and other gifts to keep up his morale. He had started writing again and a book of his poems was about to be published. His bitterness for the war spilled over into his letters and he told Ottoline he had seen a line of Turkish prisoners at work: "One was shot the other day for striking an officer—so he has escaped."[5] In May he was sent back to France. Ottoline sent him chocolates and he thanked "Lady Bountiful." He wrote: "The gas is awful bad out here and now our gallant fellas take every opportunity of availing themselves of it to get away from the line—small blame to them."[6]

Back in England Ottoline befriended two young RFC men, and one day in March, in return for hospitality at Garsington, they invited her and

Brett to watch a flying display at their airfield. The two women stared skywards as daring young men in their flying machines looped-the-loop and showed off their skill. Then, as they watched, the wings of one plane crumpled and the aircraft crashed, killing the pilot. Ottoline assumed that this would put an end to the day's aerobatics, but no; within a few minutes the aircraft resumed the display. Such demonstrations of reckless bravery increased her feeling of helplessness. But what could she do? She couldn't bring herself to "help the war," and she didn't believe that taking up lorry driving or nursing would make her feel less guilty. Later in the summer she assuaged her guilt a little by inviting groups of wounded soldiers from Oxford to come out to Garsington to sit in the garden on Sunday afternoons, mixing incongruously with Lytton Strachey and Asquith. Their clerklike signatures appear on successive pages of Ottoline's green visitor's book—S. S. Thornton (Sherwood Foresters), James Graham (Royal N. Lanc), D. Thomas (13 Batt. Tanks). But they remained symbols rather than individuals.

At the end of March Clive Bell wrote saying he had heard Ottoline had been in the thick of "the most surprising adventures."[7] What tale had reached into the wilds of Sussex to titillate Clive's ears? Maybe it was the aerobatics display, maybe something else; his letter gives no further clue. Certainly March was a worrying month for Ottoline. One worry stemmed from a meeting Philip and probably Ottoline attended early in the month at which the future Soviet Foreign Minister Litvinov spoke in praise of the Bolshevik revolution in Russia. Philip also spoke and the following day the newspapers reported that he said it would be a good thing if there were a revolution in England too. This report caused a furore and in Parliament the Home Secretary, Sir George Cave, made a virulent attack on him virtually branding him a traitor. Philip wasn't in the House to answer the attack and, the next day, he got leave to make a personal explanation. He complained about Sir George's gross impoliteness in attacking a fellow MP without notice and without checking the facts. Then Philip explained that, far from advocating revolution, he had said the exact opposite: that a revolution like the Bolsheviks' could not happen in Britain and that the only revolution the British people would accept was a revolution of opinion. Philip's reply did not attract the same publicity the original lie did and the episode turned respectable opinion further against the Morrells.

It is significant that Ottoline and Philip should have been seen flirting with socialist ideas. As the war went into its fourth year many radical Liberals had begun to turn further to the left and for a while Philip and Ottoline harboured the hope that socialism might be the answer to Britain's and the world's problems. Several of their friends joined the emerging Labour Party whose leaders including Ramsay MacDonald and Philip Snowden were welcome guests at Garsington. Here, MacDonald was often prevailed upon to do his impersonation of George V. Later in 1918 Ottoline and Philip attended a Labour Party national conference where Ottoline met Kerensky. But the flirtation was shortlived; Ottoline and Philip soon decided it was politics itself rather than its particular varieties that was at fault, and after the war ended they had little to do with active politicking.

Another worry for Ottoline that March was Russell, whose antiwar activities were starting to get him into trouble. Despite her annoyance over his infatuation with Colette, she agreed to go up to London to discuss his problems and do what she could to help him. And Russell was not the only man in her life causing her concern. In France Siegfried was facing daily death while at home Lytton and Gertler had again been threatened with call-up as the government sifted through the residue of cripples and CO's in a final effort to provide more troops. Again Lytton's "Mahomet's coffin" came to his rescue but Gertler had to wait for the decision on his appeal. Ottoline's women friends were not much consolation to her. Katherine Mansfield wrote apologising for her silence, and Brett, moping round Garsington with her ear trumpet, was getting on Ottoline's nerves. By April her headaches had reached such a pitch that she consulted a lady doctor who said that catarrh was causing her migraines and prescribed daily gargling. This didn't help and finally Ottoline and Philip went off on a driving tour around Oxfordshire and Berkshire. As they drove through the spring countryside the beauty of the fields and flowers slowly restored her spirit. Also the tour did a lot to knit up Ottoline's much-ravelled marriage. "Philip was happy," she wrote in her diary, "and I loved being alone with him."[8] They drove back by way of Sutton Courtenay where they dropped in on Asquith and Ottoline noted that her old admirer was declining into a rather boring anecdotage. "It shows such an arrested lazy mind," she wrote.[9] Asquith did, however, reveal a glimmer of interest in the current scene, evincing a marked dislike of Clive Bell, whom he described as "that fat little yellow-haired bounder."[10]

When she returned to Garsington Ottoline found Mark Gertler waiting for her. Poor Gertler had been having a rough time of it lately. Only a handful of friends and critics appreciated his work and since 1916, when he finished "The Merry-Go-Round" (probably his best painting), he had hardly sold a thing. His health wasn't good—soon tuberculosis was to be diagnosed—and, worst of all, he had at last realised that he had lost his boyhood love, Carrington, to Bloomsbury's leading homosexual. He and Lytton had actually come to blows recently and the following day Gertler apologised, thereafter confining his aggression to the composition of obscene stanzas addressed to Lytton which he never dared send. At the end of March Gertler's call-up appeal was finally granted and he fled down to Garsington where he knew he would find sympathy for his many problems.

Gertler was a particular favourite of Ottoline's and had been a welcome guest both at Bedford Square and Garsington since the day four years earlier when he first saw the tip of the ostrich feather of Ottoline's hat emerge up the stairs of his East End garrett. In a way, Ottoline discovered Gertler, introducing him into the smart world and hanging his paintings for her Thursday guests to see. Later, at Garsington, she set aside a studio for him and offered him employment on the farm should the tribunal force him to do agricultural work. But most of all she had been his staunchest ally in his pursuit of Carrington. He told Brett: "You have no idea how comforting it feels to have a sort of family and home now at Garsington. There have been moments (in London) when I sunk to the lowest pit of depression. At such moments the thought of Garsington was my only consolation." There was an element of maternalism in Ottoline's fondness for Gertler, but this was only part of their relationship. She found him an amusing and delightful companion whose swarthy good looks ("like a young Corsair") and sensitive mind stimulated her. Often they would go off alone together to galleries and theatres. "She is better to meet in the evenings than most people," he said. At Garsington Ottoline and Gertler spent many hours mulling over the turn of fate that had deprived them each of the companions of their heart. At dinner Brett would join them (Julian, now twelve, was away at boarding school, and Juliette, her governess, had gone off to work for Brett's sister, the Ranee of Sarawak) and the talk would turn to that odd household over at Tidmarsh where they imagined Lytton and Carrington were wallowing in domesticity.

Meanwhile, at Tidmarsh, over similar lunches and dinners attended by the Shoves, Clive Bell, Mary Hutchinson, and other elements of Bloomsbury, the motherly attentions Gertler was being subjected to at Garsington caused just as much comment and amusement. Carrington suspected that Ottoline's current concern for Gertler's well-being was influenced not a little by a sense of rivalry: Carrington had "got" Lytton, so Ottoline would lavish her attentions on Gertler. To all this Lytton affected indifference, though he did remark once that he was puzzled at what Ottoline and Gertler saw in each other, concluding that the clue to their relationship was that they were so different that neither ever impinged on the other. However, the rift between Tidmarsh and Garsington widened only gradually; Lytton and Ottoline continued to exchange friendly letters, and Ottoline still wrote to Carrington. In one letter she told her "Give my love to the Eminent One . . . I hope he won't become quite like Maynard—whom I find *too* far gone into the land of . . .???"[11]

Around the beginning of May Bertie went to gaol. For a long time his activities had been threatening to land him there, but the way it happened was something of a surprise. The immediate cause was a fairly innocuous article he wrote for *The Tribunal,* a weekly newspaper issued by the NCF, in which he predicted that American troops would be used to intimidate strikers in England. Apparently this struck a sore spot somewhere and Russell was arraigned and sentenced to six months' solitary confinement in Brixton Prison. Lytton, who attended the hearing, wrote to Ottoline: "It was really infamous . . . the spectacle of a louse like Sir John Dickinson [the magistrate] rating Bertie for immorality and sending him to prison! . . . James and I came away with our teeth chattering with fury."[12]

Actually Russell wasn't too perturbed about going to prison; it would be a fitting climax to his antiwar work and would focus even more attention on the stupidity of the authorities. However, he did take precautions, writing to his friends asking them to use whatever influence they had to get him classified as a First Division prisoner, which would allow him comforts like special food and plenty of books (which was granted). Ottoline was very upset by this new example of war hysteria and did her best to relieve the austerity of Bertie's incarceration. Although their love affair had by now virtually flickered out there remained between them a tie of loyalty and understanding that went beyond mere friendship; moreover, whenever one of Russell's new loves (like Colette) impinged on this friendship, some of the old possessiveness would come back. When he went into gaol Russell was very much in love with Colette, but soon she became involved with another man, causing him acute pangs of jealousy. In this situation Ottoline and Colette came to an agreement about visiting rights to Bertie: they would go to see him at Brixton prison on alternate visiting days, following a schedule drawn up by Ottoline and Russell's elder brother, Frank. In her memoirs Ottoline describes how Frank (who was an earl) would meet her and accompany her to Brixton. Lord Russell had himself been imprisoned in Brixton for bigamy and at the gate the warders would welcome him as an old habitué. "How are you my Lord?" "Quite well, thank you, Jackson, is my brother getting on?"[13] Ottoline would bring large bunches of flowers from the garden at Garsington together with lavender bags, scented soap, and toilet water—to make his cell smell sweet—and quantities of books. All these had to be first handed to a warder who presided over the visit to ensure nothing improper occurred. Ottoline would also bring a little bunch of sweet-smelling herbs which she would hold out across the table, glancing first at the warder for his permission, then handing them to Russell and saying: "I think you will find *this* bunch *very* sweet."[14] What warder could deny these unworldly descendants of two of England's greatest families this little breach of prison discipline? Rolled up inside the posy, however, was an illicit note from Ottoline. Bertie, too, soon found a way of evading prison censorship. One day Ottoline was puzzled to received from him a weighty volume entitled *The Proceedings of the London Mathematical Society*, with a note saying she might find it "more interesting than it seemed." Ottoline examined the book from every angle, holding its pages to the light to see if it contained writing in invisible ink and feeling the pages for a message pricked out with a pin. Finally she found a letter that Bertie had tucked between uncut pages in the book. Russell was quite happy during the first months of his imprisonment; he enjoyed the seclusion and was able to do a great deal of thinking and writing. But as time went on worry over Colette and her lover drove him almost mad. On one visit Ottoline was annoyed by Russell's obvious desire to see her leave so he could read a letter from Colette that Ottoline had brought him hidden in a book. He kept holding the book in his hands and fingering it impatiently. One of the high spots of Russell's time in gaol was his reading of *Eminent Victorians*, the book that Lytton had been working on for several years and which had finally been published. Russell found Lytton's sacrilegious treatment of such Victorian demigods as Florence Nightingale and General Gordon so amusing that he burst out laughing in his cell, causing one of the warders to admonish him for unprisonly behaviour. It was a major departure from Lytton's earlier specialisation in French literature, and before its publication his Bloomsbury friends had not been confident of his wisdom in undertaking it. Even Lytton seemed diffident about its chances. In March he wrote to Ottoline: "My life passes almost entirely among proof sheets, which now flow in upon me daily. It is rather exciting, but also rather harassing. All sorts of tiresome details, and minor crises . . . but my hope is that in about six weeks or so *Eminent Victorians* will burst upon an astonished world."[15] The book became a best-seller almost overnight—and no one was more astonished than Lytton and his Bloomsbury friends. Virginia and Vanessa, while accepting the brilliance of the book, felt it wasn't quite worthy of Lytton, but Clive was more enthusiastic and said Virginia was jealous.

Ottoline herself was delighted that the writer whom she regarded as her major protégé had at last achieved success, and though she and Lytton were drifting apart she could lay claim to having had a hand in the book's popularity. She gave a copy to Asquith and later she reported to Lytton that "old Squith" was very enthusiastic and was going to mention it in an important lecture he was to deliver at Oxford in June. Lytton and Ottoline drove into Oxford to hear the lecture and sat in the front row of a very colourful and distinguished audience. Asquith, who looked particularly robust and Roman, opened his lecture (which was on the Victorian age) with a discussion of Lytton's book, praising it to the skies. The former Prime Minister's public endorsement gave a distinct fillip to its sales and within a month it had gone into its third edition. Now Lytton was lionised by the very people who eight years before had scoffed at Ottoline for having such a scruffy and odd young man in her drawing room. Lytton was asked to stay with the Asquiths and was feted by Lady Colefax and Lady Cunard. At Garsington that summer *Eminent Victorians* was required reading. Lytton himself made several visits and seemed more urbane as the book went into each subsequent edition. The house appeared much the same as it had in previous summers—the crowd of friends sitting out on the lawn, the conversation, the pond—but there was still that feeling of suspended animation about it, a feeling even the presence of Ottoline's wounded soldiers from Oxford could not dispel. Bloomsbury was not much in evidence but there was an increasing number of younger guests, including T. S. Eliot and Siegfried Sassoon's friend Robert Graves. Aldous Huxley came down regularly from Eton, and Gertler was in almost permanent residence in his studio next to Brett's. Also that summer a ghost from the past, Lawrence, decided to make one last attempt to heal the split with Ottoline and in June he wrote to Gertler asking: "How is Ottoline now? Do you think she would like to see us again? Do you think we might be happy if we saw her again—if we went to Garsington? I feel, somehow, that perhaps we might. But tell me how it is—what you think."[16] Gertler didn't think it would be a wise move.*

Lytton was not the only one of Ottoline's friends to be publishing a book that summer. Katherine Mansfield's collection of short stories, *Preludes*, also appeared and was read with critical interest at Garsington. Gertler didn't think much of it himself but he said that others felt that after reading it through it somehow stuck in the mind "and then one suddenly realises that it *is* rather exquisite."[17] Siegfried Sassoon also published his book of poems and Ottoline was keen that Murry should review them in the *Nation*, but when she read what Murry wrote she exploded. Gertler reported to Kot: "Murry wrote a scathing criticism of Sassoon's poems— Ottoline furious."[18] Russell wrote to Ottoline from Brixton agreeing with her that the review was unkind: "The reviewer's safe smugness made me angry—what business has he to feel superior to one who has suffered?"[19] Russell himself was feeling restless in prison and beginning to think about his future after he was released. "The position I want for *myself* after the war is with young intellectuals—if I have that I shall be quite satisfied."[20] He envisaged himself as a latter-day Socrates—a role Ottoline playfully recognised when she named a puppy sired by her favourite pug Socrates

---

*A little later Lawrence wrote to Koteliansky: "I wrote to Gertler thinking we might see the Ott. again. . . . But I got such a stupid answer from him. . . . To Hell with the Ott & the whole Ottlerie—what am I doing temporising with them. . . . What in the name of hell do I care about the Ott's queases and qualms." (*Quest*, July 2, 1918, p. 142)

after Bertie. He was amused: "Give my love to my pug name-sake! . . . I feel it an honour to become a son of Socrates."

Ottoline's growing impatience with Brett finally boiled over in August. "I had it out with Brett about staying at Garsington for ever," Ottoline told Carrington.[21] Brett retreated to London like a hurt puppy. Ottoline soon regretted her outburst and a reconciliation followed, with Brett once again making regular visits to Garsington where she even began another picture of Ottoline, this one proving more successful than the Colossus. What it was, ear trumpet apart, that annoyed Ottoline isn't too clear. In her memoirs she says: "I give and give to Brett, all my ideas about life and literature and religion and she gives me nothing, only a clinging devotion. But I want more than that."[22] Yet Brett was still probably Ottoline's closest confidante and it was her sympathy that helped Ottoline over one of the most difficult periods in her life—a time of transition from intimate friendships with men like Russell and Lamb to the more platonic relationships of her later years. Ottoline was depressed and tetchy, and Brett did her best to get her out of one dark mood by pressing on her a new book entitled *Married Love*; its revelations could explain all Ottoline's problems, Brett assured her: "Go forward, and find a lover. S. S. is alas of no use in that way."[23] What Brett was probably hinting at here is their fear that Siegfried may have been trespassing into that land Ottoline referred to in her letter to Carrington about Lytton and Maynard Keynes. Certainly, by the time Siegfried was invalided back from France in the autumn Ottoline had given up any thought of an intimate relationship with him.

In September Russell came out of gaol, enriched mentally but both emotionally and financially broke. Colette's infidelity had caused him to denounce her "with great violence," the result being that her feelings towards him were "considerably chilled."[24] Into this emotional vacuum came Ottoline. The day he was released she took him to the Wigmore Hall to hear a Bach concert and on other days they went for long walks in Richmond Park. He told her that he felt they had come back to the intimacy of long ago: "I think that what we have now ought to last as long as we live."[25] Ottoline, too, was happier with him than for a long time. Towards the end of his prison term he had written her some particularly nice letters—some of the best he ever wrote, she thought, and she felt their friendship was now established on a new basis. "He is franker too, which

Bertrand Russell.
Courtesy George Allen & Unwin Ltd.

Above: Left to right: Ottoline, Henry H. Asquith, Philip Ritchie.

Below: Left to right: Geoffry Nelson, Dorothy Brett, Ottoline, Mr. Blay, Mark Gertler.

Vanessa Bell, 1907.
*Photograph by Beresford,
Radio Times Hulton Picture Library*

Virginia Woolf.
Portrait by Man Ray

Clive Bell and women farm workers, Garsington.

Ottoline and Cecil Beaton
at Garsington.

Left to right: Philip Ritchie,
Goldie Lowes Dickinson,
Eddie Sackville-West.

Left to right: Brett, Lytton Strachey, Ottoline, Bertrand Russell.

Peter Ralli and Julian Morrell at Garsington.

Below: Lytton Strachey and W.B. Yeats at Garsington.
Courtesy Hogarth Press

Ottoline at Garsington, 1917.

David Garnett.
Courtesy Hogarth Press

Siegfried Sassoon, 1915.
Radio Times Hulton Picture Library

Katherine Mansfield.
Radio Times Hulton Picture Library

John Middleton Murry, Frieda and D.H. Lawrence.
Courtesy Mrs. J. Middleton Murry and the Society of Authors.

Aldous Huxley.
Courtesy Hogarth Press

Below: T. S. Eliot.
Photograph by Angus McBean
Courtesy Faber & Faber Ltd.

Left to right: W. J. Turner, unidentified, H. H. Asquith, Mark Gertler, Walter Taylor.

Phillip Morrell in later life.

Ottoline Morrell in later life.

10 Gower Street (center).
Courtesy Y. Ismail

Above: Ottoline on the way to India.

Below: Left to right: Gilbert Spencer, Pilley, Kyrle Leng, Leslie Hartley, Peter Ralli, Robert Gathorne-Hardy.

Phillip, Ottoline and Julian at Garsington.

is a great comfort," she said.[26] But, as usual, Bertie wasn't being frank at all. In August he had told her: "I *must* have *some* complete holiday when I first come out of prison," but it turned out that this was so he could go away and patch up his affair with Colette.[27] While his mind was filled with thoughts of Colette, Ottoline and several other of his friends were busy organising a fund to subsidise his future work. Since he had lost his job at Trinity and bestowed gifts on the Eliots and other deserving causes his income had been so eroded that he was on the brink of poverty. Ottoline went to see one prospective donor, an old philosopher, but was embarrassed by the quite reasonable question: "Why is Mr. Russell so poor? What has he done with his money?"[28] Ottoline could hardly tell him. Eventually the money was raised and Russell was very grateful: "I am wonderfully touched by what all of you have done."[29]

That autumn Ottoline's spirits were raised considerably when Diaghilev's Russian Ballet returned to London. One night she went along to see Massine dance in *The Good Humoured Ladies* and after the performance she spied David Garnett in the foyer and bore him off backstage to meet Massine and his co-star Lydia Lopokova, the future wife of Maynard Keynes. Garnett stared at Lopokova in dumb worship and wondered if he had been "wafted into heaven by Ottoline."[30] Two tall young officers named Osbert and Sacheverell Sitwell joined them and they all went off to supper. At another performance Osbert Sitwell saw Ottoline wearing a yellow Spanish gown and looking like an oversized Infanta of Spain. For the Ballet's visit Ottoline had taken rooms at Garland's Hotel in Suffolk Street where, in an old-fashioned sitting room furnished in plush with a marble clock on the mantlepiece, she entertained the dancers to tea, the Russians eating strawberry and raspberry jam out of silver spoons which they dipped in their tea. Osbert admired Ottoline's masterly handling of the temperamental Diaghilev. One day he was at Garsington when the impresario called. Diaghilev, a born snob, was displeased to find nobody of particular genius or fame there, but Ottoline saved the situation by pointing at Brett and murmuring confidentially to Diaghilev: "That woman is sister to a Queen."[31] No matter that Brett's sister was only the Ranee of Sarawak, it was sufficient to appease Diaghilev.

In the autumn of 1918 the end of the war came where it had begun—in the Balkans. In September an Allied army broke through on the Macedonian Front and Bulgaria, Germany's ally, collapsed. On October 27

Austria also collapsed and Germany sought an armistice, which was signed in Foch's railway carriage. At eleven A. M. on November 11 a salvo of guns in London told the somewhat surprised populace that the Great War was over. That afternoon in the House of Commons Lloyd George read out the Armistice terms and concluded: "I hope we may say that thus, this fateful morning, came to an end all wars."[32] Then he and Asquith walked side by side to a nearby church to give thanks to the Almighty. Throughout the rest of London there was rejoicing. When Carrington heard the guns she thought it was a joke or some new German terror weapon. "But it soon turned out to be Peace with a big P," she said.[33] She travelled down from Hampstead and as she got closer to the city the scenes became more wild. Slum girls and coster people danced in the streets: ". . . as one [approached] Trafalgar Square office boys and girls, officers, Majors, waacs all leaped on taxis, and army vans driving around the place waving flags. In the Strand the uproar was appalling."[34] As soon as Katherine Mansfield heard the guns she sat down and wrote to Ottoline telling her that her thoughts at this moment flew to her. Siegfried was at Garsington and all he noticed was a little peal of bells from the village church and a flutter of flags from the windows of the thatched cottages. At Richmond Virginia Woolf looked out of the window when the guns went off and saw the man painting their house give one look at the sky and then go on with his job. "The rooks wheeled round and wore for a moment the symbolic look of creatures performing some ceremony, partly of thanksgiving, partly of valediction over the grave," she wrote in her diary.[35] Bertie was in Tottenham Court Road at eleven A. M. and noticed that within seconds people were pouring out on to the streets. "I saw a man and woman, complete strangers to each other meet in the middle of the road and kiss as they passed."[36] As evening came on the madness increased. Girls from the Woolwich arsenal, their bodies stained yellow from picric acid fumes, danced in the streets and embraced passersby. Ottoline, who was still in London, celebrated by going to the Adelphi flat of Montague Sherman, friend and patron of Gertler. "EVeryone was there," wrote Carrington, "the halt, the sick and the lame."[37] Even an ailing Lytton came up from Sussex to join in the merriment. The flat was filled with a constantly changing company—Clive Bell, Diaghilev, Massine, Augustus John, Roger Fry, Duncan Grant, Keynes, the Sitwells, David Garnett, and a host of others. Even Lawrence and Frieda had turned up earlier in the day. It was a strange, almost ritual occasion. While outside in the Strand people danced on the tops of automobiles and kissed in doorways, inside Sherman's flat England's intellectual elite celebrated in its own way. Lytton, looking like "a benevolent but irritable pelican," jigged about.[38] Ottoline chatted with Massine while Garnett and Bunny Carrington pranced around amid the jostling guests. Russell stayed out in the streets picking his way through the mass of people, observing their behaviour, as he had done the day war was declared four years earlier. He noted that they had learned nothing from the period of horror except to snatch at pleasure more recklessly than before; he could find nothing in common between his happiness and the crowd's, and he felt even more alone than in August, 1914.

Chapter 16

Part i
1918–1921

APART from a few postcripts, Ottoline's memoirs come to an end with 1918. She tended after this date to think of herself as a woman with a past. Partly she was right: after 1918 there are no great love affairs and few scintillating friendships. Yet the postwar period—the last twenty years of her life—was by no means dull, and it is a pity she did not take her memoirs any further. What we are left with are scraps, jigsaw pieces extracted from her correspondence, plus a rising tide of memoirs and reminiscences by other people. And these sources do not always give a very full (or very fair) picture of her later life.

When the war ended Ottoline was forty-five: no longer young. Indeed, she often seemed older than she really was. Her contemporaries—those who had shared her great days at Bedford Square—were drifting away and her postwar friendships were to be less passionate and intense; also, the element of sex had largely gone out of her life. But Bertie was just the opposite: he seemed to be getting younger and more frisky with each passing year. The loneliness he had felt on Armistice night had been partly a feeling of alienation from the common people and partly the lack of a satisfactory love life. On November 20 he pleaded to be allowed to come to Garsington; it was, he said, " a cry of distress & an appeal for help."[1] He was still seeing Colette—he had a duty towards her—but if Ottoline would let him come he would put himself in her hands. But that November Ottoline wasn't feeling gregarious and the prospect of having Bertie's long face at Garsington did not attract her. Sadly he told her that her shrinking away from intimacy would cause him to retire into his shell. "But I am ready to come out at any time," he assured her.[2]

The end of the war had left many people feeling let down. It seemed that everyone expected the prewar world to open up again, as if August, 1914, had been put into cold storage and could be taken out and warmed up now the nightmare was over; but the world went on from 1918, not 1914. What the twenties would bring no one really knew and Ottoline echoed Bertie's hope: "What is wanted is to carry over into the new time something of the gaiety and civilised outlook and general expansive love that was growing when the war came."[3] For her part she did her best to carry on and at Christmas, 1918, she organised a big house-party at Garsington, inviting Bishop Gore, Asquith, Violet, Gertler, Clive Bell, Aldous, and a number of others. But it wasn't as gay even as 1916, much less 1915. "What an appalling tale of disasters you had at Christmas," wrote Bertie early in January.[4] These disasters, according to Ottoline's letter of January 7, included: Cook ill, Julian and Ottoline colds, Millie flu, Philip toothache, and various other retainers ill. Another shadow over the festivities was the recent "coupon" election which had reduced Asquith's supporters in the House of Commons to a handful and cost him his own seat. Though Philip wasn't standing he shared the general gloom; not only did the election mark the end of his own political career but also the collapse of the cause into which he and Ottoline had put so much over the past ten years or more.

Lytton had not been among the guests at Garsington at Christmas; instead Ottoline sent him a volume of Cowper's poems and he in turn described his own quiet Christmas at Tidmarsh: "We eat large chickens which pretend to be turkeys, not very effectively."[5] For the past year he had been dabbling in Queen Victoria's correspondence and had now decided to follow up *Eminent Victorians* with "the Life of Her Late Majesty."[6] Whether this new project was the subject of the gossip at Garsington that Christmas, or whether the much more exciting news about the latest turn of events in the Lytton household had worked its way through via Gertler or Clive Bell, we do not know; certainly within a short time it became common knowledge that the menage at Tidmarsh had become a triangle—and an odd one at that. In August, 1918, Ralph Partridge, a handsome young infantry officer, arrived at the Mill House and within a few months had become established there. Carrington was mildly attracted —but Lytton was swept off his feet. For his part Partridge was not sexually attracted by Lytton: he had fallen in love with Carrington, whose interest in him was directly proportional to her fear that unless she encouraged him he would leave, thus weakening her own position in Lytton's life. This convoluted reasoning washed over Lytton: his mind was on other things. "Why am I not a rowing blue, with eyes to match, and 24? It's really dreadful not to be," he mused.[7]

In January Russell, who also hadn't been at Garsington that Christmas, went off for a holiday in the country with his friend Clifford Allen. Ottoline suspected he was hiding something and put the question to him directly, complaining also about the scrappy notes he had been sending. "I am very sorry my letters have been short," he replied. "A holiday existence leaves one so little to tell: walks, meals, sleep and a blessed cessation of the grinding wheels of one's mind. Yes, C. M. is here."[8] On January 14 he did come to Garsington and spent several days discussing with Ottoline his future plans. What he needed, they both agreed, was a wife (or rather a new wife, as officially he was still married to Alys). However for this role Colette was not a candidate. For one thing she was married to someone else, for another she had specifically ruled out the idea of having children, and Russell was becoming almost obsessed with the thought that he should start a family before it was too late. Neither Alys nor Ottoline had been able to fulfil this need and he now believed that this had been the main reason why his relationships with them had failed. A few years earlier, he had met someone else who had a different outlook. Her name was Dora Black, a young university student who surprised Russell by showing a preference not for academic pursuits but for family life. They didn't meet again until the summer of 1919 when Russell, after an argument with Colette, asked Dora to replace her as his holiday companion at a resort in Dorset. Later Colette, regretting the tiff, also turned up, placing Russell in a similar position to that of Ottoline back in 1911 at Studland, juggling two lovers and trying to keep them from meeting each other. Gradually, however, Dora, due to her willingness "not to take precautions," gained the ascendancy, and Colette gave up the field to her rival. Bertie did not break the news of his newest adventure to Ottoline until September 4 when he mentioned in passing that he had been staying in Dorset "with a Miss Black."[9]

At the beginning of 1919 Ottoline was just as unsure of the future as Bertie. The end of the war and Philip's exit from politics had robbed her of the main causes in her life. Russell was occupied elsewhere and Siegfried was not proving much of a replacement. This left her with the role of salonnière. Yet how could she hope to match the success of Bedford Square and the early days of Garsington? Now it was the platinum-plated London salons of Lady Cunard and Lady Colefax to which people like Lytton were drawn. ("Lady Cunard is rather a sport, with her frankly lower-class bounce,'' Lytton wrote in May, "she makes the rest of 'em look like the withered leaves of Autumn, poor things.''[10])

Also, now that Garsington's unique wartime function as a refuge was ended, she would have to compete with the other country establishments, like those presided over by Virginia at Rodmell and Vanessa at Charleston. For the time being however she didn't have a great deal of trouble keeping her guest rooms well stocked. Even Lytton found time to fit her in between sorties up to the glitter of London, although, like Lawrence, he found Garsington "exhaustive," as he told Virginia:

> I was often on the point of screaming from sheer despair, and the beauty of the surroundings only intensified the agony. Ott I really think is in the last stages—infinitely antique, racked in every joint, hobbling through the buttercups in cheap shoes. . . . She is rongée, too, by malevolence; every tea party in London to which she hasn't been invited is wormwood, wormwood.[11]

As usual, Lytton was exaggerating. Ottoline was far from antique, and she never much enjoyed tea parties in London. Yet no doubt there was a scintilla of truth in his observations: Ottoline's appearance around this time did cause some comment. Ever since Bertie had made that terrible remark in 1917 about her hair turning grey she had been making determined efforts to improve her looks, experimenting with brighter makeup, reddening her lips, encircling her eyes with dark shadows and employing ash-white powder. In 1919 she bobbed her hair; she refused, however, to go flapper and clung steadfastly to styles reminiscent of Beardsley that for many years had been her trademark. And though she never could have competed with the bounce of Lady Cunard, there were in 1919 extenuating circumstances for her hobbling through the buttercups, the principal of these being her almost habitual ill-health. One evening at the opera she nearly fainted; later, tonsilitis was diagnosed and in June she went into a nursing home for an operation. There she was visited by Augustine Birrell and they discussed her forthcoming trip to Ireland. After the war the cause of Irish nationalism was almost the only political activity which Ottoline supported and she looked on her holiday as something of a pilgrimage; also she was hoping to meet some of the people she had worked with on Casement's behalf. Birrell, who had resigned as Irish Secretary after the 1916 Uprising, was concerned for Ottoline's safety and warned her that parts of the countryside were dangerous even for the native Irish to travel in. This didn't deter Ottoline: It gave added spice to the trip. In Ireland she and her maid travelled around Galway and Donegal—strongholds of the Irish nationalists—in a pony trap, and far from avoiding contact with Republicans, Ottoline made efforts to seek them out, attending their meetings and dressing up in Sinn Fein colours and singing IRA songs. Though the holiday restored to her life some of the colour and romance that had been recently lacking, it had a painful and premature end. During one excursion Ottoline fell, hurting her leg, and despite the ministrations of a charming Irish doctor-poet named Oliver St. John Gogarty, complications set in. To add worry to injury Brett wrote from Garsington telling her Julian was unhappy at school and recounting excursions she had organised to London with the aim of making Julian happier. As Ottoline read about Brett's mothering activities she grew increasingly annoyed, finally despatching a stiff letter of reprimand that so shook Brett she replied by telegram: SO VERY SORRY HAVING HURT YOU. QUITE A MISTAKE. MUCH LOVE. PLEASE DON'T BE UNHAPPY. BRETTIE.[12]

Another point of friction between the two women was a consumptive part-Sioux Canadian poet named Frank Prewitt whom Siegfried Sassoon had befriended and brought back to Garsington with him. Ottoline took quite a fancy to Prewitt (whom everybody called "Toronto") and invited him to stay at Garsington while he waited to be repatriated to Canada. During Ottoline's absence in Ireland Brett had been clucking over him and trying to matchmake, to Ottoline's further chagrin, and she wrote another letter to Brett saying: "Amused at the way you have annexed Toronto & intend to organise him."[13] Toronto remained at Garsington much of 1919, revelling in the illustrious company that came and went with each passing weekend.

Later that summer the Russian Ballet returned to London and when Ottoline got back she invited its reigning stars, Picasso and Massine, to Garsington. She also made regular visits to London to see the new ballets and Picasso's sets. On one occasion she was unable to find a seat, and an usher was just about to move her on when Diaghilev spotted her. Grandly he strode up and instructed the usher: "This lady may sit wherever she wishes," and conducted Ottoline to a special seat in the front row.

When Siegfried was discharged from the army in early 1919 he hastened down to Garsington. Later he decided that he would like to take up residence somewhere near Ottoline, so she got him some rooms in Oxford which she decorated herself with multicoloured curtains. The two of them spent a lot of time in each other's company that summer, often going off to point-to-point races and other sporting events where Ottoline's presence earned for Siegfried the title "The Dowagers' Delight." Any hopes, however, Ottoline may have entertained that the end of the war would change Siegfried's apparent uninterest in her were soon dashed. She told Lytton: "I evidently do not magnetise him."[14] The reason why Ottoline went to so much trouble to seek out people like Sassoon and Toronto was her abiding love of poetry. Throughout the twenties and thirties any promising poet, old or young, homegrown or foreign, was always assured of a warm welcome at Ottoline's gatherings. And though Ottoline's taste in poetry was broad it could also be discriminating, and the two figures who dominated her postwar salons were W. B. Yeats and T. S. Eliot. That Yeats should have swung into her orbit is not surprising: He was Irish, romantic, and plainly a major figure in contemporary literature; besides, he had been a frequent guest at Bedford Square before the war and felt quite at home in Ottoline's drawing room. Their friendship however had an unfortunate beginning and an even more unfortunate ending. The former can be described here. When they first met Ottoline remarked to him: "It's wonderful how the Irish have got so much more sensible now—none of that Celtic Twilight stuff any more."[15] Yeats had to confess that he wrote *The Celtic Twilight*. After this initial setback their relationship blossomed and Yeats was to become, especially in the thirties, the leading VIP (Very Important Poet) at Ottoline's gatherings.

That Eliot and Ottoline should have got on well together is more surprising. His poetry was very complex—and not the sort of romantic verse Ottoline usually liked. Also, Eliot himself was a pretty dry stick. Yet of all Ottoline's postwar friendships the one with Eliot was probably the closest and most genuine. Between 1919 and her death in 1938 he wrote over a hundred letters to her, all of them couched in affectionate and grateful terms. And she helped him in both his career and his personal life. Once he said she was one of the few friends he had in England, and after *The Wasteland* was published he told her she had been the only person to write to him praising it. But Ottoline and Eliot did have one thing in common: religion. Despite Ottoline's partial conversion to scepticism under Russell's influence she remained devoutly spiritual, and in 1919, free now from Russell, she converted herself back to religion, though still avoiding established orthodoxy. Her reconversion did not however create much of a stir amongst her friends: they had tended to take her brand of mystical romanticism for religion anyway. When informed by Ottoline of her new frame of mind, Desmond MacCarthy told her: "I think it will suit you."[16]

Concurrent with this was Ottoline's decision to take up her memoirs again. Several times in the past she had begun to translate her daily diary into a more formal account of her life; now she began to think seriously of preparing a text for eventual publication. When Virginia heard of the project she said: "Please do it, I think it is one of the things you owe the world. Pick us all to pieces. Throw us to the dogs. It is high time you came off your heights & did a little dusting in a highminded manner."[17] Though Ottoline didn't really follow Virginia's advice about throwing people to the dogs, she did permit herself a little dusting. In writing these memoirs she consulted not only her voluminous diaries but her growing collection of letters (which she had so carefully preserved and which her maid Millie tended in their neat piles tied with pink ribbon). And though it was some time before Ottoline had any MS to show anyone, she was rather proud of the fact that she had taken up writing again; it had always been a deep regret of hers that she could not be a writer or a poet.

In the autumn of 1919 Bertie returned to London from Dorset and despite his discovery of Miss Black he was feeling rather sour. He told Ottoline that Wittgenstein had written to him from Vienna saying the city was starving and that he himself was taking up schoolteaching. Russell added: "Einstein, a German Jew, has invented a new theory of gravitation [but] our object [is] to cause these people to die of hunger, because we are afraid they will compete with our trade. It is glorious to be an Englishman, isn't it?"[18] In December Bertie went off for a reunion with Wittgenstein in Holland, where, he reported to Ottoline, he was astonished to find that his former pupil had also turned to religion. While in Holland Bertie decided to make a clean breast about the recent changes in his personal life:

Now I come to my own affairs, which I wanted to speak of sooner but on the whole decided not to. I made friends last summer with a Miss Black (I regret to say her Christian name is Dora) whom I had known for years . . . she was at Lulworth during a great part of the summer and was the cause of my being so exceedingly happy there.

He added that the present intention was to begin a common life, with the hope of children. "I believe (tho' it is rash to prophesy) that you would like her very much."[19] Ottoline replied in favourable terms, for which Bertie was almost pathetically grateful. "Thank you, thank you my dearest O."[20] A few days later he had an afterthought: "My dearest O—I forgot to say in so many words that *of course* anything that happens with regard to Dora Black will not interfere with our friendship in any way whatsoever."[21] He was planning to get a divorce from Alys—but not necessarily to marry Dora, who didn't think much of matrimony. He told Ottoline that his relations with Colette could continue, "tho' in the nature of things they will grow less intimate with time."[22] And while Ottoline made plans to go up to London for a few weeks, Russell and Dora went off to Spain together.

In London Ottoline stayed with Ethel Sands in the Vale, Chelsea, where she staged a busy series of parties and receptions. A long line of guests came—including Ezra Pound, Edith Sitwell, Murry, Keynes, Clive Bell, Vanessa, Duncan, Aldous, and Augustus John. John was about to put on a major exhibition in London which was to prove controversial, mainly because of a portrait of Ottoline. When the press saw the picture they took it to be a cruel attack on her. The *Daily News* said on March 2, 1920: "The portrait of Lady Ottoline Morrell is an unmistakable presentment, but she is not flattered."[23] *Truth* said he had made her look "rather witchlike."[24] *The Tatler* on March 10 said of it: "Not a very kind picture—in fact he's been rather hard on all women. It was Lady Ottoline's house in Bedford Square, you know, that the Asquiths took not long ago."[25] *Everyman* said: "That curiously Elizabethan Lady Ottoline Morrell is even more unpleasantly snake-like and snarling. It may puzzle one to imagine why society women should like to see themselves painted like this, even by Mr. John."[26] The *Weekly Dispatch* sent a reporter to see Ottoline and ask her what she thought. "I regret to say I have not yet seen the portrait," she replied coldly.[27] They then interviewed John, who told them he had not been intentionally cruel, but it was "the aspect he had been unfortunate enough to get." The picture dated from well before the war. When Philip went to see it at the Alpine Club Gallery he decided to write John to tell him what he thought:

> I feel I must write and tell you how greatly moved I was by that wonderful show of yours which I saw for the first time the other day—and not the least by Ottoline's portrait, which seemed to me one of the finest things there. I see that the journalists are very anxious to assure us that it is a "cruel" presentment of her, that she looks like a witch, and a snake, and an insolent aristocrat and I don't know what else besides; but whether kind or cruel it is a wonderful piece of work, and I think Ottoline (who by the way has not yet seen it) ought to feel proud to be the subject of it. She says she rather dreads going to see it, but I tell her to cheer up and not be frightened, for after all it is better any day to look wicked than feeble or commonplace.[28]

Ottoline did eventually see the picture and, though she may not have thought it flattering, she did think enough of it to eventually acquire it from John.

In May, 1920, Russell went off to Russia, there to acquire an instant dislike of Communism and all its works. He went with a group of socialists bent on seeing the good things the Russian revolutionaries had achieved, but despite his efforts to summon up all he knew about the knoutings and pogroms of the old regime, so as to have a favourable view of the new, it was no use. This almost caused a rift with Dora Black. She had followed him to Russia and, said Russell, came back "loving the Bolshies." However, this difference of opinion was patched up and Russell and Dora began preparing to go to China where Russell had been given a job lecturing. He sent £10 to Ottoline and asked her to choose some books on China he could take with him. "You are so very good at choosing," he said.[29] Ottoline consulted all her friends, including Lytton, and eventually compiled an interesting selection. Russell was now planning to marry Dora as soon as his divorce from Alys came through, and he took his wife-to-be up to Garsington to be inspected by Ottoline. It seems she approved, though later on she came to refer to the second Mrs. Russell as "that Dora." Before Russell set sail for the Orient he wrote Ottoline a farewell note: "What you and I have in common is indestructible, and what you did for me in bringing it out was a very great thing. Goodbye my Dearest O. Your B.''[30] In her next letter to Lytton thanking him for suggesting some books on China, Ottoline said: "Bertie went off in fine feather. He is accompanied by a lady sect.! He is an old rep!''[31]

In October, 1920, there reached Garsington the first trickle of what was to become, over the next few years, a stream of undergraduates from Oxford. Ottoline's nephew, Morven Bentinck (Portland's younger son), had gone up from Eton to Oxford and it was initially his friends who accompanied him to afternoon tea with his eccentric aunt and her famous guests ("Lady Vaseline Mulberry" was what one of Morven's friends called Ottoline). It soon spread round the university that any young man with a taste for literature would be welcome at Garsington, and from 1921 onwards the change in character of the gatherings in the red room and under the ilex tree was due to the presence of these groups of pink-cheeked wide-eyed young men. But in 1919 youth had two meanings: there were the new products of the schools—the real postwar generation—and there were also the young men who had left school before the war and gone straight into the army—men of Sassoon's and Toronto's generation. These were in a curious position, neither old nor young. They formed a separate strand at Garsington, making the Oxford boys seem younger and the Bloomsbury generation older. One of these "old" young men was Edmund Blunden, a poet who had been in the trenches and had come to Ottoline's attention as a promising talent. Several times in 1920 he was at Garsington and Ottoline tried to get him some work on Middleton Murry's magazine, *The Athenaeum.* She lent him books and kept up a flattering correspondence, encouraging him to bring his poems to show her. Rather embarrassed, he replied he would bring "some juvenilia."[32] Another two of this generation who turned up at Garsington after the war were Ottoline's prewar friends, Gilbert and Stanley Spencer. Both had been reluctant recruits to the armed forces, Gilbert going to Egypt and Stanley ("I could go as a brave little bugle boy," he had told Ottoline in 1914) ending up as a war artist in Greece.[33] Later Gilbert became a particularly close friend of Ottoline and Philip's, coming to work on the farm in the mid-1920's. Meanwhile, Stanley kept Ottoline informed about his projects for painting suburban ceilings with his strange visions of Biblical scenes set in his native village of Cookham. "I have just finished another biggish picture of the disciples deserting Christ among Cookham buildings and Priests falling backwards into stinging nettles," he told her.[34] In another letter he described a visit to the Tate Gallery where they had hung one of his war pictures. "They put a little gold tablet on the bottom of the frame with my name & everything *just the same* as they put on the masterpieces in the National Gall."[35]

Ottoline's most loyal correspondent in 1920 was Toronto, now exiled on the edge of a remote bay in Ontario. She kept him in touch with civilisation by sending him copies of the London newspapers and *The Times Literary Supplement*. He told her he was afraid of becoming a "veneered barbarian" in a land where "everyone becomes married and a bank clerk with slicked hair."[36] Canada, he told her, was an intellectual Siberia: "Man cannot live by bread alone, and Canada offers only the bread."[37] He couldn't return to England until he had attained a chest expansion of four inches, and he was working hard on this.

In November, 1920, Ottoline travelled across to the Continent and probably spent Christmas there. In December she got a letter from Russell describing how he and Dora were settling down to Oriental domesticity in Peking. In January Ottoline was in Italy where she had an audience with the Pope. Of this meeting Philip wrote his mother: "Ottoline is nothing if not courageous. She asked his Holiness in her best Italian for a special blessing for 'Poor Ireland!' "[38]

Early in 1921 Ottoline was horrified to read in the newspapers that Russell had died in China. Her distress at this report can be imagined. Even though they had had times of trouble and disagreement, Bertie to her was still one of the greatest and most sympathetic minds she had ever come in contact with; she had almost left Philip and gone off to live with him. For weeks she read obituaries in the papers enumerating Russell's qualities and achievements. Then it was announced that the whole thing had been a mistake: Russell had indeed been critically ill but was recovering. The mistake had occurred when Dora, exasperated with journalists asking about his condition, told them he was dead—and it was this report that had reached England. Eventually Russell was able to write to say he had recovered and that Dora was pregnant and they planned to return to England as soon as possible. Dora, who was still not married to Russell because his divorce from Alys had not yet become absolute, was very worried lest none of Bertie's friends would like her. But Ottoline wrote and reassured her, for which Russell was very grateful. On September 27 Russell and Dora arrived and on November 16 Russell's son, John Conrad, was born. In his autobiography Russell says: ". . . and from that moment my children were for many years my main interest in life."[39] For the next several years Bertie drifted out of Ottoline's life and they corresponded only irregularly. However, Ottoline still continued to receive some of the backwash of his life, and in late November, 1921, Colette wrote asking if she could come to visit Garsington. Ottoline commented: "I'll be comforting another of Bertie's cast-offs."[40]

Part ii
1921

In November, 1921, Ottoline received from Aldous Huxley an advance copy of his first novel, *Crome Yellow*. She was looking forward to reading it, for in her estimate Aldous was the cleverest of the young writers who had been at Garsington during the war, and though she had seen him only infrequently since he went off to teach at Eton in 1917, she retained a warm regard for him. As she opened the book she saw that he had written an inscription to her: "Ottoline Morrell with apologies for having borrowed some of her architecture and trees."[41] Ottoline's instincts were alerted. Surely—no, he wouldn't . . . after all, he had been just as horrified as she had been at what Lawrence did to her in *Women in Love*. But as she read, the old hurts from 1917 came flooding back. For page after page her family, her guests, everything that she held precious were portrayed. In many ways it was worse than Lawrence; the whole novel was devoted to it, not merely a few chapters. There were scenes on the lawn with guests in deck chairs under an ilex tree; people dancing to ragtime pumped out on a pianola; an almost libellous portrait of Asquith "with a face like a Roman bust" chasing young girls across the lawn.[42] There was an artist who was deaf and enigmatic—obviously Brett. There was a resident painter—Gertler. A girl whose hair hung "in a bell of elastic gold about her cheeks"—Carrington.[43] And there was Priscilla Wimbush's pianola-playing husband Henry, whose face resembled "a grey bowler hat"—a maliciously unflattering portrait of Philip.[44] There was even an incident where two of the characters slept out on the roof, to be wakened in the morning by a peacock, just as Aldous and Carrington were in 1916.

Stunned, Ottoline sent off an angry letter to Aldous. He wrote back:

DEAREST OTTOLINE,

Your letter bewildered me. I cannot understand how anyone could suppose that this little marionette performance of mine was the picture of a real *milieu*—it so obviously isn't. You might as justifiably accuse Shaw of turning Garsington into Heartbreak House or Peacock of prophesying it in Nightmare Abbey and Gryll Grange. I have made use of the country house convention because it provides a simple device for getting together a fantastic symposium.

He admitted he had erred in using some of Garsington's physical details—he should have set the book in China. But, he insisted, characters are nothing more than marionettes with voices, designed to express ideas and the parody of ideas:

My mistake, I repeat, was to have borrowed the stage setting from Garsington. I am sorry—but it never for a moment occurred to me that anyone would have so little imagination—or perhaps so much [he added tactfully]—as to read into a comedy of ideas a portrait of the life of the place in which it is laid.[45]

But Aldous' explanation did little to mollify Ottoline. To her, his action was a gross betrayal: "I was filled with dismay. I felt somehow that having given Aldous opportunities of meeting these people, I was responsible for these cruel caricatures, and that not only had he behaved dishonourably but that he had involved me in his dishonour and it might be thought that I had acquiesced in his mocking." Ottoline couldn't get over the fact that Aldous could have done to her the same hurtful thing as Lawrence had: "He already knew how much I had suffered by Lawrence having written of me and Garsington in *Women in Love,* and he had seemed to share my indignation about it, but here he had done almost the same thing. And in one way it was worse, for he had lived with us so long and had become almost one of the family, and he was quite aware that both

Philip and myself were not people who were insensitive to the actions of our friends."[46]

The publication of *Crome Yellow* caused a rift between Ottoline and Huxley which lasted for several years. When they finally met again it was at a party in London and Ottoline recalls: "He sat down by me and said with eagerness, 'I hear you've been seeing the Kaiser in Holland. What was he like?' I began to tell him, but after a few sentences I heard myself saying, 'No, no Aldous, I can't tell you about him, for you would write about it.'"[47] Ottoline added, however, that later on they patched up their friendship and spent many happy days together, especially in Italy.

Why did Huxley write what he did in *Crome Yellow*? In her biography of Aldous Huxley, Sybille Bedford says that Aldous was irritated by the practice of people trying to work out who might be who in his novels. "He felt that this whole process of writing, this process of transposing life and fiction is far from wholly conscious and a good deal more obscure and complex than putting Jack Robinson or D. H. Lawrence into a book."[48] She says Aldous did not so much put real characters into his books as use aspects of them as a starting-point for his own creations. "He had a habit," says Sybille Bedford, "of mixing up his starting points—one man's philosophy, another's sexual tastes, one trait from a member of his family, another from a character in history—and as he did not like to stop and think that any particular person might recognize fragments of himself in an otherwise outrageous context, he took little trouble to cover up his traces."[49] She explains that Huxley thought he was, if anything, complimenting his friends by putting them, or aspects of them, into his books.

The letters Huxley wrote to Ottoline after *Crome Yellow* tend to support this theory of surprised innocence. We know Ottoline was hypersensitive in such matters and it was probably unrealistic of her to expect not to be portrayed in the novels of her friends. On the other hand, she did have a point. Huxley need not have been as cruel as Ottoline thought him to be in portraying her and her milieu in *Crome Yellow*. After all, as she rightly said, he could hardly plead ignorance in the matter of her feelings about this sort of thing.

A point that should be borne in mind, however, is that over four years had passed since Aldous had been living at Garsington as one of the family. In that time much had happened in his life. In 1919 he resigned from

Eton, started work on Middleton Murry's *Athenaeum,* and finally married Maria. In 1920 they went to live in London and, after their son Matthew was born, they came to stay at Garsington. In her memoirs Ottoline says: "I was not very well and was not able to put them all up in the house, but I found them lodgings in the village and they came to meals with us . . . but somehow it was not a great success. Maria was not happy in the lodgings; she may have resented not staying with us in the house. . . . I have a feeling they were not contented."[50] And if Ottoline says they were not contented it is likely that there were some difficulties between her and the Huxleys in 1920. In addition there was an embarrassing incident the following year in Rome. Clifford Allen mentioned in Maria's presence that Ottoline had said, "Maria was a liar and could not speak the truth."[51] The relationship between Ottoline and Maria had always been extremely close. On the other hand Ottoline did not approve of the marriage between Maria and Aldous. Although we cannot be sure, it is not inconceivable that a certain coolness developed between Ottoline and the Huxleys after 1919 and before the publication of *Crome Yellow* in late 1921. This may have blunted Aldous' sensitivity to Ottoline's feelings. There is also another possibility. It may well be that Aldous felt he had to break the spell that Ottoline had cast on him when he was young. Lytton had done something similar by indulging in catty letters about her, Lamb quarrelled violently with her, and Russell deliberately hurt her so as to escape her thrall. Lawrence, too, may have cut himself loose from Ottoline and his debt to her by "writing her out of his system" in *Women in Love.*

If this is true, then by writing *Crome Yellow* Aldous did not free himself completely from Ottoline's apron strings, for, several years later, he wrote another novel, *Those Barren Leaves,* in which he did it again! In this novel he invented an Ottoline-like character in the glittering Mrs. Lilian Aldwinkle, mistress of an Italian palace in which there is a congregation of writers, poets, and hangers-on. Ottoline's reaction to this novel is not recorded, but if she recognised some aspects of herself in *Crome Yellow* there is little question she would have seen more of herself in the character of Mrs. Aldwinkle. She has sagging cheeks and a prominent chin; her lips are of a rather vague contour whose indefiniteness is enhanced by her carelessness in reddening them; her clothes are sometimes dirty; she believes in passion, passionately; she has lots of doctors and illnesses; and she has a weakness for great men. It is her greatest regret that she herself has no aptitude for any of the arts.

> Nature had endowed her with no power of self-expression; even in ordinary conversation she found it difficult to give utterance to what she wanted to say. Her letters were made up of the fragments of sentences: it was as though her thoughts had been blown to ungrammatical pieces by a bomb and scattered themselves on the page.[52]

Again there are scenes Ottoline could not but trace back to those evenings at Garsington when Aldous would put on a friendly face while absorbing detail for future use:

> For on the threshold of her bed-chamber she would halt, desperately renewing the conversation with whichever of her guests had happened to light her upstairs. Who knew? Perhaps in these last five minutes, in the intimacy, in the nocturnal silence, the important thing would really be said.[53]

Mrs. Aldwinkle also has a peculiar genius for breaking with her friends and lovers and an almost indecent interest in other people's love lives. "She liked to bring people together, to foster tender feelings, to watch the development of passion."[54]

Mrs. Aldwinkle was certainly a crueller caricature than Priscilla Wimbush. But then Ottoline never admitted she was Priscilla Wimbush. The thing that she objected to most in *Crome Yellow* was the caricature it contained of the way of life at Garsington, and, more particularly, Huxley's mockery of Philip as Henry Wimbush and Asquith as Mr. Calamy. But the fact that she did not avoid all contact with Aldous after *Those Barren Leaves* was published suggests that Ottoline may have become more reconciled to such portrayals—at least by people as talented as Aldous.

Chapter 17

Part i
1921–1927

In Oxford in the early 1920's a not infrequent sight, arousing a good deal of comment, was a well-turned-out phaeton drawn by two horses trotting splendidly up the High Street. At the reins was a tall, impressive, large-featured man and next to him an equally tall, impressive, and large-featured woman: Philip and Ottoline out shopping. Often Ottoline would drive in alone, or perhaps with Julian. She was an excellent "whip"—a legacy of her Rotten Row and Sherwood Forest days—and was one of the few people who dared take the narrow turning through the gates of Garsington at speed. Sometimes she left the phaeton behind and rode into Oxford on her bicycle, forming a little crocodile procession with Brett and Gertler and whoever else wanted to go. Her distinctive figure, sailing along the pavement, shrouded in billowing shawls and flowing dresses, darting into Hall's to buy a silk scarf or into Blackwell's to buy a book, is still remembered by some of the young men who were at Oxford during those years. Some regarded her as a comic figure, but in a handful the sight of Ottoline aroused very different emotions; to them she represented one of the most desirable of all undergraduate goals: an entree into the magic world of Garsington. One of those who watched enviously her progress up the High Street was Robert Gathorne-Hardy, then a second-year student reading English literature and to become one of Ottoline's closest friends and later editor of her memoirs. For months he tried to organise an introduction, but was far too shy. One day he was browsing in Blackwell's when Ottoline appeared beside him; phrases of introduction formed in his mind, but he didn't dare utter them. Finally another friend got permission to bring him along to one of Ottoline's Sunday afternoon teas. Millie, who took it upon herself to vet prospective guests, met them at the door. Once inside there was a blur of impressions—the cluster of pugs and pekes, the panelling, the startling colours, the paintings, and, permeating everything, the heavy sweet smell of potpourri. Then Ottoline herself: long skirts, many pearls, short auburn hair and a friendly smile on the already-known large-featured face. After that, for the first time, her unique voice. "An unkind and witty acquaintance," related Gathorne-Hardy, "once said that a cow mooing was rather like Ottoline saying 'Derain'. 'De-e-e-er-ai-ai-ain,'—a not altogether deceptive verbal caricature."[1]

Another undergraduate, L. A. G. Strong, remembered what it was like to go to Garsington in winter:

> First of all . . . one would go into the drawing room. The guest of honour would be still upstairs. There would be one or two people in the drawing room, Julian, the daughter of the house, rousing herself from a book, or Philip rising hospitably from a chair beside the fire. I remember winter afternoons, when, just in time for tea, Yeats would descend, flushed and ruffled like an eagle that had been to sleep and omitted to preen its feathers. Tea soon woke him up and set him talking. One week-end he and Bertrand Russell were there together. Doubt had been expressed beforehand as to how the two would get on, but each treated the other with the utmost respect and courtesy, the eagle speaking for a while, and then inclining his head in polite silence while the secretary-bird took up the tale.[2]

In such company many of Ottoline's young guests felt reticent, but she did her best to bring them out. Gathorne-Hardy said she orchestrated the conversation, drawing out the principal guest—whether it was Yeats, Strachey, Birrell, Asquith, or Virginia Woolf. "But," he added, "there was no question of a monologue, and no breaking-up of the talk as at a formal dinner party."[3] She would induce a shy undergraduate to say something, then cunningly lead him on with questions and comments, finally linking the boy's remarks into the general conversation. Such talk was, to the initial shock of many undergraduates, allowed to drift to topics not normally broached in polite company. "It ranged far and wide," recalled Gathorne-Hardy. But if it ranged too far, Ottoline was there to smooth over any awkward moments that resulted. Gathorne-Hardy told how once he annoyed Lytton Strachey with a priggish remark:

> A friend of mine was travelling with a character alleged to be not very reputable in his behaviour. I said that I thought this was degrading—a silly word to use. "I don't see why," piped Strachey sharply; "all I've heard about him is that he has a penchant for —"; it was a penchant that a great many people would have thought very shocking indeed.

"Not for people like you and me, Lytton," intervened Ottoline. "Not for older people like us. But for a much younger, unformed person, perhaps. . . ." And the meal became easy again.[4]

Occasionally Ottoline's efforts to bring people into the conversation were accompanied by an element of teasing. One Sunday the Asquiths turned up unexpectedly to tea. "The Asquiths! How *inconsiderate* of them!" said Ottoline.[5] There was a quick reshuffling of places at the tea table and L. A. G. Strong was placed next to Asquith's daughter Elizabeth. After the Asquiths left Ottoline turned to Strong and asked: "Does she attract you *physically*, Strong?"

The ritual of the invitation to a chat in Ottoline's private sitting room, where guests would be quizzed about their personal and literary progress, was sometimes a bit of an ordeal. Peter Quennell recalled one such interview: "*M-m-m*—Are you writing much poetry nowadays? *M-m-m-m* —Do you often fall in love?"[6] At times the undergraduates would not know how seriously to take Ottoline's questioning. C. M. Bowra recalls her saying to Anthony Powell: "Mr. Powell, do you prefer spring or autumn?" He thought for a moment and then replied that he preferred autumn, to which she commented: "At my age you'll prefer spring."[7] Invitations to Garsington were highly prized—and the degree of familiarity that did away with the need for one even more so. Yet Ottoline bestowed such treasures with a carelessness that was sometimes disconcerting. Peter Quennell remembered the first time he went. After finally managing to get invited he was in a line of young men whom Ottoline was saying good-bye to at the door. To the person in front of him she extended a cordial invitation to return, "Come back next week, *do*. . . ."; to Quennell she said a brief "Good-bye"; then to the people behind she resumed her invitations, "Come again. . . ."[8] Any slight was imaginary or unintended and Quennell returned to Garsington many times. Gathorne-Hardy described another occasion when Ottoline visited his rooms in Oxford and found a relation of his there. She couldn't stay, she said, but only came to issue an invitation to come to Garsington on such-and-such a day. "Perhaps," she droned benevolently at the relation, "you would care to come too. . . ." The young man looked up at the apparition, his mouth opening and shutting uselessly. Ottoline smiled sweetly, "Well don't trouble if you can't manage it."[9]

If Ottoline really took to someone, he—or occasionally she—was privileged with a personal brand of intimacy quite different from her public manner. Gathorne-Hardy was one of these fortunates, and he would often accompany Ottoline to Charlie Chaplin films, art galleries, and concerts. Another was A. L. Rowse. He was taken to dinner at Garsington by David Cecil, another of Ottoline's favourites, and evidently made something of a hit with his hostess. Later he was invited out alone to lunch and she took him to meet Siegfried Sassoon, who was one of his heroes. But Rowse later looked back on those visits with a tinge of regret and remembered having made a bit of a fool of himself one day by pacing up and down the yew hedge walks haranguing Desmond MacCarthy on the Marxist approach to history.

If the opportunities Garsington offered a young man of literary ambition were rich, they could also be daunting. L. A. G. Strong recalled going there in spring and wandering around the garden with Yeats and sitting by the pond with E. M. Forster. (That may have been the visit on which Forster left his vest behind and had to write, at his mother's insistence, to get it back.) On another day Strong joined the party under the ilex tree. A few people played tennis while the rest talked. Ottoline led him out to join Eliot and the Woolfs. "A rarefied silence resulted," Strong recalled, "and after five minutes Eliot excused himself. Leonard Woolf presently made a polite remark about the peacocks: Virginia gave her gentle, tortured smile. I was relieved when the party reshaped itself."[10] Except when she was incapacitated by her migraines Ottoline was a scrupulously conscientious hostess. But such was the volume of the comings and going that slights and omissions inevitably occurred. Once, when Virginia Woolf was staying at Garsington, Gathorne-Hardy, who was particularly anxious to meet her, found himself left out of the group she was in and he wandered about the house looking forlorn. Next day, after Virginia had left, he got an urgent invitation from Ottoline to come to Garsington and she showed evident anguish that he had been neglected; from that day forward she placed him next to Virginia whenever possible.

Not all the young men who went to Garsington were homosexuals, but quite a number were. It might seem poor taste to remark on this, nevertheless it is an undeniable fact of Ottoline's life in the 1920's—and one that reflects a good deal of credit on her. To their delight, these young men discovered that Ottoline not only had no objection to what most of society regarded as their perversion but that she actually entered into spirited discussions about their love lives—or, more usually, their lack of love life. She was, it must be admitted, not unlettered in such matters: she was after all an old friend of Lytton's. And, as with Lytton, she at first made efforts to bring them around to more conventional ways. One of her favourite postwar doctors was a German physician-cum-psychoanalyst named Dr. Marten, who claimed he could be of some help to these young men, and Ottoline took several parties across to Freiburg, where the doctor had a clinic, to see what could be done. The answer was virtually nothing and if there were any conversions they were of brief duration.

Lytton was rather caustic about these expeditions and when he met Marten at Garsington in 1923 he was unimpressed. "Psychoanalysis is a ludicrous fraud," he told Carrington, "the Sackville-West youth was there [at Freiburg] to be cured of homosexuality. After 4 months and an expenditure of £200, he found he could just bear the thought of going to bed with a woman."[11] At Garsington Lytton observed several undergraduates who had been through the Marten treatment wandering around the lawn looking haggard. After a while Ottoline gave up these well-meaning efforts and resumed her more natural role of den mother, discussing love affairs, suggesting liaisons, and generally being of what assistance she could. There are even hints that she may have provided at Garsington a discreet rendezvous for certain of her friends. In return they kept her well informed of their goings-on, and their letters are some of the liveliest in her correspondence.

On December 29, 1924, one of her young protégés wrote to her:

Christmas was pretty depressing, but tonight there seems to be fair prospect of entertainment of a sort. Did you know that a new beauty has arisen in the midst of our small circle? He pulls down the blinds in the office scene of "Old English," and is beautiful and tiresome, about fifty-fifty; but then he's only 17. "Is there such a place as the Zoo?" is a fairly representative remark of his! Eardley is stricken unto death. Kyrle is interested, and even Bob "sees something in him." He was produced by Rawley Leigh at a bridge party, and only appears at these functions. The formula of conduct is always the same. Whoever is dummy sits on the arm of his chair and kisses him,—and if he is dummy he selects one of the three players on whose chair to sit etc., great excitement![12]

In befriending these young men and treating them in a civilised manner

Ottoline performed a very useful service. As a sister of a duke and a friend and patroness of the great, she provided them with a feeling of acceptability that otherwise they would not have had and it is no exaggeration to say she saved many of them from part of the misery they might otherwise have been condemned to. In return she reaped many rewards. Not only did such people add a lightness and brightness to her drawing room, they also attracted more established figures like E. M. Forster, Lowes-Dickinson, and Maynard Keynes. Yet this aspect of Ottoline's life should not be exaggerated: it was a minor undercurrent, invisible to all except those with specially acute vision.

In another field Ottoline did some equally sterling work, though here she achieved less success and no reward. This involved her attempts to help some of her slightly older men friends with their matrimonial difficulties. The trouble was that some of the bright young men who came to Garsington made a habit of going off and marrying the most unsuitable women, which later led to problems. The first of these marital conflicts that Ottoline got mixed up in was between the poet Edmund Blunden and his wife Mary. At Garsington one day Blunden was looking sad and preoccupied and Ottoline asked him why; he replied in effect that his wife didn't understand him and Ottoline volunteered to write to Mary. After this she did not hear from him for several months. Finally in September 1921 he wrote apologising for his silence and explaining that he had in fact written a long letter but Mary had not allowed him to send it. He added that Ottoline's earlier letter had helped reform Mary and she had dropped the pursuing, hectoring tactics which had worried him before. He apologised for having mentioned the matter to Ottoline and said that nothing now could be "sweeter and more helpful than Mary's ways to me for weeks past."[13] Alas, the effect was short-lived, and soon Blunden was miserable again. Over the next few years Ottoline continued to try to help, inviting them separately and together to Garsington, liaising between them and offering advice, but to little effect.

Just as unsuccessful were Ottoline's efforts to help T. S. Eliot. In 1922 she was one of the prime movers, with Virginia Woolf, in organising a fund to subsidise Eliot so he would not have to do boring work in a bank. She wrote to many leading literary figures canvassing donations. Some obliged; others declined. Arnold Bennett replied: "It irks me to refuse an appeal from you; but I do not think that this kind of an appeal can be logically justified. According to my gospel the first duty of a man is to earn his living; he must be an artist afterwards."[14] Eliot thought the same way and, though tempted, he finally turned down the idea of a subsidy. In addition to his financial problems, Eliot was not getting on well with his wife and though Ottoline never had a very high opinion of Vivienne she invited her to Garsington for long talks and kept up a regular correspondence with her. At first her efforts did some good and Eliot asked her to keep it up, telling her in one of his letters that Vivienne wanted to see Ottoline, of whom she had spoken "consistently with affection." Vivienne's irritability with Eliot seemed to have some connection with her health, and Ottoline recommended that Vivienne should go and see Dr. Marten. This advice was disastrous. Eliot told Ottoline that Marten, who prescribed Draconian starvation courses and injections of animal glands, had made Vivienne even worse. It was Vivienne's deteriorating mental condition that gave Eliot most concern, and for this he partly blamed Russell for having overexcited her mind with ideas and books.

Another matrimonial tangle Ottoline became involved in was between a talented young Australian poet and critic W. J. Turner and his wife Delphine. Turner was a fairly regular visitor to Garsington from about 1919 onwards, being introduced to Ottoline by Siegfried Sassoon. How highly Ottoline came to regard Turner is shown by the fact that in September, 1922, she asked Lytton, probably her most prized guest, to come and spend a weekend at Garsington to meet Turner. Lytton described the weekend to Virginia Woolf as "pretty grim" and Turner as "a very small bird-like man with a desolating accent, and a good deal to say for himself—but punctuated by strange hesitations—impediments—rather distressing; but really a nice fellow, when one has got over the way in which he says 'count.' "[15] Ottoline continued to promote Turner and helped him with his wife, who was suspicious of the time Turner spent out of her company, particularly at Garsington. Ottoline had several long talks with Delphine and once travelled up to London to meet her on Westminster Bridge for a discussion. Turner was extremely grateful for Ottoline's interest and in 1927 he wrote to her asking if he could dedicate a book to her.

Part ii
1921–1927

Ottoline received this request from Turner with mixed feelings. The last person to ask if he could do this was Lawrence, and what that had led to was still painfully fresh in her memory. She liked Turner but suspected there might be more to his request than met the eye; she had heard rumours about the book he was writing, and didn't like what she had heard. She sent a letter back to him asking for more information:

> It is very nice of you to suggest dedicating your book to me but I feel it is rather difficult to give my consent unless I see the book first or know a little what it's all about. At present you see I really know nothing, I merely heard a kind of rumour which I hope is untrue that there was a character in it that might easily be mistaken for me.[16]

Turner was persistent. For some reason he was particularly anxious to obtain Ottoline's name on the book, and he pressed her further. Far from linking her with the book's contents, he argued, it would do the opposite. Ottoline was unimpressed:

> . . . but as to that I am afraid I don't agree. On the contrary it might put the idea into people's heads. It would certainly lead people to suppose that the book was being published with my approval and consent, which of course is not true.[17]

She concluded with the hope that Turner would leave her name out of his proposed work and wait until another time to dedicate one of his books to her "if you really want to do so." Turner replied rather sadly that he greatly regretted her decision.

The book, entitled *The Aesthetes,* was published later that year.* It was dedicated not to Ottoline but "To Cynthia," and although it did not create much of a stir—only a handful of people could have read it—it is quite easy to see why Ottoline would have objected to it and why. From

---

The Aesthetes and *Those Barren Leaves* have some similarities and it seems probable that Turner took part of his inspiration from Huxley's novel.

that moment on, Turner was persona non grata. *The Aesthetes* is a dialogue carried on by a group of guests at a country house called Wrexham over a period of three days. Their conversation centres on a well-known literary hostess, Lady Virginia Caraway, who, it is said, killed the first American poet that ever came to England. "He came to me a genius, he left me a man," she writes in her little orange book in which she records her daily struggles among the arts.[18] Lady Caraway's taste in poetry is highly coloured and she likes poets of "passion." Two of the guests, one named Esmond Darthy, the other called Dytton, give long, malicious descriptions of Lady Virginia, dwelling on her "crimson-lake" hair, her strange hats and her made-up face. Dytton refers to her collected novels of Henry James, her portraits by John and Conder, and her love of needlework. There is no doubt Turner meant Lady Virginia to be taken for a cruel portrait of Ottoline.

One day Virginia Caraway comes down to lunch with her head swathed in bandages (because of her neuralgia), followed by fifteen pugs whose pantings and gurglings so annoy one guest that he exclaims: "Virginia, I shall throw all of those horrible animals out of the window if you won't have them sent away." Virginia replies: "The darlings! They're only dreaming! aren't you Necropolis?"[19] One of the little horrors spits at her. While Virginia works at her embroidery, spasms of neuralgia and exultation struggling across her face, the conversation ebbs and flows around her. Occasionally she speaks, once venturing the theory that a landscape is "a state of mind." At this an artist called Radenlac asks sarcastically whether this didn't mean just as much as saying that a soul was a state of the landscape. Virginia replies coldly: "I don't think you care much for nature, Mr. Radenlac."[20]

The Aesthetes was as harsh an attack on Ottoline as Lawrence's had been—just as vicious and, at times, just as cruelly accurate. Ottoline's only consolation would have been that while Lawrence's book was by 1927 quite widely read, Turner's had little hope of being so—until, that is, a curious event resurrected it more than ten years later. But although it was not a best seller, in one respect Turner's caricature of Ottoline is more interesting than those of Lawrence and Huxley. In *The Aesthetes* Turner made what could be the most significant point anyone made about Ottoline.

Virginia Caraway's guests are talking about art and what it is. After conjuring up his parody of Virginia, Dytton says:

> . . . if we look upon Lady Caraway merely as a freak, a psychological sport, we are being extraordinarily superficial, because those terms don't express Lady Caraway, but only a conception of Lady Caraway. In short, we have made a mere intellectual construction which we call Lady Caraway, whereas Lady Caraway is a work of art.[21]

Dytton goes on to argue that it is possible to look at the whole of Lady Caraway—and, for the sake of argument, let's replace Virginia Caraway with Ottoline Morrell—that it is possible to look at Ottoline as being a collection of impressions, memoirs, gossip—everything known about her—all combined in the one object. He employs the simile of a painting, which is not merely canvas and dried paint but a focal point of things—its reputation, people's impressions of it, how it evokes memories, and so on. Turner says that Ottoline

> . . . is not the physical construction we may shake hands with or photograph, nor the intellectual or conceptual construction Darthy may present to us as a psychological fiction, nor the intuition-image each one of us may have, nor the work of art each one of us may experience, but the indiscernible, where all these meet.[22]

Another of Turner's puppets says that Lady Caraway is like Switzerland, or the Russian Ballet, or the Tower of Pisa: "She is known only to tourists or sight-seers. They look at her and go away—and write books about her."[23]

Turner here made an important point: Ottoline is not only a person, she is in a sense a combination of everyone's image of her. Any attempt to reconstruct what Ottoline was like is not a matter of attempting to winkle out from the morass of truth, half-truth, and fiction the supposedly "real" figure: it is more a matter of trying to catch all the diverse and scattered images at one focus.

Both Virginia Woolf and Lytton Strachey observed that in Garsington Ottoline created a work of art. Neither made the next step and described Ottoline herself as a work of art. Virginia almost did: she imagined Ottoline as something rich and wonderful: "a Spanish galleon, hung with golden coins & lovely silken sails."[24] Other writers' descriptions of her—an oversized Infanta of Spain, an enormous bird, a lion-hunting hostess—are equally picturesque and just as misleading as Hermione Roddice, Priscilla Wimbush, and Lilian Aldwinkle. The description C. M. Bowra gives of the day Violet Asquith was insulted by Lytton at Garsington differs quite a lot from Ottoline's account of the same event. Which is the more correct? Probably Ottoline's—yet much of her own descriptions and reminiscences are suspect. Later, when she moved to Gower Street, the legendary side of her character grew apace. Stephen Spender sees on her walls a misty spiritualist painting by the Irish poet, AE—yet Gathorne-Hardy said Ottoline never owned such a painting; it merely fitted in with the image Spender was trying to create. Spender also describes her going out with two or three pekinese dogs tied by ribbons to a shepherdess's crook, but they were almost certainly pugs, the ribbons were leather leashes, and she never possessed a crook. How important are such errors? Spender's image is a vivid one and has come down to us today woven inextricably into the composite image of Ottoline. And, as such—as Turner implied—it is as good as any other part of the legend.

Part iii
1921–1927

The day Lytton met Turner at Garsington was in September, 1922, and it had been Lytton's first visit for almost a year, even though Ottoline had done everything she could to lure him back. In February, 1922, she had written to him: "I hear you have a beautiful motor bed (Lytton apparently was getting about in a car). I'm wondering if your Eminence could be conveyed here on the aforesaid motor bed on Sunday in time for luncheon bringing with you your Lords and Ladies in waiting."[25] But his Eminence did not turn up for seven months, and then his letter to Virginia describing the visit indicated that such calls were becoming increasingly painful. After mentioning how bored he had been with Turner, he moved on to the subject of his hostess, whom he described in the cruellest possible terms, dwelling with relish on her bodily malfunctions. On the same day, however, he wrote to Ottoline herself in a different vein:

> It was a great pleasure to see you and to have some talks—I only wish there could have been more of them. Needless to say that I enjoyed my week-end very much. It was delightful to find Philip in such good trim, and I liked making the acquaintance of Turner. I hope your health is really taking a turn for the better at last. What a disgusting arrangement one's body does become when its machinery goes out of order.[26]

Lytton's disinclination to go to Garsington also had something to do with the fact that his own ménage was demanding more and more of his attention. The previous year Carrington had married Partridge and the three of them settled down at Tidmarsh, Carrington sleeping with Partridge, and Lytton occasionally sleeping with Partridge (but not, of course, with Carrington).* Later in 1921 Carrington fell in love with Partridge's best friend, Gerald Brenan. Then, early in 1922 while holidaying on the Continent Partridge fell in love with their hostess, a passionate woman named Clare Bollard. A little later Partridge found out about Brenan and had a furious argument with Carrington, threatening to leave Tidmarsh. Throughout that summer Lytton used all his diplomatic skill to keep Carrington and Partridge together. Later Clare turned up again only to forsake Partridge and fall in love—with, of all people, Carrington's old lover, Mark Gertler. And if this wasn't complication enough, Carrington later conceived a Lesbian affection for Clare.

Bertie's domestic life, by comparison, was uneventful. In January, 1922, Ottoline, playing an unaccustomed grandmotherly role, sent Bertie's young son a present. His father replied: "The beast you sent to John Conrad is a great joy to his parents—he will have to be a little older before he can quite appreciate him. He flourishes and I have discovered that his eyes and forehead are exactly like those of Immanuel Kant, which is a great blow, as we both regard Kant as an arch reactionary."[27] Russell reported that he spent most of his time watching John Conrad playing. Later, after he and Dora bought a cottage in Cornwall, he tried to entice Ottoline down with utopian pictures of the sea, the rocks, the bluebells, and

---

*Ottoline's comment on Carrington's marriage was: "I think this is very clever of Lytton for he will still retain his maid & attendant & he will also have a manservant too—'Married Couple' in fact!" (OM-BR, nd, McMaster)

details of John Conrad's activities. "He is full of fun and very roguish, with bright eyes which notice everything. He is altogether lovely, and I love him beyond measure."[28] Ottoline declined, sending instead a book to Bertie for his fiftieth birthday. In September he and Dora came to Garsington after which Russell went to see his aged Aunt Agatha, who, he reported back to Ottoline, told him that it had been all very well for him to have kicked up a fuss about the war, but that the pain he had caused various women was greater than all the harm wrought by the war.

Around the beginning of 1922 Ottoline's own parental responsibilities were giving some cause for concern. For three years from 1917 Julian had been boarding at school, but in 1920 she had to leave after getting whooping cough. She stayed at home for almost a year, after which Ottoline declared her formal education at an end: "You'll learn much more by sitting by the fire listening to Bertie Russell talk," she told her.[29] To supplement such fireside schooling a governess was engaged, a dumpy little German woman whom Gathorne-Hardy described as "insipid and unalluring."[30] She didn't last long and was succeeded by a tall sinister foreign lady who got off to a bad start by remarking loudly to Ottoline at the dinner table in front of Gertler that she couldn't understand how Ottoline could bring herself to have Jews to dinner. Mark got his own back later when playing cards by coining a nickname for her, saying, "It's Miss Hunka's turn."[31] After that she became known as Hunker Munker Gabber Gabber. Hunka Munka (about whom, Gathorne-Hardy felt, there was something which "faintly, horribly, suggested an evil caricature of Ottoline") would join in the games of croquet, at which she was believed to cheat, if she thought she wasn't being noticed, by kicking her ball to a more convenient position.[32] In 1921 Ottoline came to the conclusion that Julian wasn't happy and decided to take her for a holiday on the Continent where sixteen-year-old Julian won the hearts of a number of young officers. Fearing her daughter might become too precocious, Ottoline packed her off to a convent at Roehampton where Julian was thoroughly miserable. Dorothy Brett became so incensed at the way Julian was being treated that she decided to kidnap her. She sent her a rope ladder in a parcel and outlined an escape route for her, arranging to wait for her outside the school in her car ready to whisk her away. But the nuns opened Brett's suspicious-looking parcel and the plan was foiled. The incident did little to improve relations between Ottoline and Brett and in December, 1921, Brett, who apparently had been performing some sort of postal duty for Ottoline, wrote her a bitter note:

OTTOLINE DEAR,

You have the most strange ideas of friendship. Anyhow I post your letters regularly, I've no doubt it is something to be useful! but I feel a line or two at the same time thanking one for one's small services might be more polite or even friendly. I had thought of suggesting myself for a weekend but think perhaps it would be better for me to wait for you to ask me? Yrs. Brett.[33]

Soon after this the two women had a violent row during which it seems that Ottoline threw a brooch at Brett. The evidence of this incident comes from a letter written two years later by Lawrence to Mark Gertler in which he says he had seen Brett wearing a little blue chalcedony stone brooch which he (Lawrence) had given Ottoline years before. Brett had told him that "Ottoline flung it at her at the time of the row."[34] This suggests the cause of the final break between Brett and Ottoline might have been an argument over Lawrence. Brett had fallen under Lawrence's influence during the war and in 1924 joined him and Frieda to go off and establish Lawrence's Rananim in a lonely village called Taos in New Mexico.

All in all, 1922 was not a particularly happy year for Ottoline. At the start of the year she was in the hands of specialists and her ill-health continued, culminating in another operation in September, possibly to put right the trouble that Lytton had hinted at so indelicately in his letter to Virginia. There was also trouble on the farm. Philip had not yet learned his lesson about employing Ottoline's gilded amateurs, and when Toronto escaped from Canada Philip offered him a job at Garsington. Later an argument arose over accounting for milk receipts and, whatever the truth of the matter, it led to Toronto being given his marching orders. Another slightly worrying matter was a begging letter Ottoline received from Warsaw from a friend of Boris Anrep's former wife Junia informing Ottoline that Junia was on the verge of starvation. For several years after this Ottoline sent to Warsaw regular parcels of books and clothes and gifts of money. She kept such philanthropies—and, like Russell, she had more than one of them—to herself.

1923 didn't start too well either. Ottoline sent Bertie a Christmas pres-

ent and it took him some time to write to thank her. Next she received a
postcard from France, signed by Murry. It said:

MY DEAR OTTOLINE,
   Katherine died suddenly on Tuesday night: she was buried yesterday in
the cemetery here at Avin. J.M.M.[35]

It was no surprise that Katherine had died; she had been suffering from
tuberculosis for a long time. Now Murry resolved to devote the rest of his
life to her memory; he told Ottoline: ". . . the only thing that matters to
me is that she should have her rightful place as the most wonderful writer
and most beautiful spirit of our time."[36] Ottoline, too, did her best to per-
petuate Katherine's memory and composed an essay about her which she
read out to a group of friends one evening. David Cecil, who was there,
recalls Ottoline's voice purring and dipping over her words and as night
fell Philip lighting a candle and holding it over her so she could read on. It
was Ottoline's opinion that Katherine was a clever writer who struggled
constantly to escape her colonial background. Her taste, Ottoline said
once, was "Swan & Edgars" (by which she meant rather lower-middle-
class) and in her memoirs she recalled an incident concerning Katherine:

   We were playing a game after dinner when she was here, describing people by symbols, such as pictures and flowers and scents; unfortunately
   Katherine was described by some rather exotic scent such as Stephanotis or
   Patchouli, and although her name was not mentioned, we all knew and she
   knew who was meant. It was dreadful. The spite that was in the company
   maliciously flared out against her and hurt her. We all filed out of the
   drawing-room to bed very silently.[37]

After Brett's defection and Katherine's death, Ottoline's closest female
friend was Virginia Woolf, and from 1923 onwards their relationship
grew from cordiality into warm companionship. Virginia's madness was
more or less under control now and her novels beginning to attract attention. In 1924 she felt well enough to move from Richmond to Tavistock
Square in Bloomsbury and when Ottoline returned to London a few years
later they visited each other frequently and corresponded regularly. To
most of Virginia's Bloomsbury friends her consorting with Ottoline was
rather a mystery. What did Virginia see in her? Probably the same things

Lytton did—gossip and a sympathetic ear. And, like Lytton, Virginia did not let her friendship with Ottoline stand in the way of her lampooning what she regarded as some of Ottoline's more eccentric aspects. After a visit to Garsington in 1923 Virginia described the experience to Barbara Bagenal (formerly Barbara Hiles, one of the Slade cropheads) who was in hospital recovering from scarlet fever:

> I have often thought of you in hospital, as I take my way about the streets in comparative freedom. Yet I would have changed places with you last Sunday fortnight, when Ottoline completely drew the veils of illusion from me, and left me Monday morning to face a world from which all heart, charity, kindness and worth had vanished. How she does this, in ten minutes, between twelve and one, in the best spare bedroom, with the scent of dried roseleaves about, and a little powder falling on the floor, Heaven knows. Perhaps after 37 undergraduates, mostly the sons of Marquises, one's physical life is reduced, and one receives impressions merely from her drawl and crawl and smell which might be harmless in the stir of normal sunlight. Only is the sunlight ever normal at Garsington? No, I think even the sky is done up in pale yellow silk, and certainly the cabbages are scented.[38]

Although for a time Virginia toyed with the idea of incorporating Ottoline into one of her novels, it seems that she eventually decided not to, possibly because she knew of Ottoline's distaste for such things. However she did portray Philip as Hugh Whitbread in *Mrs. Dalloway*. (The name is something of a pun: both Whitbread and Morrell are English brewers.)

Lytton was at Garsington at least three times in 1923, torn between his dislike of being on display and the prospect of seeing the latest crop of pink-and-white undergraduates. Even so his patience was sorely tried. After one visit in June, 1923, (during which he had met Dr. Marten) he reported to Carrington: "Appalling! A fatal error to have come. I see now only too clearly. . . . The boredom has been indescribable. Most of the conversation is directed towards the dog when the doctor is not holding forth."[39] Dr. Marten may have been a bit of a bore, but he gave Ottoline some excellent advice, counselling her to eat plain foods and lead a simple life. Her regard for him was very high and for a time she acted as a sort of unpaid publicity agent for him, while, however, retaining a certain scepticism about his treatment, especially the amateur psychoanalysis he threw in with his more orthodox physicking. (Once when Gathorne-

Hardy asked what Marten had discovered about her, Ottoline replied seriously: "I find that my brothers play an undue part in my life."[40]) In the summer of 1923 Gathorne-Hardy and his friend Kyrle accompanied Ottoline to Freiburg for what was almost her annual pilgrimage to Dr. Marten's clinic. Even in Freiburg, a town noted for its eccentrics, Ottoline stood out. *"Die komische Engländerin"* was what the townspeople called her. Gathorne-Hardy noted that, though far away from Garsington, Ottoline managed to convert her hotel room into a kind of travelling boudoir, displaying around her room pretty little boxes and other knickknacks, some brought with her, some bought on the trip, and infusing the atmosphere with her distinctive personal perfume. Ottoline also managed to continue talent-spotting. She learned that the Russian writer Maxim Gorki was in the same hotel and, despite the language barrier, she arranged to meet him and somehow communicate her admiration, which he rewarded with his autograph. It was on a similar trip to France several years later, again accompanied by Gathorne-Hardy, that the opportunity arose for Ottoline to meet the aged painter Monet at his home at Giverny. But an efficient housekeeper refused to allow Ottoline in and she had to content herself with looking at the garden with its bridges and waterlilies.

1924 was the year Ottoline returned to the fold. Though she was again on good terms with all her brothers, and had lent one of her cats to the Duchess of Marlborough for stud purposes, she had not had any real contact with the fashionable world since 1914. But in 1924 she came to the conclusion that, although the Bohemian life might be all right for her, it was not necessarily the life that Julian would be suited to. So she decided Julian should "come out"—officially—into Society and rented Ethel Sand's house in The Vale, Chelsea, as headquarters for her campaign. Toning down her eccentric clothes, she made contact again with the houses in Mayfair and Belgravia that had been her girlhood haunts and there she found that many of the dowagers and matrons now chaperoning their daughters were the same young girls she had met at the balls back in the 1890s. She was invited to tea parties given by Ettie Desborough and the Duchess of Devonshire and other aristocratic ladies, all of whom welcomed her back as if nothing had occurred in between. Ottoline decided Julian should have a lady's maid for the Season and engaged a girl named Ivy Green, whose father was the gardener at one of the big Oxfordshire houses. She and Julian also did the rounds of the great country houses where Ivy was very impressed with the grand way of life: "There was no limit to the sport and shooting and they'd talk about nothing else than what had been shot and what had been caught," she recalled.[41] Ivy stayed on at Garsington after Julian came out to become Ottoline's personal maid and dressmaker, the latter an important position, as the sort of clothes Ottoline liked weren't to be found in the shops. Once, Ivy was sent all the way to Kenwood House in Hampstead to view a portrait of Lady Hamilton and copy details of her pink silk taffeta dress. Another time Ottoline, who had been up in London, returned home in great excitement, exclaiming: "Ivy, I've seen a coat! It was running along the street on a person, so I jumped off the bus and stopped her and asked if she would send it to us to copy it."[42] The woman obliged. Ivy recalled that Ottoline preferred very bright colours and that her shoes were bought from Pinet in Bond Street and her hats from Mrs. Wilson's in Mayfair. Ottoline liked shopping at the big stores like Marshall and Snelgrove where she would make friends with the shop assistants, asking the girls about their lives and on several occasions inviting them to Garsington.

It was Ottoline's hope that Julian would marry some well-set-up young man, and to expedite this she made a practice of inviting presentable young gentlemen to Garsington. C. M. Bowra was present one day when the main guest was a young Spanish duke whom Ottoline had summed up shrewdly and suggested a charade in which the duke would star as Napoleon. Bowra recalled: "It happened that at this moment Philip's mother was dying, and he came into the room at intervals with increasingly bad news." Ottoline would stop the charades for a moment to console Philip with a few words, then turn back to the guests, crying gaily: "Go on! Go on!"[43] On another occasion Leslie Hartley, the future author of *The Go-Between*, had come to lunch with several more eligible young men. After Ottoline carefully placed the others round the table she waved a hand at Hartley and said: "Anywhere, Mr. Hartley."[44]

After Julian's coming out, Ottoline divided her time between London, where she arranged *thé dansants* for Julian, and Garsington, where life went on more or less as always, with the usual drove of guests arriving every Friday evening and staying on till Sunday morning. On other days Ottoline would follow her routine of rising early, ordering the day's meals, attending to the household, then writing letters in her boudoir until lunch. In the afternoon she would relax and read or go into Oxford. In the evening a local village woman came to do the lamps and Mrs. Sue Wain came over from a nearby village to take up the jugs of water and turn the beds down. Usually, Ottoline did her embroidery after dinner while Julian, Philip, Gilbert Spencer, and Gertler or whoever else was staying would play bridge. Gilbert, who was now a particular friend, had come to stay at Garsington and help Philip on the farm. He was very grateful for Ottoline and Philip's friendship and once told Ottoline: "Without in any way wishing to compliment myself I think you have both helped me turn my brain into something tolerably intelligent."[45]

In 1925 Ottoline began thinking about selling Garsington. This came as a shock to all her friends, none of whom could understand how she could bear to give up such a perfect house. Exactly why she chose to leave is still not certain. Gathorne-Hardy suggested it had something to do with Mrs. Morrell's death: that Philip had "wistful longings" to live at his old home, Black Hall, and that the move to London several years later and purchase of a town house in Gower Street, Bloomsbury, was a compromise. Ottoline's daughter, on the other hand, believes money was the main reason for the move: Garsington was becoming very expensive to run and Philip and Ottoline decided to move to cheaper premises. Gathorne-Hardy, however, mentioned an incident that suggests another possible reason:

> One day I was lunching with [Ottoline and Philip at Gower Street]. Ottoline opened a letter and as she read it gave out a cry of the utmost distress. A massive limb had fallen off the great ilex tree at Garsington. I cannot recall her exact words, but she cried out that the place was ruined—that she would hardly endure to look at it again so dreadfully disfigured. And then for the only time in my life, I saw her lose her temper. Philip had been calmly sympathetic. "You drive me mad," she said suddenly and fiercely, "taking it so calmly."[46]

There is no doubt that Ottoline had come to identify Garsington with some of the greatest unhappiness in her life and it seems probable that she took the opportunity of various contingencies to make up her mind to leave it. These contingencies included Julian's growing-up, the fact that the house was now too big and too expensive to manage, and the fact that people could come to visit more easily if Ottoline were in London rather than near Oxford. One incident that did not add to her happy memories of Garsington happened in March, 1925, when Lytton paid one of his rare visits. On the day he was to leave, Carrington and Partridge arrived in their car to pick him up, and Ottoline, who hadn't seen Carrington for a long time, took her reappearance as a gesture of reconciliation. She called out her name joyfully and asked her in. But Carrington did not budge and coldly said, "No thank you, Ottoline."[47] An expression of grief came over Ottoline's face, then, pulling herself together, she managed to get out some trivial conversation about the tyres on the car. Lytton then came out, said good-bye, and drove off. This was his last visit to Garsington.

By 1926 Julian was twenty and many of the young men who now came to Garsington were there to see her, not her mother—something Ottoline would not have relished. One of these was Igor Vinogradoff, a tall and brilliant Oxford undergraduate whose father was a Russian émigré and a distinguished jurist. He became very fond of Julian but Ottoline frowned on the developing friendship, partly because she did not feel that Julian, who was used to living comfortably, would enjoy having to economise. So she went to considerable lengths to scotch the romance, even sending Julian up to London to stay with Juliette Huxley and study home science. Finally, in the summer of 1927, Julian met another young man, Victor Goodman, who was a clerk in the House of Lords and later became Clerk of the Parliaments. They married in early 1928 and set up house in Chelsea.* Julian's impending marriage was yet another factor in Ottoline's decision to return to London. At first Ottoline and Philip looked for a house near Ethel Sands's and they found one in St. Leonards Terrace, Chelsea, that suited them perfectly. But once again the past cast a pall: Logan Pearsall Smith also happened to reside in St. Leonards Terrace, and when he heard that Ottoline was planning to take a house in the same street he circulated a letter to the other residents saying that the Morrells were not at all reputable people and shouldn't be allowed to take the lease. Ottoline was cut to the quick and began looking around Bloomsbury instead. Finally she found a house at No. 10 Gower Street. It was a four-storey building and just around the corner from Bedford Square. She hurried back to Garsington and announced she had discovered somewhere for

*In 1942, after a divorce, Julian married her earlier love, Igor.

them to live: "I've found the dearest little doll's house!" she told Ivy Green.[48] Later the Morrells sold Garsington to relations of Sir John and Lady Wheeler-Bennett, the present owners. When the new purchasers inquired of Ottoline details of the local shops, and where to buy meat and fish, Ottoline intoned: "Don't talk to me of fish. You may talk to me about poetry and literature, but not fish."[49]

GOWER STREET

Chapter 18

Part i
1927–1932

IN August, 1927, Ottoline made one of her regular late-summer trips to Italy and on her return she busied herself renovating Gower Street and organising Julian's wedding, due in the New Year. This burst of activity exhausted her and, coming on top of the wrench of giving up Garsington, no one was very surprised when she began to feel ill. But this time it turned out to be something more serious than her chronic migraines and stomach disorders. First she complained of neuralgia of the jaw, then abscesses appeared. Several doctors were consulted, without much effect, then Juliette Huxley recommended an expert on tropical medicine named Dr. Rau who diagnosed necrosis of the jaw, a disease in which part of the bone marrow dies. (Apparently Ottoline was infected during her trip to Italy.) She was admitted to a nursing home in Fitzroy Square where an operation was performed to remove the diseased part of the bone, after which she had to remain in bed in a darkened room with tubes draining her jaw. For several weeks she was in constant pain and she told Juliette Huxley, who came to visit her: "At times it is so bad I just growl like a tiger."[1] The seriousness of the illness jolted all Ottoline's friends, many of whom realised how much they might miss her were she not to recover. Lytton was very worried and asked Gathorne-Hardy in hushed tones: "What is the matter with Ottoline?" When told what it was he breathed a sigh of relief: "I thought it must be cancer."[2] Her old antagonist Roger Fry felt concerned enough to visit her in hospital and Portland insisted she convalesce at Welbeck where he set aside a suite of rooms for her. There she slowly recovered, but the operation took its toll and left the lower part of her face badly scarred. She did little to hide this disfigurement, only occasionally wearing a scarf to shield her pitted jawline.

There was, however, one outcome of this ordeal that Ottoline welcomed: after twelve years she and Lawrence made up their quarrel. He learned of her illness from Aldous Huxley and wrote her immediately:

267

MY DEAR OTTOLINE,

I was so sorry to hear of you ill and in all that pain—so was Frieda. But now thank goodness you are a lot better, and soon one can think of you nicely going around again and being there in the world. I do hope you'll keep well—I consider people like you and me, we've had our whack of bodily ills, we ought to be let off a bit. . . . I trust we shall meet again one day, you and I, because I'm sure we're quite fond of one another really through all this long lapse. But the chief thing for you at the moment is to get quite well.

from us both,
D. H. LAWRENCE[3]

Ottoline replied in friendly terms and told him about giving up Garsington, adding that she felt sad their early hopes for it had not been realised. She was feeling depressed and told him she feared that her life had been largely wasted. "Don't feel you're not important," he told her. "You've been an important influence in lots of lives, as you have in mine: through being fundamentally generous, and through being Ottoline. After all, there's only one Ottoline. And she has moved one's imagination." He then went on to make what can be interpreted—and what he probably meant Ottoline to take—as an apology for Hermione Roddice:

> It doesn't matter what sort of vision comes out of a man's imagination, his vision of Ottoline. Any more than a photograph of me is me, or even "like" me. The so-called portraits of Ottoline can't possibly be Ottoline— no one knows that better than an artist.[4]

He told her he and Frieda were staying in a villa in Florence and that he was working on the final stages of a new novel (which was to be his last and most controversial novel: *Lady Chatterley's Lover*). Ottoline welcomed the reconciliation and she and Lawrence exchanged regular letters as he travelled round Italy searching for somewhere to rest between his worsening bouts of tuberculosis.

Towards the end of summer 1928 Ottoline felt sufficiently recovered to think about opening her new premises in Gower Street to the talent and intellect of London. Garsington by now was just a cluster of memories— good and bad—and a weekly hamper of flowers and vegetables sent up by the gardener, while Bedford Square, where twenty years ago she first launched herself on an unsuspecting capital, was distant history. Yet it had partly been the memory of Bedford Square that had lured her back to London, and, as she stood on the threshold of another new era in her life, she hoped that Gower Street might help her recapture some of the magic of those prewar days. She especially hoped that people like Lytton, who had excused themselves from the long journey to Garsington, would feel more inclined to accept invitations to the Thursday at homes she now began holding at regular intervals.

In Lytton's case she reinforced her invitation with a little bit of nostalgia. She sent him a postcard showing a photograph of the pond at Garsington and on the back told him how much she envied his cottage in the country, adding: "I believe I once had such a place where there was an ilex tree and statues where you used to come and talk to your admirers. But perhaps I am dreaming. I must have been in another existence (a tear!) for it has all vanished now."[5] Whether it was the photograph or the tear, the approach had the desired effect and that autumn Lytton turned up to one of Ottoline's first Thursday tea parties where he met Aldous Huxley, Yeats, and several other old friends. The occasion, however, was considerably spoilt by the presence of "a little gnome-like Irishman" named James Stephens whom Ottoline had acquired somewhere.[6] Though a poet, Stephens was better known as an almost unstoppable chatterbox:

> On and on he went [Lytton told his friend Roger Senhouse] inveighing against "destructive criticism" (that tedious old story), pointing out that no one could write about love, but only about sex, lamenting that there were no epics. . . . Ethel Sands filled up gaps with her appreciative shiny teeth, and Pipsey interrupted and floundered as usual. . . . I was suddenly asked to give my opinion upon some long-winded dictum of Mr. J. S.'s on medieval clothes—the differences between the sexes—beauty of women—love—and all the rest of it. I was rather at a loss and could only shriek "Armour: I'm in favour of armour!" . . . Mr. J. S. condemned me, of course, as destructive.[7]

Ottoline must have noted Lytton's unease, for she wrote saying how good it was to see him again: "It was such a real, real, real pleasure! I hope the little Irish gnome didn't weary you—I was afraid he might."[8] Yet it was almost two months before she could lure Lytton back again and this time, despite the gnome, things went off rather better, though, as Lytton again reported to Roger Senhouse, his entrance created more of a stir than he had planned: "I made a pompous entry—late—everyone sitting around the table—a general remuement, etc. and some slightly dazed looks. I didn't know why but on at last taking my seat found that *all* my front buttons were undone from top to bottom."[9]

Ottoline's hopes for Gower Street were realised and soon most of the old Garsington habitués—Aldous, Yeats, Siegfried, Eliot, Gilbert Spencer and the rest were coming regularly. Even Bertie called in occasionally, though like Eliot and Siegfried he preferred tête-à-têtes to the larger, noisier gatherings. To supplement the old faces was a stream of new talent, including a new generation of young poets and writers like Stephen Spender and William Plomer, plus a sprinkling of bright young women such as the poet Ruth Pitter. In the past women had been almost a rarity at Ottoline's gatherings for she had little patience with the usual female pursuits, and only those rare individuals with special gifts—or with special male friends—had found their way to Garsington or Bedford Square. But at Gower Street an older, more placid Ottoline began to actively seek out female companionship, often finding in these shallower friendships more comfort and fewer problems.

Indeed, the Ottoline who received her guests at Gower Street was altogether a quieter, less neurasthenic figure. She had, she said, consciously chosen to "mute herself down" in order to survive, and this muting down was reflected in the more conventional decor she chose for her new house.[10] Veterans of Garsington recognised the boxes, the familiar knick-knacks, the china, pictures, books, the silk cushions and the all-pervading perfume, but there was no longer anything especially startling or dramatic: the hall was plain white and the reception rooms exceptional only for the beautiful pink and silver curtains Ottoline's maid Ivy ran up.

The Gower Street at homes were even more informal than before, with everyone sitting round the large dining room table tossing conversation and ideas around like Ping-Pong balls. Portland called whenever he was in London, though he didn't join the round-table discussions. (David Cecil remembers coming across Portland sitting in his Rolls-Royce outside 10 Gower Street and when he mentioned this to Ottoline she replied, "Oh yes, Portland's outside, reading."[11]) Another reason for Ottoline's more placid aspect was the contentment of her newfound relationship with Philip—a relationship that Maria Huxley characterised as "Darby and

Joan.''[12] For though they led lives that were mainly separate, with Philip spending much of his time at his clubs and playing bridge, as time went on he assumed a more dominant role in their partnership. He advised her with the more complicated areas of her personal affairs and shielded her from people who might make trouble for her. If there was a difficult letter to write it was Philip who would draft a tactful reply and Ottoline would then copy it out in her inimitable handwriting.

Ottoline's health continued to be poor and she was plagued increasingly by deafness; this was another reason for the more subdued character of Gower Street. Also, the worsening economic situation did little to engender an atmosphere of gaity, though Ottoline remained very comfortably off—thanks to Portland's allowance—and the ''doll's house'' in Gower Street ran to a full-time staff of five. Even so, Ottoline's life generally was in keeping with her more modest establishment. She and Philip did not go out often and then it was usually to see a film or more rarely a play or an opera. Sometimes she would call on Ethel Sands in Chelsea, or Virginia Woolf in nearby Tavistock Square, or have tea with one of her new friends, such as Dame Ethel Smythe, a voluble ex-suffragette and composer who was a sort of female James Stephens. Ottoline almost always dined at home—except on Sundays, which was Cook's day off. Then the Morrells would go out to eat at a restaurant, mostly to the Etoile in nearby Charlotte Street, which Ottoline described as ''a charming little restaurant—so cheap.''[13] She herself could hardly boil a kettle unaided, and Julian recalls going down to the basement of Gower Street to make a cup of tea and a maid rushing up to stop her, then saying, ''Oh, I forgot—you're not as helpless as her Ladyship.''[14]

Some time during 1928 Ottoline obtained an illicit copy of Lawrence's new novel, *Lady Chatterley's Lover*. She wrote him praising it and gently taking him to task over his ideas on sex. He told her that he wasn't advocating perpetual sex—nothing nauseated him more than sex in and out of season—rather he was trying to promote a healthy attitude to it.

> . . . one of the reasons why the common people often keep—or kept the good natural *natural glow* of life, just warm life, longer than educated people, was because it was still possible for them to say shit! or fuck! without either a shudder or a sensation. If a man had been able to say to you when you were young and in love: an' if tha shits, an' if tha pisses, I'm glad, I shouldna want a woman who couldna shit nor piss—surely it would

have been a liberation to you, and it would have helped to keep your heart warm.[15]

Ottoline showed this letter to Gathorne-Hardy and waited for his reaction with a straight face, but he was rather at a loss as to what to say, so she said: "I don't think it would," then, shaking her head and laughing, added, "In fact, I'm quite *sure* it wouldn't."[16] The letters that Ottoline and Lawrence exchanged have an air of two elderly ladies musing and reminiscing about old friends and acquaintances. Ottoline told him she didn't think much of Huxley's books, particularly his latest work, *Point Counter Point,* and Lawrence agreed, though he had to confess to a grudging admiration for the way Huxley could describe things. The two exchanged symptoms and Lawrence suggested that perhaps a little burgundy might help her headaches. He told her that all he wanted now was a few people around him that he could really be fond of, and he wished he and Frieda could live nearer to Ottoline and Philip. He recalled the day in 1915 when Ottoline visited him in Greatham in Sussex, "stepping out of an old four-wheeler in all your pearls, and a purple velvet frock."[17] What a pity, he added, that something had come across it all and prevented them keeping a nice harmony. He urged Ottoline to see the exhibition of his pictures that Dorothy Warren was putting on in London in the summer of 1929, "because some of them you will surely like—there is a suggestion of Blake sometimes."[18]

Unfortunately there was also a suggestion of something else in the paintings, and after the exhibition opened it was raided by the police and a number of the works seized on grounds of obscenity. In August, 1929, a court sat to decide if the seized paintings should be destroyed and the hearing was attended by many luminaries from the artistic and literary world. Lawrence wasn't there (he was ill in Italy; besides he would have probably been arrested on his arrival for sending copies of *Lady Chatterley* through the post) but Ottoline attended, and her entrance created a stir in the courtoom. The proceedings halted as her tall resplendent figure wove through the public gallery, and the magistrate, impatient to get on with the case, began to fidget. At last he asked testily, "Can nobody find that lady at the back a seat?" There was a shuffle of chairs and muffled voices said, "Please sit here, Lady Ottoline." But Ottoline had already found a seat and now rose to her full height and, pointing her long forefinger at the Bench, intoned in her best droning voice, "He ought to be burned. He ought to be burned."[19] In the event, the court refused to grant an order for the paintings to be destroyed. Frieda also resumed writing to Ottoline, and about the time of the court hearing wrote that she had always appreciated Ottoline's "bigness and real spirit," adding: "I think the tragedy of your life has been that it was a small age you lived in and the men were small beer & the women too."[20]

In 1929 Philip launched into print with a potted version of the Greville diaries. Ottoline was very proud of this production—Greville was a remote ancestor of hers—and sent a copy to Lawrence, who told her he enjoyed it. She also sent a copy to Lytton but he was rather taken aback as he was at that moment in the process of getting out an edition of the same diaries. Ottoline assured him that had Philip known he had embarked on such a project he wouldn't have bothered. Lytton, however, was very nice and said that Philip's work had underlined the need for a full edition of the diaries and would spur him and his helpers to complete their task.

In April, 1929, Ottoline acquired a new doctor who put her on to a starch diet which, she remarked to Lytton, was probably why she felt stiff. In May she was feeling no better and was admitted to Preston Deanery Hall, a curious establishment near Northampton which specialised in starvation cures and where silver platters of nuts and caraway seeds were served to patients by footmen. The new doctor responsible for her incarceration there was a society quack called Cameron, who was to become over the next nine years her favourite physician—and the man who eventually, through his ineptitude, killed her.

Around this time three of Ottoline's old lovers drifted back briefly into her life. The first was Augustus John, who was also an habitué of Preston Deanery Hall, being sent there, Ottoline suspected, to remove him from within reach of too much food and wine. In 1929 John wrote thanking her for buying one of his drawings. He was grateful that she was still collecting him: "I was rather afraid you were beginning to think I was dead."[21] The second old flame was Henry Lamb, who Ottoline was distressed to hear was having similar trouble to Augustus John's. In recent years Lamb had fallen into a state of *dégringolade* and Dorelia remarked in a letter to Ottoline that "his case was more serious than John's."[22] The third old flame was the oldest of the lot—Axel Munthe, who arrived in London in May, 1929, in a pathetic state. He wrote Ottoline telling her that he was almost blind and begged her to find him a decent hotel near Hyde Park and someone who would come and read to him. He signed his letter "Your Old Friend."[23] Ottoline did her best to help, asking him to one of her Thursdays but when he came it turned out that he wasn't as decrepit as he made out.

Probably it was Munthe's reappearance that caused Ottoline to start pondering her current beliefs. Late in 1929 she exchanged several letters with Gathorne-Hardy on the subject of religion, explaining to him that she believed the Divine Spirit was at the back of all life. "The best human relationships—indeed all—have something divine in them," she wrote, "and that one can possess the spirit of someone by really *understanding* them—as one can possess a poem or flower, or anything beautiful one absorbs and loves."[24] In another letter she harkened back to her disappointment that she was not creative. "I wish, I wish, one could *express* some new expression of the Divine. It is so humiliating that one is so uncreative. Perhaps in another existence I may be able to. I don't know quite what I would rather be, a mystic or a poet. In this life I have learned to be content."[25]

In January, 1930, Ottoline received her last letter from Lawrence. He told her he had had a bad winter and that there was a possibility he might have to go to a sanatorium for a few months. "Perhaps I will," he said, "I am tired of always being defeated by bad health."[26] Two months later Ottoline opened a telegram from Aldous telling her Lawrence was dead. She wrote in her diary: "I had always thought that we should have a time to laugh over our old quarrels, to disagree and argue, and to plan a new Elysian world."[27] Ottoline later wrote an essay about Lawrence, entitled *Recollections of D. H. Lawrence by O. M.*, which was published in *The Athenaeum*. In it she said Lawrence was obsessed with titles, that he was extremely sensitive to women's emotions, that his "dark gods" philosophy was claptrap, and that despite his rejection of England he remained until his death profoundly English. She also had much to say about Frieda, some of which was valid—for example that Frieda was jealous of any other female influence in Lawrence's life, even that of his mother. Ottoline regarded Frieda as Lawrence's refuge from the rest of the female world. "He had great fear, and like a frightened dog he could dash out from his kennel and bark and bark,'' Ottoline wrote.[28] And Frieda was his kennel.*

Frieda sailed back briefly into the Morrells' life in 1931 when she sought Philip's help to sort out the financial mess Lawrence's death had left her in. Lawrence's will, in which he left everything to Frieda, had been mislaid and his other relations, principally his brother George and sister Ada, were contesting Frieda's claim to be sole beneficiary of the now substantial estate. Philip did his best to help and spent some time straightening out the tangle with agents and lawyers and negotiating on Frieda's behalf with George and Ada. But his efforts were completely undone by Frieda's irrational behaviour. Philip went to see George Lawrence and arranged a reasonable settlement, then wrote to Frieda explaining the arrangement and warning her to restrain her natural inclination to write a "blister" to Lawrence's family. Frieda ignored his advice, and duly wrote a blister telling George and Ada and all the other Lawrences not only what she thought of them and this shabby haggling but also revealing everything Philip had told her in confidence about the tactics he was using in the case. Thereafter Philip washed his hands of the whole business. Frieda eventually succeeded in having her rights confirmed— but only after a court case—and she bore Philip and Ottoline no grudge.† Later she wrote Philip saying: "I wish Lawrence had known you for I believe he only saw a rather swanky, conceited Philip, well I know better!" and she signed it "Yours, Frieda (the poor widow in distress)."[29] Frieda also wrote to Ottoline telling her not to think that Lawrence had said nasty things about her: "You meant so much to him—and I thought Hermione was such a noble & splendid figure in *Women in Love,* greek and moving."[30] When Frieda subsequently went off to America and Taos with her Italian lover, Ottoline gave her a grudging tribute: "I wish I had her vitality," she said.[31]

Between 1928 and 1933 Ottoline again became embroiled with T. S. Eliot and his wife. Vivienne's mental condition had declined further, but

*Ottoline blamed Frieda for turning Lawrence against her and inspiring Hermione Roddice. In October, 1932, Ottoline told Virginia Woolf: "I am trying to do a sketch of [Lawrence] for my memoirs but I find my fury against Frieda runs away with me & burns up all else." (OM-VW, October 15, 1932, Sussex)

†During the hearing Frieda's lawyer rather oversentimentalised her life with Lawrence—years of poverty, a model of concord, etc. Suddenly Frieda jumped up and cried, "But that's not true—we fought like hell!"

Eliot was loyally staying with her, even though he realised she restricted his relationships with other people. He was particularly anxious to stay friends with Ottoline. Some time earlier, when a cloud had passed over their friendship, he had written saying he had a sure conviction that he had offended her and begging her to write and tell him how he could patch things up. On another occasion he wrote saying he was afraid she was ill and asking if somebody could send him a card to say how she was. "It would be a great relief," he added. Vivienne, too, was writing to Ottoline, and in January, 1928, she told her that "Tom hates the sight of me."[32] Later on Vivienne conceived a suspicion that Ottoline was seeing too much of her husband and Eliot was forced to write to Ottoline explaining that though he wanted to see her he couldn't because of Vivienne. He suggested that Ottoline write to them both saying that she wasn't well and could only see one at a time and would like to see them both separately. The following year matters worsened. Vivienne, who was coming to Gower Street quite a lot, told Eliot that Ottoline was upset because she thought Eliot had "dropped" her. Eliot wrote to assure Ottoline that it wasn't so and begged her to come and dine with them alone. This misunderstanding was ironed out and the following Christmas Eliot wrote thanking Ottoline for the diary she made a practice of giving him each year. Vivienne's condition deteriorated further and in 1932 Eliot thanked Ottoline for her kindness to Vivienne throughout the past year. Not long after this Eliot abandoned Vivienne and went to America where he begged Ottoline to keep an eye on his wife. Though Ottoline didn't like this task she went to see Vivienne and reported back to Eliot on her state, advising him that it might be better if he did not return to her. Eliot had already decided this was the best course anyway. He still blamed Russell for a lot of what had happened and told Ottoline, "He has done Evil."[33] Vivienne continued to write to Ottoline and in March, 1933, told her that she was running down and had taken only two or three baths since Tom had left. Later she went into an asylum where she died insane. Eliot returned to England in 1933 and his friendship with Ottoline continued.

What were Ottoline's motives in helping Vivienne? The answer is simply that Ottoline was a generous person who always put herself out to help people. For many years it was—and still is—fashionable to wax sarcastic about this aspect of her nature; many people have put Ottoline's motives down to "lion hunting." But this epithet is neither subtle nor particularly apt. It is, for instance, understandable if she were a "lion hunter" that she should have gone out of her way to befriend Thomas Hardy—yet why did she bother to make friends with his widow, Florence, who had very little greatness in her, and why, long after Hardy's death, did she continue to invite and write to Florence? This example could be repeated many times. Nor does any simple lion-hunting theory explain why André Gide should ask Ottoline to the theatre in Paris, nor why art collector Samuel Courtauld would invite her to dinner and a show at the Golders Green Hippodrome, nor why Lord Beaverbrook, whose views Ottoline could hardly have agreed with, should write to her hoping she was recovering from her jaw operation. It seems that Ottoline had a genuine sympathy if not regard for Vivienne Eliot: one might ask a mad-woman to tea once out of pity, but not twice and more.* And Vivienne was not the only one; Ottoline's kindness to her was echoed in another case, this one involving Lawrence's old friend, Koteliansky. Kot, a trans-lator of Tolstoy and a friend not only of Lawrence but of Katherine Mans-field, Murry, and the Woolfs, was not particularly close to Ottoline, but she was friend enough to have him both at Garsington and Gower Street fairly frequently. At Gower Street his sombre, intense face is sometimes seen recorded in group snapshots taken in the garden. In the early thirties his mental state began to deteriorate and he became subject to black depressions, these eventually getting so severe that he couldn't leave his house in Swiss Cottage, and from there would write sad letters to Ottoline describing his state. Beatrice Campbell, a friend of both Kot and Otto-line, wrote asking if she could help him, and Ottoline visited Kot several times and kept up a correspondence with him. She would act like a moth-er to him and he told her "your severity is very helpful."[34] Occasionally his mood would lift and he would be able to visit Ottoline at Gower Street. In 1933 he wrote telling her about arriving at her place and, as soon as he saw her, her understanding smile lifted his depression. "It is good to understand and be understood. . . . Ottoline, thank you so much for all your presents; and I do admire you for what you are."[35] Lat-

*On one occasion Ottoline told Virginia Woolf: "Obviously I was endowed with an ex-tra amount of interest in human beings—an absurd overdose of 'kindness'—I suppose a sort of extended maternal instinct." (OM-VW, November 20, 1933, Sussex) But on another occasion Ottoline told Virginia she felt "that people are just vampires—sucking one's life. I am a magnet for egoists." (OM-VW, December 28, 1928, Sussex)

er, when he was sent to a nursing home, Ottoline visited him. He was very miserable and to brighten him up she conjured up madcap schemes to kidnap him. He could dress up in one of her hats, impersonate her, and walk out of the hospital unaccosted. In 1936 he wrote to Ottoline recalling being photographed in her garden with James Stephens and several others, and he added: "I think now that it would be worth my getting well again for one more photograph in your garden."[36]

Ottoline had seen very little of Russell for some time—he was too busy bringing up and educating his two children (Dora had also given birth to a daughter). He and Dora had actually started a school in a disused semaphore station high on the Sussex downs where they instructed their own children and a small group of others along progressive lines. He was also occupied lecturing and writing and could only infrequently spare time for a visit to Gower Street. Even his letters were few and far between. But he did find time to dictate his memories. He entitled this work *My First Fifty Years* and sent a copy of the manuscript to Ottoline for her comments as it contained some mention of those apocalyptic events that began in March, 1911. Ottoline reacted to what Russell had written—virtually what was later published in 1968 in his autobiography—in the same way she did the caricatures of Lawrence, Huxley, and Turner. She was irate. On the MS she angrily scratched out several references—in particular his description of her as having a face rather like a horse—and was generally unenthusiastic about the whole project, suggesting that it shouldn't be published for many years. There is even a hint she may have threatened to publish or somehow expose his love letters if he went ahead and brought out his own version of their affair. And in one way her reaction is understandable—the publicity would have caused a great fuss and much hurt, particularly to Julian and Philip. In the end Russell concurred and promised he would not publish until after he and Ottoline were both dead.

Meanwhile Russell's marriage was breaking up. He told Ottoline that he had decided to leave Dora, as she was pregnant by another man.

While checking through Bertie's letters Ottoline also came across Lytton's old letters and in April, 1931, she wrote him:

> I like occasionally to plunge into the past & to relive it again—to walk in
> that mysterious wood—but it is fatal to do it often for it fades away.

I think really in those days I was too "overdone." Too worried to appreciate *all* its delights.[37]

She added that she felt steadier and wiser now. He replied with an amount of sentiment suitable for Ottoline's mood:

> For me, getting to know you was a wonderful experience—ah! those days at Peppard—those evenings in Bedford Square! I cannot help surmising that if H[enry] L[amb] had been a *little* different—things would have been *very* different, but perhaps that is an impossible notion. Perhaps we are all so deeply what we are that the slightest shift is out of the question. I don't think I want to go back. It was thrilling, enchanting, devastating, all at once—one was in a special (a very special) train, tearing along at breakneck speed—where?—once could only dimly guess—one might be off the rails—at any moment. Once is enough! . . . I have been astonishingly happy now for a long time—if only life were a good deal longer—and the sunshine less precarious![38]

This was the last letter he wrote to Ottoline. But it was not the last time she saw him. In October or November, 1931, he was one of the special guests invited to Gower Street for a tea party in honour of Charlie Chaplin, Ottoline's favourite screen hero. She regarded his acceptance of her invitation as a great coup and all her oldest and dearest friends were invited along to meet him, including Russell, Gathorne-Hardy, Duncan Grant, and Augustus John. Ottoline also found excuses for Millie, Ivy, and the other servants to come into the room and catch a glimpse of the famous star. The conversation was about Chaplin's East End background and the life of the working class people who grew up there, and Ottoline told him about her visits to Burnley. Then she startled Chaplin by turning to him and saying intensely: "Those people have no poetry. You don't feel that anyone ever felt ecstasy in Burnley."[39]

Soon after this party Lytton became gravely ill and by early January, 1932, it was obvious he would probably not recover. Ottoline wrote to Carrington advising her to call in a certain eminent specialist and in turn Carrington kept Ottoline informed of Lytton's weakening condition. Carrington told Ottoline that each time Lytton was washed with the scented water she had sent, he asked: "Is this Ottoline's?"[40] On January 21 Lytton died and a few days later Carrington wrote to Ottoline saying: "It is to you I owe the happiness, probably of my life with Lytton. I thank you for those days at Garsington where I grew to love him."[41] In March she sent Ottoline a packet of photographs of Lytton taken in Cornwall in 1916. On the envelope Ottoline wrote: "She shot herself two days later."

Part ii
1932–1943

———

Ottoline's life, Philip apart, was based on three great friendships—Lawrence, Lytton, and Russell. Though there were other friendships and love affairs, the great intellectual and spiritual moments of her life centred on these three men. Now two were dead and the third not much more to her than some memories and a bundle of letters. She could not but have felt melancholy. Each of the three had given her something unique. With Lawrence she had a genius who shared her intuitive love of life and nature; with Russell she had access to a great mind and an intense passion—but it was Lytton who had given her the most fun. She confessed after his death that there had been nobody with whom she had been more intimate. She had in fact, she suspected, been in love with him, and though she had suffered because of his apparent forsaking her in later years, she never believed he forsook her in his heart.

In this mood of retrospection Ottoline began to think about polishing up her own memoirs. She was also gaining more satisfaction from spiritual reflection and for a while flirted with Eastern mysticism, once going so far as seeing a swami. Now nearing sixty she felt she was an anachronism, that her day had passed. "I don't suit the modern mind," she told a new young friend, Sebastian Sprott.[42] In another letter she revealed to him her current thoughts on friendship:

> Somehow I never feel now that anyone cares to know me. I think it is partly because I have been very ill and have had to live so retired. But it is also my old Inferiority Complex, that crops up in full vigour from time to time. It is depressing reading old letters. It makes one feel that one's life is

all over and past—and too that awful realisation of how quickly the sand of friendship and love runs through the hourglass. . . . One may keep a friendship . . . but it seems a thin little trickle. I am I believe more faithful than most people. Also I am *much more interested in other people* and other lives than anyone else that I know.[43]

So the search for new minds and fresh talent went on. One day Ottoline read an article on T. S. Eliot which she enjoyed and wrote to its author, a young writer named Dilys Powell. The two women became friends and often went out to films together. They also attended the opening night of Eliot's play *Murder in the Cathedral* together and afterwards Ottoline suggested: "Let's go and have a doughnut!"[44] They went to a Lyon's Corner House where Ottoline's unusual clothes and aristocratic manner caused some consternation. Another new friend whom Ottoline met through Eliot was the crippled writer and critic John Hayward. Ottoline embarked on a campaign to get Hayward out into society, visiting him, giving him a pheasant for Christmas, and trying to entice him to *Così Fan Tutte*. Philip would come for him in the car . . . their dining room was on the ground floor, so there wouldn't be any problem with stairs, and there was a side door at the theatre that didn't involve stairs either. Ottoline even tried to marry him off to Frieda's daughter, Barbara Weekley. Hayward gradually responded and began to go out more and his letters to her show both appreciation for her generosity and an insight into her own situation. In 1933, when Philip was ill and about to have his teeth out, Hayward wrote remarking that Philip had always been her anchor. "Yes," Ottoline replied, "you are right. I have had Philip—and whatever the difficulties and complications 'that' entails. . . . It is a rare and wonderful thing and I am *unspeakably grateful*. . . . The inner centre of everyone's life must go on alone but it is so very very hard to be alone in the other chambers of one's life."[45] By December, 1933, Ottoline was on such good terms with Hayward that she was able to reveal her most sensitive thoughts to him—even her regrets about the passing of her looks. She had been to Elizabeth Arden's to buy a handkerchief and found herself surrounded by shop assistants, "paroquets," who started pecking at her face and telling her that her skin was dry: "I came out feeling a hag."[46]

Another acquaintance who became a regular at Gower Street in the thirties was the poet Thomas Sturge Moore (brother of Russell's friend

G. E. Moore). Ottoline showed him her memoirs but she wasn't pleased with the advice he gave her about them. Concerning her version of the troubles with Lawrence and Frieda he said: "I do not doubt your accuracy, but you are up against one of the oldest prejudices which will long outlast any of us. Namely that what two women fond of the same man say of each other must not be believed.''[47] He told her that the repetition of words like "tigress," "violent," and "jealous" four or five times would tend to impress people in the opposite sense to that intended and he added that her ideas on modern art would date. He criticised some of the more flowery passages in her memoirs: "Perhaps you indulge a little too much in descriptions of spring and country. Such things have nearly always been done so well in the classics that they can be taken very much for granted.''[48]

A younger friend was Francis Needham, one of Ottoline's university young men, whom she helped to get a job at Welbeck Abbey as historian and librarian. Ottoline had had him to dinner several times and occasionally gave discreet assistance to his love life. In his case, however, her aid did carry a small charge. For some reason Ottoline was in need of money around 1931 and she asked Needham if he would be interested in buying several Lawrence first editions from her for the Welbeck library. This put poor Needham in rather a difficult position. How could he deal equitably with his friend who was also the half-sister of his employer? He replied doubtfully that the library might not need her Lawrence editions and, seeing she had two copies of *Sons and Lovers,* might not she donate one anyhow? Ottoline was persistent and finally sent him two Lawrence books for appraisal, one of which he kept, returning the other with a rather uncomfortable letter saying that he never thought money would matter to her. She replied that she needed the money to buy a new coat. Earlier Ottoline had been trying to sell off some other books and manuscripts through Gathorne-Hardy. She sold some letters of Katherine Mansfield's to his firm for £40, but complained later that they cheated her on the deal. These are not the only instances of what might seem meanness on Ottoline's part. Sometimes she would sell things, then forget she had been paid for them; or demand books back that had been returned already. Much of this can be put down to simple forgetfulness, or an aristocratic inability to be too precise in such matters. Yet put beside all her philanthropies and kindnesses, such incidents are insignificant. The money and other help she lavished on several generations of poets, painters, and writers would add up to uncounted thousands of pounds—not to mention the cost of her hospitality generally. She was always either giving money to, or getting up appeals for, destitute poets and artists. In 1935, for example, Eliot was getting some money together to help a young poet called George Barker; not only did Ottoline give generously, she also worked on Barker's behalf for several years. She had many charities, among them the Women's Public Lodging House Fund, whose secretary wrote gratefully to her after receiving a gift of £20. 5s: "You were the first to give us a hand." And Ottoline never forgot her old friends at Welbeck. One of them wrote to her from Laundry Lodge, Welbeck, thanking her for some photographs of Julian she had sent him:

> My Lady,
> I beg to offer my thanks for the charming photographs. . . .I'm afraid your Ladyship would not find many members of your bible class still at Welbeck, they have got scattered about, and I know of two at least who made the great sacrifice in the war. One was poor G. Marples of Holbeck Woodhouse, and the other was Joe Willies of Holbeck. I thank God that I was spared to return to my wife and boys of whom we have been blessed with three, and I was away from the day we mobilised until March, 1919. I was in Gallipoli, Salonica, Palestine and Syria.
> > Thanking your Ladyship once again,
> > I beg the honour to remain
> > Your Ladyship's humble servant,
> > > F. HANCOCK

Gathorne-Hardy mentions several other examples of Ottoline's kindness towards former servants. He quotes a letter an old servant wrote to Philip after Ottoline's death: "It's strange how often I think of her. Sometimes at the station when I'm trying to get my change, I put my ticket in my mouth and then I think 'Her Ladyship would not do that,' and I desist."[49] When Virginia Woolf was shown this letter she said it was the most touching tribute she had ever read.

In some quarters, however, Ottoline remained the figure of fun she had become to many of her former friends. In January, 1931, Roger Fry wrote Clive Bell describing a masked children's party Vanessa had held at which her daughter Angelica gave an "almost alarmingly good" impersonation of Ottoline. There is no doubt that Ottoline did leave herself open to such parodies. Sybille Bedford remembered an incident at the Aldous Huxleys' when Ottoline's string of pearls broke and bounced and rolled over the floor like peas, disappearing under the furniture and carpet. The younger guests went down on their hands and knees scavenging for the pearls, which they placed one by one in a saucer in front of Ottoline. Quite unruffled, she refused to count them (obviously they were not her best pearls) and presently took her leave, pearls in a paper bag. Stephen Spender recalled another occasion when, in the middle of a sentence, a large earring fell off Ottoline's ear and dropped into her teacup. Without interrupting what she was saying, she fished it out and attached it to her ear again. "I once saw far worse things happen," he recalled, "but she was not at all embarrassed as with a diving, pulling motion, she set herself to rights."[50]

In her later life, travelling became one of Ottoline's main pleasures. She always seemed to be off somewhere, to Germany, Holland, France—and, of course, her beloved Italy. In 1931 it was to the Low Countries where she toured galleries and was converted to Franz Hals, which pleased Augustus John, as Hals had always been one of his favorite painters. In 1932 it was Freiburg again. Here she didn't like the other tourists: "There are some *awful* people here mostly, smart, rich and insolent . . . they are the type of people one sees in the stalls at a *silly* play in London."[51] In 1933 she went to Sicily, reporting to Gathorne-Hardy: "We went and returned by *sea*—wasn't that *brave of me!* Who do you think got on board at Palma—but Godfrey Winn!! . . . I did my best to put away prejudice and I liked him *fairly* but got so tired of him and his voice—and ended up by never wishing to see the silly lad again . . . and to think he makes £2000 writing!"[52] In 1934 it was Athens. Then in 1935 Ottoline and Philip undertook a major expedition to India, partly because Philip was thinking of writing a book about Ottoline's ancestor William Bentinck, the Governor-General who abolished suttee. They set out in January by P & O steamer with Ottoline spending most of the voyage lying in a deckchair and reading Indian books. In India their progress was like a royal tour in miniature. Indians travelled long distances to see "Lady Ottoline Bentinck," descendent of the great Governor-General, and they were feted by local princelings, governors, and even the Viceroy himself. Oddly enough, Ottoline—stern foe of British Imperialism during the First World War and in Ireland—thought very highly of the Raj and of the hundreds of loyal Englishmen working all their lives out as magistrates and clerks to help "civilise" India.

In 1935 Maynard Keynes tried to organise a presentation dinner in Ottoline's honour at the Café Royal, but Ottoline, though grateful, scotched the idea. "I'm too shy," she said. She preferred to meet her friends in less formal circumstances. But it should not be thought that all these friends were present or future celebrities: many of the people she devoted most attention to were anything but raging successes. There was a Frenchman called Jean de Menasce who exchanged scores of letters with Ottoline and ended up taking the cloth and immuring himself in a monastery. Another comparative flop was a New Zealand poet called D'Arcy Cresswell who came over to England on the basis of a book he had published called *The Poet's Progress*. He called Ottoline "Dear Lady Ginger" and after he returned to New Zealand they kept up a correspondence for many years. But it was not Cresswell's lot to become famous, and he ended up a radio announcer. With others she was more successful. She patronised a young novelist called Graham Greene and helped him get a job. Someone else she helped was the poet William Plomer and it was he who first brought Stephen Spender along to one of her Thursdays. Spender made quite a hit with Ottoline and for some time it was not Yeats or Virginia Woolf who were dangled as bait for other guests, but the good-looking Spender. "We have had one or two newcomers . . . Stephen Spender who is so lovely to look at," she wrote to one prospective guest. Plomer said Ottoline was the occasion of one of the most feudal remarks he had ever heard. It came from an old noblewoman who, hearing Ottoline praised as a patron of the arts, said severely: "But she has betrayed our Order."[53]

From 1935 on Ottoline's health declined steadily. For much of the time she was in nursing homes and clinics and her letters of the period are filled with discussions of symptoms and doctors. One of the last good doctors she had was Dr. Rau, who had saved her life with the jaw operation. Later, when she went to him with a whole ragbag of symptoms, he told her bluntly: "Sack your cook."[54] But Ottoline enjoyed her food and refused to give up the quantities of butter and cream and other rich things. So instead of sacking her cook she sacked Rau, and from then on it was Dr.

Cameron with his nice bedside manner and easy cures who held sway. Ottoline went to his clinic at Tunbridge Wells many times and no doubt the rest did her some good. "I had to retire to my clinic at Tunbridge Wells—I had a lovely quiet time there," she told a friend.[55] In 1936 she was struck down with a severe illness and was so sick she decided to compose a last message to all her friends. However, she recovered and what she wrote was later circulated among her friends after she did die:

> Don't mourn for me, dear friends. When you are quiet and alone remember me kindly, and when you are in lovely country—in England or Italy or Greece—give an affectionate thought to one who drank in the beauty and poetry of the lands that you are gazing at . . . and when you walk the streets of London, remember one who passed in and out amongst the crowds trying only to understand. . . . I should like to call to my side and wave good-bye to the many friends I had in the shops. I could name them all . . . and then to those friends who came on Thursdays. Remember I have watched you all and tried to understand what you are like underneath, and when possible I have tried to help you and encourage you to do your best in life.[56]

After recovering from this illness she resumed her Thursdays. Virginia would come round for private chats, their "owling sessions." Both were involved in encouraging younger poets and one day Virginia asked Ottoline to help a young friend of hers by coming round to one of Virginia's functions and making friends with him "The world requires the presence of your golden wing," she said.[57] At this time Ottoline's other main friend was Yeats, but in 1936 their friendship ended abruptly. Yeats had made friends with W. J. Turner, who prevailed on him to write an introduction to a collection of poems Turner was bringing out. In this introduction Yeats mentioned *The Aesthetes*, praising it highly. When Ottoline learned about this she was outraged, and her actions soon made it clear to Yeats that something was wrong. He wrote to her asking rather bewilderedly what he had done to offend her. She wrote back telling him. In several letters he tried to appease her, but her anger would not be abated. On March 10, 1937, she told him:

> I am afraid your letter makes matters worse! I had hoped that you had not read through "The Aesthetes" and so were unaware of the repulsive caricature that Turner had drawn of me in it—but obviously you knew all about

it and you knew that it was intended to be my portrait . . . this leaves me all the more astonished that you should have singled it out of all of Turner's prose works to mention in your preface and introduction. In fact you rescued it from oblivion—the oblivion into which I was thankful it had fallen. . . . That Mr. Turner should have written it did not surprise me very much, for though I liked him and found him clever I had never regarded him, to put it plainly, as much of a gentleman. . . . I still cannot understand what induced you to write as you did. The book after all was not poetry. There was no need for you to mention it at all.[58]

Yeats was dumbfounded and made vain attempts to make light of the matter. But Ottoline wrote back coldly and on his last letter she scrawled at the bottom "Yeats fini!"

Yeats' "betrayal" soured Ottoline greatly and she began to believe that all her efforts at friendship had been wasted. But in 1936 she met two people who were to help her regain her trust. They were Francis Hackett, an Irish historian and novelist, and his Danish wife Signe, also a writer, and from 1936 on they were possibly Ottoline's closest friends. She visited them in Ireland and sent them her memoirs to read, together with her articles on Lawrence and Katherine Mansfield. Hackett gave her the sort of praise she needed after the split with Yeats: "I liked so much what you said about Henry James," he wrote, "at times I feel he was exactly—well, one of us!"[59] In another letter he said: "You are the most deeply appreciative human being I ever knew. To have been in love with you must have been very dangerous."[60]

At the beginning of 1937 Ottoline went up to Liverpool to have some medical tests and a few months later entered a clinic with suspected gall bladder trouble. She continued to correspond with people but her Thursdays at Gower Street were suspended. She wrote to Gathorne-Hardy asking him to drop the "Lady" when he addressed her and he in turn told her that at a party he had been at recently there had been a discussion about whether her street was pronounced Gower or Gore and that Max Beerbohm had said the correct name was "Lady Ottoline Street." In May she was put on a starvation cure for a month. Later the same month Philip saw a doctor who told him he had a bad heart. The doctor also told Ottoline, and at this news she suffered a stroke which partially paralysed her. She was sent to Dr. Cameron's Tunbridge Wells Clinic where a "diseased heart" was diagnosed. Amongst all this illness she still found time to try to help Russell, whose finances were now in a mess. In June she wrote to the philosopher George Santayana asking if he could use his influence to get Russell a post somewhere, " . . . For through perhaps his own impetuous altruistic fault he is now very poor and there seems no way here in England for him to get a post as he is over age for a university job . . . he has to pay a good amount yearly to one of his brother's widows and also a good deal to that dreadful Dora."[61] Santayana replied that he couldn't do much, but Ottoline thanked him anyway: "He perhaps has done foolish things but he has such fine integrity & courage that is rare," she wrote.[62] In August, 1937, Ottoline had partially recovered. She wrote to Dora Sanger: "Yes I was very ill and nearly died. I was paralysed but thanks to my dear Dr. Cameron at Tunbridge Wells in whose clinic I was for nearly 3 months I am alive."[63] Ottoline returned to London and made an attempt to recommence her Thursdays. She also visited Juliette Huxley, who now lived with her husband at the Regents Park Zoo. Juliette noticed how ill Ottoline looked—her skin was not merely white but grey. "I don't think Philip realises just how ill I am,"Ottoline told her.[64] In December Ottoline had some "X-ray treatment" and was also ill with a heavy cold. In January, 1938, she was making plans for a trip to France but was too ill to leave. Again Cameron was called in and injected her with a powerful antibiotic called Prontosil. Apparently Cameron had been administering Prontosil to other of his patients, with results that were bringing threats of investigation by the medical authorities. In April Ottoline entered his clinic again and soon after was told that Cameron had committed suicide. A few days later, on April 21, a nurse was administering her usual Prontosil injection when Ottoline fell back on her pillow. When a doctor was brought in he pronounced her dead. The official cause of her death was given as heart failure.

Four days later Ottoline was buried at Holbeck church on the Welbeck estate and the next day a memorial service was held in St. Martin's in the Field, Trafalgar Square. Virginia Woolf and Margot Asquith both wrote obituaries which were published in *The Times* on April 21. Virginia wrote: "A life-long struggle'against ill health had impeded the literary productiveness which she desired."[65] She added that Ottoline had held fast to her deeply rooted Christian mysticism. Margot Asquith said that Ottoline's·appearance was considered eccentric by those who did not know her well, but that she herself was unconscious of this. "We delighted in her distinguished carriage, beautiful countenance and original clothes. In spite of an admirable sense of humour I never heard her utter an unkind word—of how many clever women can we say the same?'' [66] Hundreds of people wrote to Philip expressing their sympathy—and not just the conventional polite note, for some letters were several pages long, extolling Ottoline's virtues with a warmth that reflected genuine fondness. Philip ordered an inscribed slab and a memorial plaque for Ottoline and engaged their friend the sculptor and typographer Eric Gill to inscribe them. When Virginia heard of this plan she said: "How could anyone get Ottoline on to a slab?" When Gill's memorial plaque was ready, Portland—who had been so upset at Ottoline's death that he retired to his bed for three days—refused to allow it to be hung because he didn't approve of its design. Finally it was placed in the parish church at Garsington.

After Ottoline's death Philip continued to live at Gower Street, going to his club to play bridge and devoting much of his time to collecting blue-and-white china, the hobby he had begun at Eton as a boy. He also decided to edit and rewrite Ottoline's memoirs. Gathorne-Hardy made a point of visiting Philip after Ottoline's death. Sometimes Philip would take him upstairs where Ottoline's clothes still hung, her unique scent clinging to them, and he would gently lift the silks and velvets in an attempt to get in touch with her again. Soon after the war began, the house at Gower Street was damaged by a bomb and Philip went to live in various hotels on the south coast of England where he whiled away his time playing bridge. He returned to London occasionally and was back at Gower Street in February, 1943, when he suffered a heart attack. As he lay dying his last words were: "Partner, we can't make it. We haven't enough hearts." [67] He was buried next to Ottoline in the graveyard at Holbeck, his simple sanserif gravestone identical with hers, the two monuments contrasting oddly with the traditional Gothic script on the rest of the Bentinck graves.

APPENDIX 1

There are two main strands in Ottoline's genealogy: the Cavendish and the Bentinck. The Cavendish line goes back to Tudor times and Bess of Hardwick, whose second husband was Sir William Cavendish and whose last husband was the sixth Earl of Shrewsbury. Bess' second-youngest son, William Cavendish, founded the Devonshire, or senior side of the Cavendish line, and her youngest son, Charles, founded the junior or Newcastle line which descended through a series of heiresses until 1734 when William Bentinck, the second Duke of Portland, married Margeret Cavendish-Holles-Harley, Ottoline's great-great-grandmother. William Bentinck was the grandson of Hans Willem Bentinck, who came over to England in 1688 with William of Orange (William III of England). Hans Willem, a younger member of an old Dutch family, was a close friend of William III, who created him Earl of Portland. Hans Willem's son Henry was made First Duke of Portland by George I (mainly because of Hans Willem's efforts in the Hanovarian cause). (Source: Turberville)

APPENDIX 2

The Lady and the Pug
by Aldous Huxley

There was a Lady loved a Pug
    "Honey," said she
"I long to kiss your ugly mug!"
    "Gr-r-rumph," said he.

"I'll give you red morocco shoes,
    "Honey," said she
"And little hats and tartan trews."
    "Gr-r-rumph," said he.

"I'll make you pants of purple plush,
    "Honey," said she.
Pug turned aside to hide a blush:
    "Gr-r-rumph," said he.

"To make your figure slim and sveldt,
    "Honey," said she
"I'll give you an abdominal belt,"
    "Gr-r-rumph," said he.

"I'll give you sixteen meals a day,
    "Honey," said she.
Pug would have liked to shout Hurray
    But Grumph was all that he could say,
    So "Gr-r-rumph, Gr-r-rumph, Gr-r-rumph,
    Gr-r-rumph!!" said he.

APPENDIX 3

[An example of Ottoline's letter-writing style.]

MY DEAR MR STRONG,

It was very nice of you to send me your poems as you know I like and admire them *very much.* I showed them to Mr. Desmond MacCarthy who was here and I am pleased that he also liked them *very* much and I know he is a good judge.

I only suggested another day except Sunday as there is generally such a crowd here that day. But now Lent is over there won't be. So do come on Sunday, perhaps next Sunday if you like. I should like to talk about different things.

It would be a great pleasure if you would.

Thanking you so much for your poems,

Yours very sincerely

OTTOLINE MORRELL

KEY TO ABBREVIATIONS OF SOURCES
IN NOTES

Charleston: Charleston Papers
HRC: Humanities Research Center
Holroyd: Michael Holroyd's Biography of Lytton Strachey
Huxley: Aldous Huxley's Edition of Lawrence's Letters
King's College: King's College Library
McMaster: Bertrand Russell Archives, McMaster University
Memoirs: Memoirs of Lady Ottoline Morrell
Moore: Harry F. Moore's Collected Letters of Lawrence
Strachey Trust: Miscellaneous Letters of Lytton Strachey, Dora Carrington, and James Strachey
Sussex: Letter From Ottoline to Virginia Woolf, Sussex University

NOTES

(Brackets indicate postmark date)

CHAPTER ONE

1. Virginia Woolf (VW)—Ottoline Morrell (OM) (nd) HRC.
2. D. H. Lawrence (DHL)—Mark Gertler (MG) (May 24, 1928) Huxley.
3. Osbert Sitwell, *Laughter in the Next Room*, p. 16.
4. Dorothy Brett (Brett)—Sybille Bedford, quoted in *Aldous Huxley*, Vol. 1, p. 71.
5. Peter Quennell, *Sign of the Fish*, p. 123.
6. Stephen Spender, *World Within World*, p. 162.
7. Leonard Woolf, *Beginning Again*, p. 199.
8. Vanessa Bell (VB)—Roger Fry (RF) (October, 1917) Charleston.
9. Lytton Strachey (LS)—VW (May 27, 1919) Holroyd, p. 771.
10. David Garnett (DG), *Flowers of the Forest*, pp. 36–39.
11. DG, interview with author (interview).
12. Mrs. Bentinck to Henry Bentinck. Copy in possession of Mrs. Vinogradoff (Mrs. V).
13. OM—Lord Henry Bentinck (nd) Mrs. V.
14. *Memoirs*, Vol. 1, p. 77.
15. Unpublished memoirs.
16. *Memoirs*, Vol. 1, p. 94.
17. *Ibid.*, p. 96.

CHAPTER TWO

1. William Maclagan—OM (nd) HRC.
2. *Memoirs*, Vol. 1, p. 98.
3. Maclagan—OM (June 3, 1897) HRC.
4. Maclagan—OM (July 9, 1897) HRC.
5. *Memoirs*, Vol. 1, p. 95.
6. *Ibid.*, p. 99.
7. *Ibid.*
8. *Ibid.*, p. 101.
9. *Ibid.*, p. 102.
10. H. H. Asquith—OM (August 25, 1898) HRC.
11. Hilda Douglas-Pennant—OM (January 1, 1918)HRC.
12. *Memoirs*, Vol. 1, p. 106.
13. *Ibid.*, p. 106.
14. *Ibid.*, p.107.
15. *Ibid.*
16. Lady Huxley, interview.
17. Unpublished memoirs.
18. *Memoirs*, Vol. 1, p. 113.
19. *Ibid.*, p. 114.
20. Asquith—OM (Easter, 1900) HRC.
21. Asquith—OM (May 1, 1900) HRC.
22. Asquith—OM (June 14, 1900) HRC.
23. Asquith—OM (June 21, 1900) HRC.
24. Asquith—OM (December 26, 1900) HRC.
25. Letter to author (November 14, 1973).
26. Essay on Asquith by Lytton Strachey published in *The Times*. Introduction by Michael Holroyd. (January 15, 1972).

27. *Ibid.*
28. *Memoirs*, Vol. 1, p. 114.
29. *Ibid.*

CHAPTER THREE

1. *Memoirs*, Vol. 1, p. 120.
2. OM—Philip Morrell (PM) (nd) Mrs. V.
3. *Memoirs*, Vol. 1, p. 121.
4. *Ibid.*,
5. *Ibid.*, p. 147.
6. *Cuthbert Learmont*, p. 80.
7. *Memoirs*, Vol. 2, p. 148.
8. OM—LS (November 2, 1913) Mrs. V.
9. J. A. Cramb (JAC)—OM (nd) HRC.
10. JAC—OM (May 20, 1904) HRC.
11. *Cuthbert Learmont*, p. 94.
12. JAC—OM (May, 1904) HRC.
13. JAC—OM (June 4, 1904) HRC.
14. JAC—OM (June 9, 1904) HRC.
15. JAC—OM (November 18, 1904) HRC.
16. *Memoirs*, Vol. 1, p. 132.
17. *Ibid.*, p. 148.
18. Unpublished memoirs.

CHAPTER FOUR

1. Leonard Woolf, *Beginning Again*, p. 36.
2. Unpublished memoirs.
3. *Memoirs*, Vol. 1, p. 155.
4. William Rothenstein—OM (December, 1908) HRC.
5. *Memoirs*, Vol. 1, p. 161.
6. Michael Holroyd, *Augustus John*, p. 280.
7. *Memoirs*, Vol. 1, p. 141.

8. *Ibid.*, p. 156.
9. Augustus John (AJ)—OM (April 22, 1908) HRC.
10. AJ—OM (May 3, 1908) HRC.
11. AJ—OM (May 30, 1908) HRC.
12. *Memoirs*, Vol. 1., p. 158.
13. *Ibid.*, p. 159.
14. Jacob Epstein—OM (October 22, 1908) HRC.
15. AJ—OM (November 30, 1908) HRC.
16. AJ—OM (December 18, 1908) HRC.
17. Dorelia McNeill—OM (nd) HRC.
18. AJ—OM (December 18, 1908) HRC.
19. AJ—OM (January 8, 1909) HRC.
20. *Memoirs*, Vol. 1, p. 163.
21. *Ibid.*, p. 165.
22. AJ—OM (July 23, 1909) HRC.
23. Augustus John, *Chiaroscuro*, p. 83.
24. *Virginia Woolf*, Vol. 1, p. 144.
25. *Ibid.*, p. 124.
26. *Ibid.*, p. 144.
27. *Ibid.*, p. 145.
28. *Ibid.*
29. *Ibid.*
30. RF—D. S. MacColl (March, 1909) *Fry Letters.*
31. *BR Auto.*, Vol. 1, p. 202.
32. Gertrude Stein, *Autobiography.*

CHAPTER FIVE

1. *Memoirs*, Vol. 1, p. 186.
2. Henry Lamb (HL)—OM (nd) HRC.
3. HL—OM (nd) HRC.
4. *Memoirs*, Vol. 1, p. 194.
5. HL—OM (April 25, 1910) HRC.
6. *Memoirs*, Vol. 1, p. 195.
7. HL—OM (May 26, 1910) HRC.
8. HL—OM (June 14, 1910) HRC.
9. HL—OM (June 18, 1910) HRC.
10. HL—OM (July 7, 1910) HRC.
11. RF—G. L. Dickinson, *Fry Letters.*

12. *Memoirs*, Vol. 1, p. 202.
13. LS to L. Woolf (October, 1905) Holroyd, p. 448.
14. *Memoirs*, Vol. 1, p. 202.
15. OM—LS (November 16, 1910) Mrs. V.
16. *Memoirs*, Vol. 1, p. 203.
17. LS—James Strachey (November 18, 1910) Holroyd, p. 451.
18. HL—OM (November 28, 1910) HRC.
19. LS—OM (December 8, 1910) HRC.
20. Unpublished memoirs.
21. OM jotting on envelope (January, 1911) HRC.
22. Unpublished memoirs.
23. HL—OM (January 25, 1911) HRC.
24. HL—OM (March 8, 1911) HRC.

23. BR—OM [March 28, 1911] HRC.
24. BR—OM [March 29, 1911] HRC.
25. BR—OM [March 31, 1911] HRC.
26. BR—OM [April 2, 1911] HRC.
27. BR—OM [April 3, 1911] HRC.
28. BR—OM [April 4, 1911] HRC.
29. BR—OM [April 6, 1911].
30. BR—OM [April 7, 1911] HRC.
31. BR—OM [April 8, 1911] HRC.
32. BR—OM [April 8, 1911] HRC.
33. BR—OM [April 8, 1911] HRC.
34. BR—OM [April 10, 1911] HRC.
35. BR—OM [April 10, 1911] HRC.
36. BR—OM (nd) HRC.
37. BR—OM [April 14, 1911] HRC.
38. BR—OM [April 15, 1911] HRC.
39. *BR Auto.*, Vol. 1, p. 204.

CHAPTER SIX

CHAPTER SEVEN

1. *Memoirs*, Vol. 2, p. 266.
2. *BR Auto.*, Vol. 1, p. 203.
3. *Ibid.*, p. 151.
4. BR Diary, HRC.
5. *Ibid.*
6. *Ibid.*
7. *Ibid.*
8. *Ibid.*
9. *Ibid.*
10. *Ibid.*
11. *Ibid.*
12. *Ibid.*
13. *Ibid.*
14. *Ibid.*
15. *Ibid.*
16. *BR Auto.*, Vol. 1, p. 151.
17. BR—OM [March 21, 1911] HRC.
18. BR—OM [March 22, 1911] HRC.
19. BR—OM [March 23, 1911] HRC.
20. BR—OM [March 25, 1911] HRC.
21. *Memoirs*, Vol. 2, p. 267.
22. BR—OM [March 28, 1911] HRC.

1. RF—OM (nd) HRC.
2. RF—OM [April 3, 1911] HRC.
3. RF—OM [April 4, 1911] HRC.
4. *BR Auto.*, Vol. 1, p. 204.
5. *Memoirs*, Vol. 2, p. 272.
6. *Ibid.*, p. 273.
7. *BR Auto.*, Vol. 1, p. 205.
8. *Memoirs*, Vol. 2, p. 273.
9. BR—OM [April 4, 1911] HRC.
10. Unpublished memoirs (see *Memoirs*, Vol. 2, p. 267 for published version).
11. *Memoirs*, Vol. 2, p. 268.
12. HL—OM [April 8, 1911] HRC.
13. HL—OM [April 11, 1911] HRC.
14. HL—OM [May 6, 1911] HRC.
15. HL—OM [May 10, 1911] HRC.
16. HL—OM [May 16, 1911] HRC.
17. *V. Woolf*, Vol. 1, p. 145.
18. BR—OM [May 29, 1911] HRC.
19. BR—OM [June 1, 1911] HRC.
20. *Memoirs*, Vol. 1, p. 213.
21. HL—OM [May 22, 1911] HRC.

CHAPTER EIGHT

1. LS—George Mallory (nd) Holroyd, p. 459.
2. LS—Clive Bell (CB) [October 21, 1909] Holroyd, p. 454.
3. *Ibid.*
4. *Ibid.*, p. 453.
5. OM—LS (nd) Mrs. V.
6. *Memoirs,* Vol. 1, p. 214 (first sentence from unpublished memoirs).
7. BR—OM [June 3, 1911] HRC.
8. LS—OM (nd) HRC.
9. LS—OM (July 28, 1911) HRC.
10. VB—RF (June 28, 1911) Charleston.
11. BR—OM [June 6, 1911] HRC.
12. HL—OM [June 22, 1911] HRC.
13. *Memoirs,* Vol. 1, p. 216 (last sentence from unpublished memoirs).
14. BR—OM [June 20, 1911] HRC.
15. *Memoirs,* Vol. 2, p. 278 (last 15 words from unpublished memoirs).
16. BR—OM [June 9, 1911] HRC.
17. BR—OM [July 17, 1911] HRC.
18. BR—OM [July 16, 1911] HRC.
19. BR—OM [July 9, 1911] HRC.
20. BR—OM (nd) HRC.
21. BR—OM (September, 1911) HRC.
22. BR—OM (nd) HRC.
23. VB—RF (August 15, 1911) Charleston.
24. BR—OM (August, 1911) HRC.
25. BR—OM (October, 1911) HRC.
26. OM—BR (nd) McM.
27. BR—OM (nd) HRC.
28. *Memoirs,* Vol. 2, p. 279 (with corrections from unpublished memoirs).
29. BR—OM [November 13, 1911] HRC.
30. HL—OM [November 21, 1911] HRC.
31. LS—OM (December 26, 1911) HRC.
32. BR—OM [December 27, 1911] HRC.
33. BR—OM [December 27, 1911] HRC.
34. BR—OM [December 29, 1911] HRC.
35. HL—OM [February 23, 1912] HRC.
36. BR—OM [March 18, 1912] HRC.
37. HL—OM (March, 1912) HRC.
38. HL—OM [March 20, 1912] HRC.
39. BR—OM [April 15, 1912] HRC.
40. BR—OM [April 6, 1912] HRC.
41. BR—OM (April 20, 1912) HRC.
42. BR—OM [May 31, 1912] HRC.
43. HL—OM (April, 1912) HRC.
44. HL—OM [May 27, 1912] HRC.
45. LS—OM (June 12, 1912) HRC.
46. HL—OM (July, 1912) HRC.
47. HL—OM [July 19, 1912] HRC.

CHAPTER NINE

1. *Memoirs,* Vol. 1, p. 228.
2. Romola Nijinsky, *Nijinsky,* p. 155.
3. OM—LS (June 7, 1912) Mrs. V.
4. OM—LS (nd) Mrs. V.
5. BR—OM [August 1, 1912] HRC.
6. BR—OM [July 26, 1912] HRC.
7. BR—OM [May 23, 1912] HRC.
8. BR—OM [July 25, 1912] HRC.
9. *Memoirs,* Vol. 1, p. 231.
10. LS—OM. (August 19, 1912) HRC.
11. LS—OM (August, 1912) HRC.
12. BR—OM (August, 1912) HRC.
13. LS—OM [September 25, 1912] HRC.
14. LS—OM (September 27, 1912) HRC.
15. *Memoirs,* Vol. 2, p. 281 (first 12 words from unpublished memoirs).
16. LS—OM (October, 1912) HRC.
17. LS—OM (October 18, 1912) HRC.
18. Molly MacCarthy—CB (November 23, 1912) Charleston.
19. BR—OM (nd) HRC.
20. Unpublished memoirs (see *Memoirs,* Vol. 2, p. 281 for edited version).
21. *Memoirs,* Vol. 2, p. 281.
22. LS—OM (October 18, 1912) HRC.
23. LS—OM (April 4, 1913) HRC.

24. VB—RF (April 8, 1913) Charleston.
25. OM—LS (nd) Mrs. V.
26. OM—LS (nd) Mrs. V.
27. BR—OM [May 4, 1913] HRC.
28. BR—OM [May 23, 1913] HRC.
29. BR—OM [May 28, 1913] HRC.
30. BR—OM [June 17, 1913] HRC.
31. BR—OM (June, 1913) HRC.
32. *Memoirs,* Vol. 1, p. 240.
33. Holroyd, p. 561.
34. BR—OM (August 10, 1913) HRC.
35. Bessie Burrows—OM (January 9, 1914) HRC.
36. LS—OM (November 21, 1913) HRC.
37. LS—OM (nd) HRC.
38. *Memoirs,* Vol. 1, p. 251.
39. BR—OM [February 13, 1914] HRC.
40. BR—OM (February 25, 1914) HRC.
41. BR—OM (March 19, 1914) HRC.
42. BR—OM (April 6, 1914) HRC.
43. BR—OM (June 1, 1914) HRC.
44. LS—CB (May 4, 1914) Charleston.
45. *Memoirs,* Vol. 1, p. 253.
46. *Ibid.,* p. 254.
47. LS—OM (May 19, 1914) HRC.
48. E. M. Forster—OM (May 25, 1914) HRC.
49. *BR Auto.,* Vol. 1, p. 213.
50. Unpublished memoirs.
51. BR—OM [July 3, 1914] HRC.
52. *Memoirs,* Vol. 1, p. 258.

CHAPTER TEN

1. BR—OM [August 1, 1914] HRC.
2. Hansard (August 3, 1914).
3. BR—OM [August 1, 1914] HRC.
4. BR—OM [August 5, 1914] HRC.
5. *Memoirs,* Vol. 1, p. 262.
6. Max Gieland—OM (nd) HRC.
7. Violet Asquith—OM (May 27, 1914) HRC.
8. Violet Asquith—OM (August 29, 1914) HRC.
9. BR—OM (August, 1914) HRC.
10. Unpublished memoirs (for edited quote see *Memoirs,* Vol. 2, p. 286).
11. BR—OM [August 29, 1914] HRC.
12. Unpublished memoirs.
13. Unpublished memoirs (for edited quote see *Memoirs,* Vol. 2, p. 287).
14. *Memoirs,* Vol. 1, p. 277.
15. BR—OM (December 26, 1914) HRC.
16. *Memoirs,* Vol. 1, p. 272.
17. D. H. Lawrence (DHL)—OM (January 3, 1915) Huxley, p. 213.
18. DHL—OM (January 27, 1915), Huxley, p. 215.
19. DHL—OM (nd) HRC.
20. *Memoirs,* Vol. 1, p. 272.
21. DHL—OM (nd) HRC.
22. *Memoirs,* Vol. 1, p. 272.
23. DHL—OM (February 1, 1915) Huxley.
24. BR—OM [January 8, 1915] HRC.
25. BR—OM [January 20, 1915] HRC.
26. *Memoirs,* Vol. 1, p. 273.
27. H. T. Moore, *Intelligent Heart,* p. 183.
28. DHL—OM (nd), *London Magazine* (February, 1956, Vol. 3, No. 2).
29. Frieda Lawrence (FL)—S. S. Koteliansky (Kot) (nd) *M and C,* p. 208.
30. DHL—OM (February 22, 1915) *London Magazine,* Vol. 3, No. 2, p. 48.
31. BR—OM (March, 1915) HRC.
32. BR—OM (March, 1915) HRC.
33. BR—OM (March, 1915) HRC.
34. DHL—OM [April 4, 1915] *New York Review of Books* (April 23, 1970).
35. DHL—OM (nd) Huxley.
36. DHL—OM (nd) HRC.
37. DHL—OM (nd) HRC.
38. DHL—OM (nd) Huxley, p. 231.
39. DHL—PM (April 20, 1915) *London Magazine,* Vol. 3, No. 2, p. 51.
40. DHL—Kot (nd) Moore, p. 333.

41. Unpublished memoirs.
42. DHL—OM (April 23, 1915) *London Magazine,* Vol. 3, No. 2.
43. BR—OM [May 1, 1915] HRC.
44. DHL—OM (nd) Huxley, p. 228.

CHAPTER ELEVEN

1. *Memoirs,* Vol. 2, p. 32.
2. *Ibid.,* p. 36.
3. *Ibid.*
4. *Intelligent Heart,* p. 213.
5. DHL—Cynthia Asquith (nd) Moore, p. 349.
6. BR—OM (nd) HRC.
7. BR—OM [July 19, 1915] HRC.
8. DHL—OM (nd) Moore, p. 349.
9. *Ibid.*
10. LS—OM (June 8, 1915) HRC.
11. LS—DG (July 14, 1915) Holroyd, p. 599.
12. LS—DG (July 25, 1915) Holroyd, p. 600.
13. LS—OM (July 31, 1915) HRC.
14. *Memoirs,* Vol. 2, p. 40.
15. BR—OM (nd) HRC.
16. DHL—BR (nd) *Memoirs,* Vol. 2, p. 67.
17. *Ibid.,* p. 69.
18. Brett, *Lawrence and Brett.*
19. DHL—OM (December 12, 1915) HRC.
20. DHL—Cynthia Asquith (December 3, 1915) Huxley, p. 283.
21. DHL—Cynthia Asquith (nd) Moore, p. 381.
22. *Memoirs,* Vol. 2. p. 48.
23. BR—OM (nd) HRC.
24. VB—RF (nd) Charleston.
25. LS—Lady Strachey (December 28, 1915) Holroyd, p. 613.
26. Philip Heseltine—OM (January 28, 1916) HRC.
27. DHL—OM (February 25, 1916) Moore, p. 437.

CHAPTER TWELVE

1. BR—OM [November 10, 1915] HRC.
2. BR—OM [November 10, 1915] HRC.
3. BR—OM (nd) HRC.
4. BR—OM [March 18, 1916] HRC.
5. BR—OM (nd) HRC.
6. LS—DG (March 10, 1916) Holroyd, p. 629.
7. *Ibid.*
8. LS—VW (April 15, 1916) *Ibid.,* p. 629.
9. *Memoirs,* Vol. 2, p. 98.
10. *Ibid.,* p. 102.
11. OM—LS (April 27, 1927) Mrs. V.
12. VB—RF (nd) Charleston.
13. RF—VB (nd) Charleston.
14. LS—Barbara Hiles (July 17, 1916) Holroyd, p. 661.
15. *Memoirs,* Vol. 2, p. 84.
16. Dora Carrington (DC)-MG (nd) *Letters and Extracts,* p. 21.
17. LS—OM (April 23, 1916) Holroyd, p. 630.
18. DG, interview.
19. DC (nd) *Letters and Extracts,* p. 33.
20. Holroyd, p. 635.
21. *Memoirs,* Vol. 1, p. 279.
22. OM—Maynard Keynes (Keynes) (May 2, 1916) Charleston.
23. *Memoirs,* Vol. 2., p. 106.
24. *Ibid.,* p. 107.
25. LS—OM (July 3, 1916) HRC.
26. OM—Keynes (July 11, 1916) Charleston.
27. Asquith—OM (nd) HRC.
28. *Memoirs,* Vol. 2, p. 121.
29. *Siegfried's Journey,* p. 11.
30. VB—RF (nd) Charleston.
31. *Flowers of the Forest,* p. 116.
32. *Memoirs,* Vol. 2, p. 123.
33. DC, *Letters and Extracts,* p. 34.
34. Draft of prospectus, HRC.
35. PM Minutes Burnley (October 5, 1916).
36. OM—Keynes (October 5, 1916) Charleston.

37. Aldous Huxley (AH)—OM (nd) HRC.
38. *Siegfried's Journey*, p. 22.

CHAPTER THIRTEEN

1. DHL—OM (nd) Moore, p. 422.
2. DHL—OM (April 17, 1916) Huxley, p. 343.
3. FL—Cynthia Asquith (May 24, 1916) *M and C*, p. 212.
4. FL—OM (nd) HRC.
5. FL—OM (nd) HRC.
6. DHL—Kot (November 7, 1916) Moore, p. 482.
7. DHL—Catherine Carswell (November 27, 1916) Moore, p. 488.
8. *Women in Love*, p. 16.
9. *Ibid.*
10. *Ibid.*
11. *Ibid.*, p. 95.
12. *Ibid.*, p. 178.
13. *Ibid.*
14. *Ibid.*, p. 92.
15. *Ibid.*, p. 46.
16. DHL—OM (April 23, 1915) *London Magazine*, Vol. 3, No. 2.
17. CB—VB (February 2, 1917) Charleston.
18. *Memoirs*, Vol. 2, p. 128.
19. *Ibid.*
20. *Ibid.*
21. *Ibid.*
22. Marginal comments on Ottoline's copy of *Women in Love*. Report filed at HRC.
23. *Women in Love*, p. 18.
24. *Memoirs*, Vol. 2, p. 128.
25. CB—OM (nd) HRC.
26. CB—VB (January 20, 1917) Charleston.
27. *Memoirs*, Vol. 2. 129.
28. *Ibid.*
29. FL—Kot (February 6, 1917) *M and C*, p. 219.
30. DHL—J. B. Pinker (February 20, 1917) Moore, p. 502.
31. DHL—MG (April 1, 1917) Moore, p. 508.
32. Cynthia Asquith, *Diaries*, p. 294.
33. DHL—Kot (February, 1918) Moore, p. 542.
34. DHL—MG (February 21, 1918) Moore, p. 543.
35. Cynthia Asquith, *Diaries*, p. 417.
36. DHL—MG (March, 1918) Moore, p. 548.
37. DHL—OM (Easter Monday, 1918) HRC.
38. *Memoirs*, Vol. 2, p. 129.

CHAPTER FOURTEEN

1. *BR Auto.*, Vol. 2, p. 25.
2. *Ibid.*, p. 26.
3. BR—OM [September 5, 1916] HRC.
4. BR—OM (nd) HRC.
5. BR—OM [December 3, 1916] HRC.
6. *BR Auto.*, Vol. 2, p. 27.
7. Unpublished memoirs.
8. *Ibid.*
9. *Memoirs*, Vol. 2, p. 178.
10. On envelope, BR—OM (nd) HRC.
11. Brett—OM (January 15, 1917) HRC.
12. *Siegfried's Journey*.
13. LS—VW (February 21, 1917) Holroyd, p. 675.
14. *Memoirs*, Vol. 2, p. 175.
15. Brett—OM (January 21, 1917) HRC.
16. Brett—OM (nd) HRC.
17. *Memoirs*, Vol. 2, p. 180.
18. BR—OM [May 5, 1917] HRC.
19. BR—OM [May 11, 1917] HRC.
20. *Siegfried's Journey*.
21. CB—VB (nd) Charleston.
22. *Memoirs*, Vol. 2, p. 182.
23. Unpublished memoirs.
24. BR—OM (June, 1917) HRC.
25. BR—OM (June, 1917) HRC.

26. BR—OM (June, 1917) HRC.
27. BR—OM (July, 1917) HRC.
28. John Middleton Murry (Murry)—OM (nd) HRC.
29. *Memoirs*, Vol. 2. p. 187.
30. *Ibid.*, p. 188.
31. *Ibid.*, p. 190.
32. *Ibid.*
33. *Ibid.*, p. 191.
34. *Ibid.*
35. Murry—OM (nd) HRC.
36. *Memoirs*, Vol. 2, p. 192.
37. Siegfried Sassoon (SS)—OM (November 13, 1917) HRC.
38. *Memoirs*, Vol. 2., p. 230.
39. *Ibid.*, p. 231.
40. MG—OM (November 10, 1917) HRC.
41. *Memoirs*, Vol. 2., p. 224.
42. *Ibid.*
43. *Ibid.*
44. Note on BR—OM [September 20, 1917] HRC.
45. BR—OM [September 17, 1917] HRC.
46. BR—OM [September 20, 1917] HRC.
47. Unpublished memoirs.
48. *Memoirs*, Vol. 2., p. 199.
49. *Ibid.*, p. 203.
50. *V. Woolf*, Vol. 2, p. 51.
51. *Ibid.*, p. 52.
52. *Memoirs*, Vol. 2, p. 232.
53. VB—RF (January 22, 1918) Charleston.
54. *Memoirs*, Vol. 2, p. 232.

8. *Memoirs*, Vol. 2, p. 247.
9. *Ibid.*, p. 248.
10. MG—OM (nd) HRC.
11. OM—DC (nd) HRC.
12. LS—OM (March 3, 1918) Holroyd, p. 720.
13. *Memoirs*, Vol. 2, p. 251.
14. *Ibid.*, p. 252.
15. LS—OM (March 3, 1918) Holroyd, p. 718.
16. DHL—MG (June 26, 1918) huxley, p. 448.
17. MG—Kot [July 15, 1918] *Selected Letters*, p. 160.
18. *Ibid.*
19. BR—OM [July 14, 1918] HRC.
20. *Ibid.*
21. OM—DC (nd) HRC.
22. Unpublished memoirs.
23. Brett—OM (nd) HRC.
24. *BR Auto.*, Vol. 2, p. 37.
25. BR—OM (nd) HRC.
26. *Memoirs*, Vol. 2, p. 254.
27. BR—OM (nd) HRC.
28. *Memoirs*, Vol. 2., p. 254.
29. BR—OM (nd) HRC.
30. *Flowers of the Forest*, p. 185.
31. *Laughter in the Next Room*, p. 17.
32. Hansard (November 11, 1918).
33. DC—Noel Carrington (NC) (November 18, 1918) Holroyd, p. 748.
34. DC—NC, Holroyd, p. 748–49.
35. *V. Woolf*, Vol. 2, p. 62.
36. *BR Auto.*, Vol. 2, p. 37.
37. DC—NC (November 18, 1918) Holroyd, p. 749.
38. *Laughter in the Next Room*, p. 24.

CHAPTER FIFTEEN

1. *Memoirs*, Vol. 2, p. 233.
2. *Ibid.*, p. 237.
3. *Ibid.*, p. 241.
4. SS—OM (March 6, 1918) HRC.
5. *Ibid.*
6. SS—OM (June 7, 1918) HRC.
7. CB—OM (nd) HRC.

CHAPTER SIXTEEN

1. BR—OM [November 20, 1918] HRC.
2. BR—OM [February 18, 1919] HRC.
3. BR—OM (nd) HRC.
4. BR—OM [January 8, 1919] HRC.

5. LS—OM (December 27, 1918) Holroyd, p. 750.
6. *Ibid.*, p. 752.
7. LS—DC (July 11, 1919) *Ibid.*, p. 765.
8. BR—OM [January 1, 1919] HRC.
9. BR—OM (September 4, 1919) HRC.
10. LS—Mary Hutchinson (May 15, 1919) Holroyd, p. 769.
11. LS—VW (May 27, 1919) *Ibid.*, p. 771.
12. Brett—OM (September 15, 1919) HRC.
13. OM—Brett (October 10, 1919) HRC.
14. OM—LS (nd) Mrs. V.
15. Mrs. V., interview.
16. Desmond MacCarthy—OM (nd) HRC.
17. VW—OM (nd) HRC.
18. BR—OM (nd) HRC.
19. BR—OM (December 20, 1919) HRC.
20. BR—OM (December 27, 1919) HRC.
21. BR—OM (January 1, 1920) HRC.
22. *Ibid.*
23. *Daily News* (February 3, 1920).
24. *Truth* (March 6, 1920).
25. *The Tatler* (March 10, 1920).
26. *Everyman* (March 13, 1920).
27. *The Weekly Dispatch* (March 14, 1920).
28. PM—AJ (March 22, 1920) (copy) Mrs. V.
29. BR—OM (nd) HRC.
30. BR—OM (August 14, 1920) HRC.
31. OM—LS (nd) Mrs. V.
32. Edmund Blunden—OM (nd) HRC.
33. Stanley Spencer—OM (nd) HRC.
34. Stanley Spencer—OM (March 10, 1923) HRC.
35. Stanley Spencer—OM (June 17, 1921) HRC.
36. Frank Prewitt—OM (October 17, 1919) HRC.
37. Prewitt—OM (nd) HRC.
38. PM—Mrs. Frederic Morrell (nd) Mrs. V.
39. *BR Auto.*, Vol. 2, p. 136.
40. OM—PM (nd) Mrs. V.
41. Copy of *Crome Yellow*, Mrs. V.
42. *Crome Yellow*, p. 187.
43. *Ibid.*, p. 14.
44. *Ibid.*, p. 13.
45. AH—OM (December 3, 1921) HRC.
46. *Memoirs*, Vol. 2, p. 215.
47. *Ibid.*, p. 218.
48. Sybille Bedford, *Aldous Huxley*, Vol. 1, p. 122.
49. *Ibid.*, p. 123.
50. *Memoirs*, Vol. 2, p. 214.
51. *Ibid.*, p. 215.
52. *Those Barren Leaves*, p. 58.
53. *Ibid.*, p. 63.
54. *Ibid.*, p. 77.

CHAPTER SEVENTEEN

1. *Memoirs*, Vol. 1, p. 20.
2. L. A. G. Strong, *Green Memory*, p. 237.
3. *Memoirs*, Vol. 1, p. 27.
4. *Ibid.*
5. *Green Memory*, p. 237.
6. Peter Quennell, *The Sign of the Fish*, p. 125.
7. C. M. Bowra, *Memories*, p. 195.
8. Quennell, interview.
9. *Memoirs*, Vol. 1, p. 21.
10. *Green Memory*, p. 239.
11. LS—DC (June 3, 1923) Holroyd, p. 856.
12. PR—OM (December 29, 1924) HRC.
13. Blunden—OM (nd) HRC.
14. Arnold Bennett—OM (November 21, 1922) HRC.
15. LS—VW (September 19, 1922) Holroyd, p. 851.
16. OM—W. J. Turner (WJT) (draft) (April 23, 1927) HRC.
17. OM—WJT (draft) (nd) HRC.
18. WJT, *Aesthetes*, p. 36.
19. *Ibid.*, p. 65.
20. *Ibid.*, p. 67.
21. *Ibid.*, p. 41.

22. *Ibid.*, p. 47.
23. *Ibid.*, p. 50.
24. VW—OM (nd) HRC.
25. OM—LS (February, 1922) Mrs. V.
26. LS—OM (September 19, 1922) Holroyd, p. 85.
27. BR—OM (January 2, 1922) HRC.
28. BR—OM (May 11, 1922) HRC.
29. Mrs. V. interview.
30. *Memoirs,* Vol. 1, p. 29.
31. *Ibid.*
32. *Ibid.*
33. Brett—OM (December 29, 1921) HRC.
34. DHL—MG (March 10, 1924) *Intelligent Heart,* p. 327.
35. Murry—OM (January 13, 1923) HRC.
36. Murry—OM (nd) HRC.
37. *Memoirs,* Vol. 2, p. 150.
38. VW—Barbara Bagenal (June 24, 1923) C. Bell, *Old Friends,* p. 103.
39. LS—DC (June 3, 1923) Holroyd, p. 856.
40. *Memoirs,* Vol. 1, p. 37.
41. Ivy Green, Interview.
42. *Ibid.*
43. C. M. Bowra, *Memories,* p. 196.
44. *Ibid.*
45. Gilbert Spencer—OM (nd) HRC.
46. *Memoirs,* Vol. 1, p. 51.
47. *Ibid.*, p. 56.
48. Ivy Green, interview.
49. Sir John Wheeler-Bennett, interview.

CHAPTER EIGHTEEN

1. Lady Huxley, interview.
2. *Memoirs,* Vol. 1, p. 17.
3. DHL—OM (May 8, 1928) *Memoirs,* Vol. 2, p. 129.
4. DHL—OM (May 24, 1928) HRC.
5. OM—LS (nd) Strachey Trust.
6. LS—Roger Senhouse (November 9, 1928) Holroyd, p. 970.
7. *Ibid.*
8. OM—LS (nd) Mrs. V.
9. LS—Roger Senhouse (January 8, 1929), Holroyd, p. 971.
10. OM—Sebastian Sprott (nd) King's College.
11. Lord David Cecil, interview.
12. Lady Huxley, interview.
13. Mrs. V., interview.
14. Mrs. V, interview.
15. DHL—OM (December 28, 1928) Huxley, p. 772.
16. *Memoirs,* Vol. 1, p. 55.
17. DHL—OM (April 3, 1929) *Memoirs,* Vol. 2, p. 136.
18. DHL—OM (April 3, 1929) *Ibid.*, p. 137.
19. *Nehls, A Composite Biography,* Vol. 3, p. 383.
20. FL—OM (nd) HRC.
21. AJ—OM (nd) HRC.
22. Dorelia McNeill—OM (nd) HRC.
23. Axel Munthe—OM (nd) HRC.
24. OM—Gathorne-Hardy (GH) (copy) (June 5, 1929) Mrs. V.
25. OM—GH (copy) (June 5, 1929) Mrs. V.
26. DHL—OM (January 21, 1930) *Memoirs,* Vol. 2, p. 137.
27. *Ibid.*, p. 138.
28. *Ibid.*, p. 142.
29. FL—PM (nd) HRC.
30. FL—OM (March 2, 1932) HRC.
31. OM—Sebastian Sprott (nd) King's College.
32. Vivienne Eliot—OM (nd) HRC.
33. TSE—OM (March 14, 1933) HRC.
34. Kot—OM (nd) HRC.
35. Kot—OM (nd) HRC
36. Kot—OM (September 8, 1936) HRC.
37. OM—LS (nd) Mrs. V.
38. LS—OM (April 8, 1931) HRC.
39. *Memoirs,* Vol. 1, p. 56 and interview, Dilys Powell.
40. DC—OM (nd) HRC.

41. DC—OM (nd) HRC.
42. OM—Sebastian Sprott (November 23, 1931) King's College.
43. OM—Sprott (June 6, 1931) King's College.
44. Dilys Powell, interview.
45. OM—J. Hayward (February 17, 1933) King's College.
46. OM—Hayward (December 28, 1933) King's College.
47. T. S. Moore (TSM)—OM (February 21, 1938) HRC.
48. TSM—OM (March 14, 1938) HRC.
49. *Memoirs,* Vol. 1, p. 16.
50. Stephen Spender, *World Within World,* p. 161.
51. OM—GH (copy) (August 13, 1932) Mrs. V.
52. OM—GH (copy) (June 13, 1933) Mrs. V.
53. William Plomer, *At Home,* p. 50.
54. Lady Huxley, interview.
55. OM—Dora Sanger (nd), possession Daphne Sanger.
56. Mrs. V.
57. VW—OM (nd) HRC.
58. OM—W. B. Yeats (draft) (March 10, 1937) HRC.
59. Francis Hackett—OM (nd) HRC.
60. Hackett—OM (nd) HRC.
61. OM—George Santayana (copy) (nd) HRC.
62. OM—Santayana (copy) (June 28, 1937) HRC.
63. OM—D. Sanger (August 25, 1937), Daphne Sanger.
64. Lady Huxley, interview.
65. VW, *The Times,* (April 21, 1938).
66. Margot Asquith, *ibid.*
67. Lady Huxley, interview.

BIBLIOGRAPHY

Asquith, Cynthia. *Diaries 1915–1918,* E. M. Horsley, editor. London: Hutchinson, 1968. New York: Alfred A. Knopf, Inc., 1968.

Bedford, Sybille. *Aldous Huxley: Vol. I, 1894–1939.* London: Chatto & Windus, 1973.

———. *Aldous Huxley.* New York: Alfred A. Knopf, Inc., 1974.

Bell, Clive. *Civilization* and *Old Friends.* Chicago: University of Chicago Press, 1974.

———. *Old Friends: Personal Recollections.* London: Chatto & Windus, 1956.

Bell, Quentin. *Bloomsbury.* London: Weidenfeld & Nicolson, 1968.

———. *Virginia Woolf: Vol. I, 1882–1912.* London: The Hogarth Press, 1972.

———. *Virginia Woolf: Vol. II, 1912–1941.* London: The Hogarth Press, 1972.

———. *Virginia Woolf.* New York: Harcourt Brace Jovanovich, Inc., 1972.

Bowra, Cecil M. *Memories: 1898–1939.* London: Weidenfeld & Nicolson, 1966. Cambridge: Harvard University Press, 1966.

Brett, Dorothy. *Lawrence and Brett.* Philadelphia: Lippincott, 1933.

Cecil, David. Entry on Lady Ottoline Morrell, *Dictionary of National Biography.*

Delavenay, Emile. *D. H. Lawrence: The Man and His Work 1885–1919.* London: Heinemann, 1969.

Fry, Roger. *Letters,* Denys Sutton, editor. London: Chatto & Windus, 1973. New York: Random House, 1973.

Garnett, David, editor. *Carrington Letters and Extracts from her Diaries.* Introduction by David Garnett. London: Cape, 1970. New York: Holt, Rinehart and Winston, 1970.

Garnett, David. *The Flowers of the Forest.* London: Chatto & Windus, 1955. New York: Harcourt Brace Jovanovich, 1954–1963.

Gertler, Mark. *Selected Letters*, Noel Carrington, editor. Introduction by Quentin Bell. London: Hart-Davis, 1965.

Glenavy, Beatrice. *Today We Will Only Gossip.* London: Constable, 1964.

Holroyd, Michael. *Augustus John: Vol. I, The Years of Innocence.* London: Heinemann, 1974.

———. *Augustus John*. New York: Holt, Rinehart and Winston, 1975.

———. *Lytton Strachey*, a Biography: London, Penguin, 1971.

———. *Lytton Strachey*. New York: Holt, Rinehart and Winston, 1968.

Huxley, Aldous. *Crome Yellow*. London: Chatto & Windus, 1969. New York: Harper & Row, 1965.

———. *Those Barren Leaves*. London: Chatto & Windus, 1951. New York: Avon, 1964.

Jenkins, Roy. *Asquith*. London: Collins, 1964.

———. *Asquith: Portrait of a Man and an Era*. New York: Chilmark Press, 1965.

John, Augustus. *Chiaroscuro: Fragments of Autobiography*. London: Cape, 1952. Philadelphia: Richard West, 1952.

Lawrence, D. H. *Collected Letters*, 2 vols, Harry T. Moore, editor. London: Heinemann, 1962. New York: Viking Press, 1962.

———. "I Will Send: Address: New Letters of D. H. Lawrence," by Mark Schorer, *The London Magazine* , Vol. 3, No. 2 (February, 1956).

———. *The Quest for Rananim: Letters from and to S. S. Koteliansky*, G. Zytaruk, editor. Montreal and London: McGill-Queens University Press, 1970.

———. *The Rainbow and Women in Love*, Colin Clarke, editor. Introductory Note by George H. Ford. London: Macmillan, 1969. Nashville: Aurora, 1970.

———. *Selected Letters*, Aldous Huxley, editor. London: Heinemann, 1932.

———. *Women in Love*. London: Penguin, 1971. New York: Viking Press, 1960.

Lawrence, Frieda. *Memoirs and Correspondence*, E. W. Tedlock, Jr., editor. London: Heinemann, 1961. New York: Alfred A. Knopf, Inc., 1964.

———. *Not I but the Wind*. New York: Viking Press, 1934.

Moore, Harry T. *The Intelligent Heart*. London: Heinemann, 1955. New York: Farrar, Straus & Giroux, 1974 (retitled *The Priest of Love: A Life of D. H. Lawrence*).

———. *The Life and Works of D. H. Lawrence*. London: George Allen & Unwin, 1951. New York: Twayne, 1964.

Morrell, Lady Ottoline. *Ottoline*, Vol. 1, *The Early Memoirs 1873–1915*, Robert Gathorne-Hardy, editor. London: Faber, 1963.

———.Vol. 2, *Ottoline at Garsington 1915-1918*, Robert Gathorne-Hardy, editor. London: Faber, 1974.

———. *Ottoline: The Early Memoirs of Lady Ottoline Morrell*, Robert Gathorne-Hardy, editor. New York: Alfred A. Knopf, 1946.

Nehls, Edward H. *D. H. Lawrence: A Composite Biography*. Milwaukee: University of Wisconsin Press, 1957.

Nijinsky, Romola. *Nijinsky*. London: Gollancz, 1933. New York: Simon & Schuster, 1934.

Plomer, William. *At Home: Memoirs*. London: Cape, 1958.

Portland, Sixth Duke of. *Men, Women and Things*. London: Faber, 1937.

Quennell, Peter. *The Sign of the Fish*. London: Collins, 1960.

Revermort, J. A. *Cuthbert Learmont*. London: Constable, 1910.

Rowse, A. L. *A Cornishman at Oxford*. London: Cape, 1965.

Russell, Bertrand. *The Autobiography*, Vols. 1 and 2. London: George Allen & Unwin, 1971. Boston: Little, Brown and Company, 1968.

Sassoon, Siegfried. *Siegfried's Journey*. London: Faber, 1945.

Sitwell, Osbert. *Laughter in the Next Room*. London: Macmillan, 1949. Boston: Little, Brown and Company, 1948.

Spender, Stephen. *World Within World*. London: Hamish Hamilton, 1951. Berkeley: University of California Press, 1951.

Stein, Gertrude. *The Autobiography of Alice B. Toklas*. London: John Lane, 1933. New York: Harcourt Brace, 1933.

Strachey, Lytton. Article on H. H. Asquith, Introduction by Michael Holroyd, *London Times*, January 1, 1972.

Strong, L. A. G. *Green Memory*. London: McThuen, 1961.

Turberville, Arthur S. *A History of Welbeck Abbey and Its Owners*, 2 vols. London: Faber, 1938.

Turner, W. J. *The Aesthetes*. London: Wishart, 1927.

Victoria, Queen. *Letters*. Third Series, 1862–1883. London, John Murry, 1928.

Wilson, Trevor. *The Downfall of the Liberal Party*. London: Fontana, 1968. Ithaca: Cornell University Press, 1966.

Woolf, Leonard. *Beginning Again*. London: The Hogarth Press, 1964. New York: Harcourt Brace Jovanovich, 1964.

––––––. *Downhill All the Way*. London: The Hogarth Press, 1970.

Woolf, Virginia, and Strachey, Lytton. *Letters: Virginia Woolf and Lytton Strachey*, Leonard Woolf and James Strachey, editors. London: Chatto & Windus, 1956.

INDEX